KING'S INNS AND THE BATTLE
OF THE BOOKS, 1972

Christopher Robinson, king's counsel, 1750. By Benjamin Wilson.
© Leeds Museum and Galleries (Temple Newsam House).

King's Inns and the Battle of the Books, 1972

Cultural Controversy at a Dublin Library

COLUM KENNY

FOUR COURTS PRESS

in association with

THE IRISH LEGAL HISTORY SOCIETY

Typeset in 11 pt on 13 pt Plantin by
Carrigboy Typesetting Services, County Cork for
FOUR COURTS PRESS LTD
Fumbally Court, Fumbally Lane, Dublin 8, Ireland
e-mail: info@four-courts-press.ie
and in North America for
FOUR COURTS PRESS
c/o ISBS, 5824 N.E. Hassalo Street, Portland, OR 97213.

A catalogue record for this title is available
from the British Library.

ISBN 1–85182–686–6

Printed in Great Britain by
MPG Books, Bodmin, Cornwall.

To my sister, May

For books are not absolutely dead things, but do contain a potency of life in them to be as active as that soul was whose progeny they are; nay, they do preserve as in a vial, the pure efficacy and extraction of that living intellect that bred them. I know they are as lively, and as vigorously productive, as those fabulous dragon's teeth; and being sown up and down, may chance to spring up armed men. And yet on the other hand, unless wariness be used, as good almost kill a man as kill a good book; who kills a man kills a reasonable creature, God's image; but he who destroys a good book, kills reason itself, kills the image of God, as it were in the eye. Many a man lives a burden to the earth; but a good book is the precious life-blood of a master-spirit, embalmed and treasured up on purpose to a life beyond life.

John Milton

Of making many books there is no end, and much study is a weariness of the flesh.

Ecclesiastes

Foreword

by Mr Justice Hugh Geoghegan

IN 1972 THE BENCHERS of the Honorable Society of King's Inns ran out of money and were faced with a large overdraft. At the same time they had sole responsibility for the training and education of barristers who in practice were the sole advocates in the higher courts. There was no outside source of funding. It would not have been proper or practical to increase student fees to any kind of level which would be relevant to resolving the financial problems nor was it viable at that time for the barristers' profession to come to the rescue. Earnings were low and the Bar Council had no surplus funds. What were the benchers to do? With great reluctance they decided that they must sell some valuable books in their library which were not law books and which were 'not of Irish interest'.

This decision led to a tragic story brilliantly recounted by Dr Colum Kenny in the ensuing pages. The reader will be anticipating excellence having regard to the previous extraordinary output of Dr Kenny in relation to the history of King's Inns. His definitive history of King's Inns from its early beginnings in 1541 up until 1800 was published in 1992, and that was followed in 1996 by a fascinating account of Irish legal training in the mid-nineteenth century entitled *Tristram Kennedy and the Revival of Irish Legal Training, 1835–1885*. This third volume is a worthy successor.

Understandably, scholars and librarians in particular but also many members of the general public were outraged at the decision to sell. The King's Inns Library had originally been a copyright library entitled to receive a copy of any book published. Partly for this reason and partly due to other circumstances there were housed in the King's Inns Library, itself a separate and beautiful building, several thousand valuable books. The value arose from their subject matter or their rarity or their printing or for many other reasons. The benchers availed themselves of the services of Sotheby's of London who auctioned the books in the course of several sales. The benchers were subjected to severe criticism on the grounds that they were selling out of the country part of our national heritage. Thirty years on, in an era of economic prosperity in Ireland and of far greater sensitivity about preservation of our heritage, it is easy to condemn the benchers both for the decision to sell part of that heritage and for the wholly inefficient manner in which the sale was carried through as graphically described by Dr Kenny, but it would be anachronistic and wrong to be over critical. Criticism is certainly warranted and, indeed, was made at the time both within and outside legal circles, but balance is required in measuring the legitimate extent of such criticism.

As is clear from Dr Kenny's well researched book there is no one person who can be blamed. Ironically, the prime mover among the benchers for proceeding with the sale was the late Mr Justice George Murnaghan, a dominant figure within the judiciary but not the most popular judge among practitioners. Some members of the Bar took fiendish pleasure in pointing the finger of blame at him, but Dr Kenny quite rightly does not do so, and even at the time there was an acknowledgement among those in the know that the King's Inns would not have survived but for the service, time and energy which Mr Justice Murnaghan applied to the management of it. Furthermore neither the decision to sell nor the manner of its execution was in any sense his sole responsibility. The problems of the sale and the public criticism of it were discussed at meetings of the benchers where men of letters such as the former chief justice, Cearbhall Ó Dálaigh, constantly tried to find alternative solutions. The eminent and highly respected senior counsel, Raymond O'Neill, assisted Mr Justice Murnaghan in the carrying out of the decision, and although they can be criticised for excessively relying on the advice of Sotheby's, it is only fair to say that the retired director of the National Library, Dr Richard Hayes, had encouraged the benchers to sell many of their books as clearly emerges from Dr Kenny's book. Interestingly, Dr Hayes had apparently been consulted at a much earlier stage by the former chief justice, Conor Maguire, and at that time also he was in favour of a sale.

Even if legitimate criticism can be levelled at the benchers much more blame must be placed on the government of the time. None of the eminent scholars and librarians who were objecting to the sale was insisting that the books had to remain in the King's Inns Library. What they were objecting to was the loss to Ireland of the valuable heritage. If, therefore, funds had been provided to the National Library or one of the university libraries to have purchased the books, a solution would have been found.

Alternatively, there might have been ways by which the state could have provided funds to the King's Inns as they have done both before and since in the form of uncollected suitors' funds. Good advocacy is essential for the smooth administration of justice in the courts, and there was, therefore, a public interest in the maintenance of the King's Inns as an educational institution. There was, at the same time, a public interest in preventing these unique books leaving the country. Without assistance it was impossible for the benchers to reconcile both public interests.

I have merely concentrated on the background to the sale. What is even more interesting are the details as to how it was carried out and the problems that arose particularly as to the definition of 'Irish interest'. Dr Kenny has given us a very fair account of what happened. He has not excessively criticised the benchers, but he has levelled criticism where it appeared to be warranted, and he has done likewise in relation to the government of the time.

As the current chairman of the King's Inns Library Committee, I am happy to confirm that the computerised cataloguing of the library is at last in progress. I welcome this book, not least because of the defensive ammunition it provides against any future proposal to sell.

Contents

List of Illustrations

Frontispiece. Christopher Robinson, king's counsel, 1750. By Benjamin Wilson. Courtesy of Leeds Museum and Galleries (Temple Newsam House).

Plate section between p. 142 and p. 143

1 Portrait of Henrietta Somerset (1690–1726). By Enoch Seeman. Private Collection. Photograph: Photographic Survey, Courtauld Institute of Art.

2 Oval portrait of a man, seated, with books, 1771. By the Dublin artist, Francis Robert West. Courtesy The Pierpoint Morgan Library, New York, 1971.6.

3 (a and b) Unsigned plan of buildings intended for the King's Inns, proposed but never built behind the Four Courts, 1790. Courtesy King's Inns, MS H4/6–1.

4 Benchers' Council Room, King's Inns, 1958. Courtesy Irish Architectural Archive and Smurfit Publications.

5 a) Elevation of King's Inns, 1813. From *Rec. comm. Ire. Reps.*
   b) Entrance to the intended library of King's Inns, taken instead for the Registry of Deeds. Courtesy Irish Architectural Archive.

6 a) Exterior of King's Inns Library, Henrietta Street, 1981, showing also part of the Registry of Deeds. Courtesy Irish Architectural Archive.
   b) Ground floor of King's Inns Library, 1981. Courtesy Irish Architectural Archive.

7 a) Reading room of King's Inns Library, 1981. Courtesy Irish Architectural Archive.
   b) King's Inns Library, 1981, showing the entry to the annex and gallery. Courtesy Irish Architectural Archive.

8 Richard Hayes. Courtesy the National Library of Ireland (R.12984).

9 Portrait of Conor A. Maguire, by David Hone, 1963. Courtesy King's Inns.

xiii

Acknowledgements

THIS ACCOUNT OF A signal controversy relating to the cultural heritage of Ireland could not have been written without the assistance and cooperation of others. In particular, I wish to thank the benchers of the Honorable Society of King's Inns for allowing me to reproduce certain images in their possession and to publish extracts from the minutes and records of that society. I am grateful, especially, to their librarian, Jonathan Armstong, and to his staff, for their assistance. Reports by Sotheby's relating to the society's library, as well as correspondence between Sotheby's and the benchers, are quoted in full or in part with the permission of both parties. An Taisce, the National Trust for Ireland, kindly allowed me to view and to quote from its files.

Helpful, too, was Nicholas Robinson, who played a leading role in the campaign to save for Ireland some of the books put on sale at Sotheby's, in 1972, and who permitted me to read certain papers in the possession of himself and Mary Robinson. Another of those deeply involved in the controversy was the late T.P. O'Neill, an historian. His widow, Marie O'Neill, was of assistance to me. Both Roger Kenny and Eoin Murnaghan kindly searched for any personal papers of their late fathers, judges John Kenny and George Murnaghan, that might be relevant to the story told below, although none were found by them. James Feisenberger of Surrey provided a photograph of his late father, Hellmut, who visited King's Inns on behalf of Sotheby's. Aidan Clarke has allowed me to reproduce a satirical poem that Austin, his father, then wrote. Mary Pollard has given her permission for the inclusion of special verses that she composed about the affair. Chief Justice Ronan Keane shared some reminiscences.

In the course of my research, I was pleased to discover a portrait of Christopher Robinson, which was painted in 1750 by Benjamin Wilson, a renowned English artist. Robinson later became a judge, and his books formed the nucleus of the new King's Inns Library when they were purchased by the benchers after his death. The portrait, hitherto generally unknown in Ireland, is believed to be the only extant image of Robinson. I am indebted to Erika Ingham of the National Portrait Gallery, London, for directing me from her files to Temple Newsam House, Leeds, where the portrait of Robinson has hung since 1951. The staff of Temple Newsam House generously cleaned and photographed it, so that the painting might be reproduced as the frontispiece of this volume. The curator of Temple Newsam House, James Lomax, provided information about the portrait and its provenance. Wilson visited Dublin in 1750, when he also painted Robinson's father.[1]

It proved possible, too, to locate a portrait of the woman in whose honour, it is said, Henrietta Street, Dublin, was named. At the top of that historic street today stands King's Inns Library. Henrietta Somerset (1690–1726), wife of the second duke of Grafton, lord lieutenant of Ireland, 1724–27, died in childbirth. Her portrait, by Enoch Seeman, still hangs with one of her husband in a room at Euston Hall, Suffolk, home of the present duke of Grafton. I am grateful to Melanie Blake of the Courtauld Institute of Art, London, for furnishing me with a photograph of Henrietta's portrait, and to the duke of Grafton for his permission to reproduce it below. I know of no other image of Henrietta, and believe that this is the first publication to include Seeman's painting of her.

A fine drawing of an unnamed man with book, by the Dublin artist, Francis Robert West (*c*.1749-1809), is reproduced courtesy of the Pierpoint Morgan Library, New York. The Irish Architectural Archive and King's Inns have provided me with photographs of King's Inns Library and of the present librarians, respectively, by David Davison. David Evans kindly gave me permission to reproduce his depiction of the interior of the reading room, which has been included recently by the benchers in their short series of prints and which features here in colour on the back of the dust jacket. I wish to thank the *Irish Times* for its picture of Nicholas Robinson and Noel Jameson at Dublin Airport, by Eddie Kelly, and that of Maura Neylon and Christine Lysaght at King's Inns Library, by Peter Thursfield. Kennys Bookshops and Art Galleries Ltd., Galway, have allowed me to reproduce the photograph of T.P. O'Neill, while the board of Trinity College Dublin granted permission for the publication of that of Mary Pollard and Mary Robinson. University College Galway provided photographs of books that are now its library, but that formerly belonged to the benchers.

1 Strickland, *Dictionary of Irish artists*, ii, 544.

Among the archivists, curators and librarians who have helped me were those of the Advocates' Library, Edinburgh; Bray Public Library, Co. Wicklow; Chester Beatty Library; Dublin City University; Irish Architectural Archive; King's Inns; Marsh's Library; National Archives; National Gallery of Ireland; National Library of Ireland; National Photographic Archive, Dublin; National University of Ireland, Galway; National University of Ireland, Maynooth; Queen's University of Belfast; Royal Irish Academy; Signet Library, Edinburgh; Trinity College Dublin; University College Cork; University College Dublin; University of Ulster, Coleraine.

Once again, in the course of my research, I have found W.N. Osborough, the professor of legal history at University College Dublin and a founding member of the Irish Legal History Society, to be a source of inspiration and assistance. As usual too, my wife Catherine Curran and ours sons, Oisín, Conor and Samuel, have been very supportive and understanding.

CHAPTER ONE

'A memorable series of sales'

DURING 1972 A SERIES of highly controversial auctions took place in London. The society of King's Inns, Dublin, sold at Sotheby's thousands of books of literary, scientific, religious and ethnographic interest, as well as many rare maps. The sale was criticised as the 'random dispersal of an irreplaceable collection' and it raises vital questions about the proper care of libraries, about the relationship of general knowledge to professional expertise and about the problematic nature of Irish identity in a post-colonial era. Sotheby's had promised King's Inns 'a memorable series of sales', and that is certainly what occurred, albeit not for the reasons anticipated.

King's Inns is the association of judges and barristers which governs admission to the degree of barrister-at-law in the Republic of Ireland. Since 1850 the 'benchers', or ruling council of the society, have also provided courses of education and training for law students. While the society in 1972 was roundly condemned by bibliophiles and academics for selling books from one of Ireland's oldest libraries, it may be noted that the Irish government was informed in advance of the intended auctions and failed to intervene or to express concern. Other Irish libraries were so poorly funded that they were powerless to purchase the collection, and were at first slow even to comment on its cultural value to Ireland. The sale itself was represented by the benchers as a modernising initiative, allowing them to get rid of certain books which they believed to be seldom or never read and of no obvious interest to Ireland so that they might repair their premises and improve their service to the legal profession. As Ireland prepared to join the European Economic Community, it was a time for looking to the future. Elsewhere in Dublin substantial damage was inflicted on the architectural heritage of the city as the state emerged from a period of poverty, and its newly enriched entrepreneurs pulled down Georgian and Victorian buildings to make way for shiny office blocks such as had risen in other countries. Many citizens associated certain aspects of Ireland's heritage with English or 'protestant' oppression and were emotionally indifferent to its fate. However, before long, an increasingly prosperous state would develop a more nuanced appreciation of its past, and the very controversy which developed when the benchers sent their books to London was itself an indication of the evolution of that more sophisticated awareness. One sign of the changing times was the fact that there were three women in the small band of protestors who actively opposed the sale, while all of those promoting it were men.

The manner in which the benchers set about disposing of part of their collection was not best calculated to win friends and influence people. No attempt was made to compile a full list of the books prior to their removal from King's Inns to England. The benchers were accused of breaking Irish law by exporting certain old volumes without a licence. They had deemed the sale necessary because King's Inns was drifting into ever greater debt, notwithstanding an earlier grant by the government of funds intended to meet their needs. The debt arose partly from a refurbishment of their kitchen, where dinners are prepared for lawyers and for students, the latter being obliged to eat in the society's dining-hall before qualifying for practice at the Irish bar. The benchers chose to auction off their books rather than seeking more money from members of the legal profession, or increasing considerably the fees which students of the society were obliged to pay, and they failed to explain clearly to the public their reasons for doing so. The chief architect of the sale was George Murnaghan, chairman of the benchers' Standing Committee and a judge of the High Court whose manner was formidable. However, Murnaghan undoubtedly had a mandate from his colleagues, even if some were less enthusiastic than others about the decision to meet their debts by means of a sale of books. In executing their decision, the benchers were discreetly advised and encouraged by Dr Richard Hayes, then curator of the Chester Beatty Library and formerly director of the National Library of Ireland.

Taoiseach Jack Lynch was invited by King's Inns to take whatever steps might be necessary to keep the books in Ireland but, busy attending to the inflamed circumstances of Northern Ireland in 1971 and 1972, the prime minister of the republic found no time to interest himself deeply in the matter. One of his junior ministers mistakenly informed Dáil Éireann that no works of any special interest to Ireland had been included in the auctions. The sales were resisted most notably by An Taisce, the National Trust for Ireland, as well as by a small number of academics, librarians, journalists and politicians. Amongst those involved in the controversy which erupted were two future presidents of Ireland (Ó Dálaigh and Robinson), five sometime taoisigh (Costello, Lynch, Cosgrave, Haughey and Bruton), a future European commissioner (O'Kennedy) and an English lord (John Kerr). Campaigners prevented some valuable books from being lost to Ireland, mainly by raising money to acquire them for Irish libraries. All of the other volumes sent to London were auctioned off by Sotheby's.

During 1972 a total of almost 7,000 volumes, some being parts of annual series or of other multi-volume works, were sold by King's Inns in approximately 1,450 lots, comprising between 2,700 and 2,800 titles. At least twenty of the books were published before 1501 and were, for that reason, known as 'incunables' (or, in the Latin form sometimes used, 'incunabula'). Many others were printed prior to 1800. The single most valuable book sold by the benchers in London was a first printed edition of Augustine's *Confessiones*, for which they might well have earned at open auction a sum in excess of £10,000, that being equivalent in purchasing power to approximately IR£86,000, or €109,000, at the start of 2002. However, they eventually permitted An Taisce to buy the Augustine volume for a lesser sum and it was saved for Ireland. The appendices below give readers some idea of the richness of the collection in King's Inns Library, and indicate which of the volumes put on sale were of the greatest importance in the opinion of that small number of protestors who objected to the sale. In Chapter Thirteen below, the present author also discusses some of the titles sold which received little publicity but which are notable for other reasons. It is intended that such lists and references prompt an awareness of the value and range of works that still remain in the library, rather than merely serve as a memorial roll of honour. For, by no means were all of the benchers' best or non-law books sold.

The row that erupted in 1972 was not the first 'battle of the books' in Ireland. Appropriately, given the benefits which successive Copyright Acts have brought to King's Inns in enriching its library, one of the earliest Irish disputes that is known to have arisen over the control of books involved the formal adjudication of a matter of intellectual property. Central to that dispute of the sixth century was what is believed to have been the first copy of

St Jerome's psalter to reach Ireland. It was in the care of Finnian of Moville, at whose great school Columcille (also known as Columba), the future saint of Iona, had spent a number of years. The younger man loved books so much that he surreptitiously borrowed the psalter to make a copy of it for himself. Finnian laid claim to the transcript, but Columcille refused to give it up. Judgment was delivered by the king, who found against Columcille. 'To every cow her calf', said that judge famously, 'and to every book its son-book.' In 1972, among the volumes that King's Inns sold at Sotheby's, were a number of old psalters, or books of psalms.

The work of monks in illuminating and caring for great books is generally regarded by Irish people as one of the distinctive features of a golden age of learning, brought to a brutal and shameful end partly by the Vikings. From the close of the eighth century, these fierce warriors swept down on 'the island of saints and scholars', raiding monasteries and burning manuscripts that they did not steal to bring home. Some of their booty later enriched libraries in other parts of Europe. The tale of foreign intrusion and native loss has been kept alive in Irish schools and provides a conscious or unconscious reference point whenever books are taken from Ireland, against the wishes of Irish scholars, to be distributed abroad for the benefit of others. That a privileged class or profession in Ireland may benefit financially from such exportation is unlikely to discourage objections to it.

One thousand years after Columcille's clash with Finnian, Jonathan Swift wielded his pen in another notable dispute. This was between those intellectuals who believed that works of classical learning were generally superior to the works of modern authors, and those who did not. Swift, whose nominal father had been the steward of King's Inns, turned his attention to the disagreement in an essay entitled *The battle of the books*. His satire took the form of an account of books, written by famous authors, clashing in the Royal Library at St James's Palace, when someone was so careless as to slap the works of Descartes next to Aristotle and when poor Plato got inadvertently lodged next to Hobbes. At one point, in Swift's essay, both sides halt to listen to a quarrel between a resident spider and an errant bee. The bee had entered the library through a broken pane of glass and boasted a view of the world which purported to be more universal than that of the weaver of webs. Readers may find an echo of their quarrel below, in statements made by persons who argued over the sale of certain non-law books by King's Inns in 1972. However, I will leave it to others to cast parties to that clash in the respective roles of spider and bee. One may note, with some amusement, that while Hippocrates and Descartes were on opposite sides in Swift's battle of the books, both authors found themselves in the same van on the journey from King's Inns Library to Sotheby's.

Although, in 1976, the benchers again contemplated selling certain books, they quickly dropped the idea when it became clear that such an auction might be even more controversial than the sales of 1972. Yet, King's Inns Library is not necessarily the best place for any such unwanted volumes to be kept, and it may be in the interests of the public and of scholars to move at least some of them to other libraries which would welcome them. Any possible loss to the benchers in terms of a depreciation on the notional sale value of their collection might be offset by savings in necessary upkeep and the freeing of space for new law titles. A punitive attitude which insists that the benchers simply keep all of their volumes, including those perceived by lawyers to be of little or no relevance to professional training or practice, tends towards the reification of heritage and fails to ensure the preservation of particularly valuable volumes in the best possible condition. However, in advance of any relocation it would be desirable to make available to interested parties a satisfactory catalogue of the entire King's Inns collection and to avoid the errors and misunderstandings which occurred in 1972. How this might best be achieved will be considered later.

Moreover, before turning to the controversial sales themselves, it is useful to understand the context in which they took place. This requires a brief review of the history of King's Inns Library, as well as some examination of the significance of the copyright privilege which the society once enjoyed. There follows a tale that includes reference to drunkenness, arson and neglect, but also to patriotism, professionalisation and a love of learning. It serves to remind us of the necessity of policies intended to safeguard, for the future, valuable collections of books and manuscripts.

CHAPTER TWO

Christopher Robinson and the foundation of King's Inns Library

THE SOCIETY OF KING'S INNS is one of Ireland's oldest institutions. Its present home was designed over 200 years ago by that great architect, James Gandon, and is set in plain and peaceful gardens at Constitution Hill, on the north side of Dublin. King's Inns shares its building with the Registry of Deeds, which occupies a wing originally intended to house the lawyers' books but subsequently used for other purposes. There is no evidence that the benchers had ever kept a library at their first and former home on the northern bank of the River Liffey, which premises became ruinous and were abandoned in the middle of the eighteenth century. King's Inns had been founded in 1541, but for over three hundred years the society appears not to have provided courses of study or legal education of any kind and to have lacked law books of its own. It functioned principally as a meeting place for busy practitioners and as a mechanism for supervising admissions to legal practice in Ireland. In that respect it was inferior to the English inns, for between 1542 and 1885 the law required any Irishman wishing to become a counsellor in Ireland first to attend also an inn of court in London. In the late eighteenth century, having allowed the government to occupy their lands by the Liffey for the purposes of erecting new courts and a records office, the benchers began to consider where they might construct new premises for the society of King's Inns.[1]

Even before they had selected a suitable location for their intended buildings, the benchers took steps to acquire books for a

1 Kenny, *King's Inns, passim*; ibid., pp. 167–8 for Sir Patrick Dun. Until his death, in 1713, Dun, an eminent physician, maintained a famous library at his house, which stood between King's Inns dining–hall and the River Liffey, on ground sublet from a tenant of the benchers. From 1717, this library was used by members of the Royal College of Physicians and became the basis for their permanent collection (Wheeler, 'Libraries in Ireland before 1855', 110).

6

new library. At a meeting on 29 January 1788, they were informed that a committee which they had asked to 'inspect and look into the library of the books of the late Mr Justice [Christopher] Robinson [of the court of King's Bench]' was of the opinion that, 'the law part of the said library, and such parts thereof as have been particularly viewed, selected and chosen by them are worthy of the attention of the society for the time being, so soon as a library or proper room can be provided by the society for that purpose'. It was immediately agreed to purchase the books which had been viewed and to have these, until such time as a proper space became available, 'carefully ... packed up in strong boxes and deposited in the large record room or depository, a part of or near the rolls office in the new buildings or offices provided for the preservation of the public records', adjacent to the site of the present Four Courts. The benchers may have been influenced in their decision to pro- ceed by their knowledge that the Royal College of Surgeons in Dublin had established a library at the time of its foundation in 1784, and had purchased its first books as recently as 1787. There was also the fact that the Scottish legal profession enjoyed an outstanding legal and general library, founded at Edinburgh in 1682 by the Faculty of Advocates. The importance of the benchers' acquisition of Robinson's collection, in terms of its cultural and professional symbolism, is marked by the unusual fact that the relevant order was signed by the chancellor, ten judges, the attorney general, the third serjeant and fifteen king's counsel. The most senior of these king's counsel was George Hart, who subsequently became the society's first known and salaried librarian. Of the purchase of Robinson's books it has been said by W.N. Osborough that, 'a gesture designed, in part, to relieve the distress visited upon Robinson's widow thus secured for the benchers of the inns a collection of outstanding interest which reflected Robinson's wide reading and deserved reputation amongst his peers for historical erudition'.[2]

By 1790, a ground-plan had been drawn for King's Inns which shows that a library, dining-hall and council chamber were then intended to be located for the use of the society immediately

2 Admissions of Benchers, 1741–92 (King's Inns MS), pp. 177–8; Benchers' minute book (King's Inns MS, hereafter BMB), 1792–1803, ff. 25, 30v; Wheeler, 'Libraries in Ireland', 109; Osborough, 'In praise of law books', 35. Robinson's manuscripts, which Osborough describes as 'a major source of enlightenment on facets of eighteenth century Irish law', were not bought by the benchers. They are in the Gilbert Library of Dublin Corporation.

behind the new Four Courts and on or adjacent to a portion of
the society's old site. In 1792, in order to reconstitute their society,
the benchers secured a royal charter extending their authority over
the profession and empowering them 'to promote the study of the
science of the law'. The charter allowed the society, among other
entitlements, to 'make, have and use a common seal'. The seal which
the benchers then adopted, and continued to use even after the
charter was later revoked, had as its centrepiece an open book with
the motto '*nolumus mutari*' inscribed on its pages. An open book is an
obvious emblem for institutions dedicated to learning and is found,
for example, in the seals of the universities of Dublin, Oxford and
Harvard. Upon receipt of their charter, the benchers also drafted
ambitious bye-laws which would have provided Ireland with a system
of legal education at least as florid and extensive as that which the
English inns of court had provided in their heyday. Because of
opposition from within the legal profession to the benchers'
increased powers, that charter was revoked and the elaborate bye-
laws lapsed. One of the draft bye-laws indicates that the benchers
were particularly concerned about the preservation and good order
of their new collection of books, and that they were committed to
maintaining an excellent catalogue of their collection and to opening
a library as soon as possible. There is nothing to suggest that this
particular bye-law was controversial. It stated,

That the librarian shall be elected by the benchers who shall choose for that
office one who is fond of home, given to study and a lover of books, and
when elected, he shall continue in office until further order. He alone shall
keep the keys of the library ... He shall take care that the books are properly
and scientifically arranged, that a proper catalogue be made, and all books
entered therein immediately upon their being received into the library, and
shall cause a duplicate of the said catalogue to be made and lodged in the
treasury of the society; and shall keep the said duplicate compleat [*sic*]. That
once in every year the books shall be all taken from their places, carefully
wiped, dusted and immediately returned ... And that no person shall be
suffered to walk idly about the library, but that as soon as he has obtained
the book he wants, he shall sit down and read in silence, and having finished
his study he shall return the book in its proper place.[3]

3 Plan of courts and society's [proposed] buildings, 1790 (King's Inns MS). This
   plan is unsigned but may be attributed to Gandon (Duhigg, *King's Inns*, p. 511);
   Draft of bye-laws, 1792 (King's Inns MS), pp. 22–4 (no. vii); *Saunders's Newsletter*,
   14 June 1798. The words '*nolumus mutari*' are ambiguous and may have been
   intended to mean 'we do not wish to change' or 'we do not wish to be changed'.
   They echo the declaration of the English barons, in 1236, '*nolumus leges Angliae
   mutari*' (see Kenny, *King's Inns*, pp. 243–5).

Although their draft bye-laws were superseded by a set of simpler rules, the benchers pressed on with their plans for a library and, by January 1792, had appointed George Hart as the society's librarian. That same month, having for reasons that are not known abandoned the plan to build behind the Four Courts, they decided to rent the indoor tennis court in Townsend Street 'and fit the same up for a temporary hall and library'. Then, they turned their attention to finding a permanent home. Shortly afterwards, they identified a site at Galway's Walk on the south side of the Liffey, bounded by James's Street and Watling Street, as the most proper location 'for erecting a dining-hall, library, chapel and inns of court for the accommodation of such members of the society as shall choose to reside therein'. It was decided too that the librarian would be allowed £50 yearly to provide one or more persons as may be necessary 'for cleaning and placing the books and attending him in the library'. On 14 December 1792 the carriage of books to the room prepared in Townsend Street for the temporary library was recorded. Hart, the society's librarian, died the following year and, on 21 November 1793, was succeeded in that position by Stephen Dickson, another bencher, who was permitted to appoint as his deputy one Bartholomew Duhigg. Dickson was asked to prepare a list of such titles as were most wanted in the library and was given money to purchase books. On the same day as Dickson was appointed librarian, the benchers selected for their new permanent premises a site on Constitution Hill, instead of that previously chosen at Galway's Walk across the Liffey. In the summer of 1794, at their temporary library in Townsend Street, they discussed a plan and elevation of their proposed new dining-hall and library, apparently drawn up by the society's own treasurer. However, it was James Gandon who designed the premises that they actually built at Constitution Hill. In architectural style these premises were intended to reflect the current social ambitions of the benchers' own class. The Irish parliament, albeit exclusively protestant, was increasingly showing signs of independence and the fabric of the city of Dublin was being greatly enhanced by architects such as Gandon. First, the benchers erected at Constitution Hill another temporary library and dining-hall, this being ready in time for commons to commence on 14 June 1798. Then, on 1 August 1800, Lord Chancellor John Fitzgibbon laid the foundation stone of the present King's Inns building. The following year, the benchers published a catalogue of their books which shows that the society possessed about 3,100 titles. A reading of this catalogue alongside that prepared earlier for the sale of Robinson's library of 2,746 titles suggests that the bulk of the King's Inns collection had come from the latter source, although the benchers had also acquired other works in the interim.[4]

Subsequent to their appointments as librarian and deputy librarian, respectively, Dickson and Duhigg fell out. The former accused the latter of neglect and disobedience in failing to attend 'at the society's public library at the days and time prescribed', and in other matters. He accused Duhigg of lending the keys to persons not responsible for any injury or embezzlement which might occur thereby. On 14 February 1801 the benchers opted for a diplomatic solution to the dispute, blaming themselves for any ambiguity in the relationship between a librarian and deputy librarian, and re-appointing Dickson and Duhigg as senior librarian and junior librarian, respectively.[5]

The building work at Constitution Hill proceeded very slowly. Unfortunately for the benchers, the structure which James Gandon designed and which they intended for the sole use of their society came to be shared upon completion. The north wing was built first, with more than six years passing before the dining-hall was ready for use. In 1811, the temporary library building at Constitution Hill was taken down and its materials sold. With little sign of further progress, the government subsequently decided to intervene and provided funds to complete the entire building. However, this was only after the benchers ceded ownership of the south wing, which was wanted by the state both for the storage of public records and deeds and for the use of the Prerogative Court. Between 1811 and 1832, the society was reduced to storing its

4 Admission of benchers, 1741–92 (King's Inns MS), p.189; Treasurers' account book, 1789–1803, 'A' (King's Inns MS), ff. 13, 16–20, 22, 26; Treasurers' account book, 1797–1802, 'K' (King's Inns MS), ff. 13, 14; BMB, 1792–1803, ff. 1–2, 7, 20v, 21v, 25, 28, 30v-31, 33, 33v, 34v, 36v, 42v, 47–47v, 149, 163. The date of Hart's appointment is not recorded, but receipts for payments made to him from January 1792 onwards survive. His only known purchase was an unidentified work in three volumes, by William Prynne (Receipt Book, 1781–99 (King's Inns MS), *passim*, unpaginated); on 3 February 1794, when Duhigg was appointed deputy librarian, Henry Watts was appointed bookseller to the society. Duhigg claimed to have prepared the catalogue published in 1801.
5 BMB, 1792–1803, ff. 171–3. Duhigg may also have defaced some of the society's records that suggested a version of the society's history inconsistent with that related by him in his *History of the King's Inns* (Kenny, 'Counsellor Duhigg, antiquarian and activist', 318–20).

A

CATALOGUE

OF THE

LIBRARY

BELONGING TO

The Honourable Society of King's Inns, Dublin;

To Trinity Term 1801.

DUBLIN:

PRINTED BY R. E. MERCIER, NO. 31, ANGLESEA-STREET, BOOKSELLER, PRINTER, AND STATIONER TO THE SOCIETY.

1801.

Title-page of the first catalogue of King's Inns Library, 1801. Probably compiled by Bartholomew Duhigg, deputy librarian.

books in the present 'Benchers' Council Room', above the vestibule of the dining-hall, an arrangement which was wholly unsatisfactory.[6] In 1822, a committee of the benchers reported that,

Upon the subject of the library and the inadequacy of the present temporary room to afford the necessary accommodation, the committee have ascertained that there are large parcels of miscellaneous books upon the floor, and heaped on each other for want of room; and therefore there cannot be any useful arrangement, or a general catalogue made, without considerably further accommodation.

Although the committee recommended that the society should proceed 'without delay to erect a building suitable to so important an object', another ten years were to pass before the proposed 'further accommodation' was ready to welcome readers. In 1832, the benchers completed the fitting out of their present library at the top of Henrietta Street, behind the Registry of Deeds, and the society's books were removed to it from the crammed room above the vestibule of the nearby dining-hall. After four decades of temporary arrangements, and for the first time in its long history, the society of King's Inns now had a permanent library building.[7]

Between 1794 and 1813 Bartholomew Duhigg, the junior librarian, had acquired many pamphlets for King's Inns and these came to form the basis of the society's present substantial collection of such tracts. In 1806, the year in which his *History of the King's Inns* was published, he noted that 'considerable additions' had been made to the library since its inception in 1788, but added that King's Inns 'cannot, however, boast of many scarce or valuable books'. Duhigg died in 1813, and Dickson retired in 1815. From 1815 until 1851 Henry Joseph Monck Mason (1778–1858), barrister and writer, served the society as its librarian. The sometime Examiner of the Prerogative Court, Monck Mason is said to have been mainly instrumental in the establishment of a professorship of

6 BMB, 1792–1803, f. 180v, f. 200; Caterer's account book (King's Inns MS), Michaelmas term 1811, unpaginated; Sale by auction of building material (King's Inns MS); Kenny, *King's Inns*, p. 265; Warburton, Whitelaw and Walsh, *Dublin*, p. 1019; Wright, *Dublin*, p. 293. Final decoration of the dining-hall and western façade, by Edward Smyth, appears to have followed only upon completion of both wings.
7 BMB, 1804–19, f. 104, and ff. 130–2 for 'Report of the Standing Committee, June 1822', which also responds to a petition from some barristers that the library room at King's Inns stay open longer hours, by recommending that it be accessible between 9.00 a.m. and 5.00 p.m.

Irish at Trinity College Dublin. The collection of Irish manuscripts in the library of King's Inns may owe its origin to him. In the library's 'department of Irish literature' Monck Mason's 'patriotism and special predilections' were said to have been particularly manifested: 'one of the traditions in King's Inns Library is that he was extremely scrupulous about recommending the taking in of any work which was infidel or immoral in tendency, however popular or instructive it might otherwise be.' His main purpose in promoting the study of Irish appears to have been to see it used as a means of persuading people to abandon their native tongue, to learn English and to become protestants.[8]

From early in the nineteenth century, there was also a small but growing law library at the Four Courts. In 1818, the benchers agreed to pay Valentine Delany £30 yearly, 'as a salary for his trouble in supplying the courts with the books'. Delaney described himself as 'the librarian to said Law Library'. His salary may be compared to the £200 yearly that Monck Mason then received at King's Inns. In 1832, as the new library at King's Inns opened its doors to readers, the committee of the Law Library at the Four Courts petitioned the benchers to allocate part of their funds 'in paying for the erection of a more suitable and healthful place of accommodation' for the Law Library itself. This committee noted 'the great inconvenience felt by the subscribers from the small and inconvenient size of the reading room and the state of the atmosphere from the number who attend'. It may be observed that cholera was prevalent in Dublin that year, making some barristers reluctant even to dine at King's Inns.[9]

8 From April 1814, Monck Mason had served as junior librarian under Dickson. When promoted, the former was given a salary twice that paid previously to Dickson (BMB, 1804–19, ff. 83, 88–90); *DNB*, xxxvi, 423–4; Canon O'Hanlon, 'Life of the author', in Monck Mason, *Essay*, pp. 16–17; de Brún, *Irish manuscripts in King's Inns*, p. viii. The library of the Faculty of Advocates in Edinburgh had earlier amassed a fine collection of Scots Gaelic manuscripts (St Clair and Craik, *The Advocates' Library*, pp. 27–9); Inis Cealtra, 'The proselytisers and Irish', 108–13.
9 BMB, 1804–19, f. 103 (8 April 1818); BMB, 1830–35, pp. 63–4 (26 May 1832); Hogan, *Legal profession*, pp. 55–6.

CHAPTER THREE

'Anxious to increase': 1832–1892

IT WAS DURING MONCK MASON'S term of office as librarian that the society, as indicated above, built its present library. This stands at the top of Henrietta Street, just behind the inns itself. Henrietta Street was laid out in the 1720s by Luke Gardiner, and is thought to have been named in honour of the wife of the duke of Grafton, lord lieutenant from 1724 to 1727. To make way for their library, the benchers demolished the oldest house on the street. This had served as the Dublin residence of Hugh Boulter (1672–1742) and later Church of Ireland archbishops. Hence, for a while, the street became known also as 'Primate's Hill'. More recently, the large house had been 'for many years occupied as the Prerogative Office, and was suffered to go very much out of repair. And after the office was removed to the King's Inns the said house and premises became nearly a ruin'. In 1859, Littledale wrote that the site was chosen by the society because it stood exactly opposite the residence of a judge and bencher, who was very displeased at a proposal that the large house be converted into a mendicity institute. However, the location was also close to the dining-hall, and the benchers wished to keep their open ground in front of the new King's Inns free for the construction of chambers. It was said that, in digging the foundation of the new library, workmen came upon a brick-vaulted wine-cellar with old bottles of wine still in it, but that the wine had turned to water. They found, too, a chest containing 124 guineas.[1]

The construction of King's Inns Library was commenced in 1826 and its furnishing completed in 1832. Designed in Greek Revival

---

1 Duhigg, *King's Inns*, p. 323; Purchase of library premises: opinion of Francis Blackburne (King's Inns MS), pp. 6–7 (who states that, when the Prerogative Office moved out, the landlord conveyed the old house to a pauper in order to avoid property tax); Wright, *Dublin*, pp. 293–4; Littledale, *King's Inns*, p. 27; *Ir. Times*, 30 Aug. 1886; Anon. (1), 'Henrietta Street'; Anon. (2), 'Henrietta Street'; *Georgian Society records of domestic architecture*, ii, 12–13, where it is noted that Archbishop George Stone was laid in state in the house; O'Mahony, 'Some Henrietta Street residents', 15–16. For the chambers never built see 'King's Inns and Queen's Inns Chambers', in Kenny, *Tristram Kennedy*, pp. 218–35.

style by the architect Frederick Darley, it has been described by Maurice Craig as 'bleak and uninspired'. Others find that 'the interior of the library is very handsome with remarkable cast-iron tables especially created for it', and that 'the lay-out has functional merits'.[2]

During the early 1840s, King's Inns Library opened daily from 7.00 a.m. to 6.00 p.m. between April and October (except August, when it remained closed), and from 8.00 a.m. to 6.00 p.m. for the rest of the year. By 1849 it was opening only from 9.00 a.m. to 6.00 p.m., the latter being the hour of dinner at King's Inns. It was little used before 10.00 a.m., yet several barristers, law students and solicitors petitioned to have it remain open every day from 7.00 a.m. to 10.00 p.m., as they had 'experienced the inconvenience of not having the library accessible during the hours in the day at which professional men could attend to it'. However, the Library Committee discovered that the library of King's Inns was already open far longer every day than the libraries of the inns of court in London and that of the Faculty of Advocates in Edinburgh. The benchers rejected the petition. One particular concern of theirs was the danger of fire from the flames used for illumination at that time.[3]

Monck Mason and his family were allowed living quarters on the ground floor of the new library building, a concession which had its complications:

2 Craig, *Dublin*, p. 298; O'Brien and Guinness, *Dublin*, p. 187; King's Inns grant, etc., 1957–59 (National Archives) at the memorandum for government, 26 November 1958, p. 5. In 1824, the benchers ordered their treasurer to advertise for proposals for building the intended library conforming with the plans drawn by Frederick Darley. By late 1831 the librarian was in a position to proceed with shelving and, in April 1832, was given leave to move the books from the room over the vestibule of the dining-hall, to classify them and to print a catalogue whenever they might be arranged for the use of the profession. In May 1832, he was granted permission to provide furniture and a clock, and to acquire 15 tables, including those two large circular tables 'from Mr Mallet' which remain such a striking feature of the reading-room. Soon afterwards, the stained-glass window on the library stairs was completed, each bencher individually contributing three guineas for his coat of arms to be included in it (Library construction, contracts, accounts, etc., 1822–35 (King's Inns MSS)); BMB, 1819–30, pp. 97, 138, 146; BMB, 1830–35, pp. 21, 44–5, 58–9, 60, 65, 71, 135–6, 171). The Faculty of Advocates in Edinburgh also opened its present library premises in the 1830s.
3 In 1852, the benchers decided that, henceforth, between 1 September and 1 March the library need not open until 10 a.m., it appearing that the average number of readers before that hour was not more than one (BMB, 1835–44,

for finding that Henry Monck Mason, their former librarian, about forty years ago, then dwelling in the library, had some very fine girls for daughters, they thought their beauty troubled the studies of the young barristers, and for the future (after his demise) they required the librarians to dwell in the adjacent house, taken by them for that purpose.[4]

About 1890 Monck Mason was described to Canon O'Hanlon, by a person who remembered him, 'as wearing a velvet cap, and as frequently pacing around the stalls in soft slippers and with noise-less tread, intent upon some literary quest'. O'Hanlon paints a rosy picture of Monck Mason's commitment to the library. However, the latter's relationship with his employer was, at times, somewhat fraught. This may have been due, to some extent, to a want of tact on his part, but the benchers also suspected that he neglected his duties in favour of other interests. When, in 1848, he announced his intention of retiring, members of the library committee complained to the bench that,

They have themselves been obliged to perform for years duties properly within the province of the librarian and to devote in their discharge much time, labour and research to their own great inconvenience in many respects, a sacrifice too great to be imposed upon, or to be expected from any of your committee.[5]

On one occasion, this committee visited their library and found in attendance a Mr Langrishe, who was a friend of Monck Mason and who told the benchers that Monck Mason 'was then at Rome for the benefit of his health' and was not expected back for about two months. The committee passed over this state of affairs with-out official comment, but vented their spleen on the library porter,

---

p. 215 (14 June 1843); BMB, 1844–49, pp. 103–5; BMB, 1849–56, p. 102; *Return on public libraries*, p. 22; *Select committee on legal education*, p. x, q. 1048).

4 BMB, 1804–1819, ff. 83, 88–90; BMB, 1830–35, pp. 4, 11; BMB, 1844–49, p. 215; BMB, 1849–56, pp. 81, 103; Anon. (2), 'Henrietta Street'. Mason was married to Anne, daughter of Sir Robert Langrishe with whom he had two sons and four daughters (*DNB* at Monck Mason). Until 1865, some private rooms continued to be set aside for his successors as librarian ('but not for a family'). These were, 'on the right hand side of the entrance hall, with three apartments, viz: – kitchen, store-room, and bedroom' (Librarian: rules for selection, 1856 (King's Inns MS)).

5 BMB, 1844–49, pp. 214–5; *DNB* says he made many enemies; O'Hanlon, at Monck Mason, *Essay*, pp. 45–6, adds that Monck Mason built at King's Inns a stable and coach-house for his horse and a 'shay' (or chaise, a type of light carriage 'which was fashionable at the period'), and on summer evenings drove home to Dargle Cottage near Bray.

recommending his removal as soon as convenient, and his replacement by 'a person of superior class in society to those who have hitherto acted in that capacity' and of 'respectable appearance and decent manners' and 'a tolerably good education'. He should also be under thirty years of age when appointed.[6]

The Library Committee recommended in 1848 that any person appointed to succeed Monck Mason should

> be a practical working man of business, willing and desirous to exert his own intelligence, knowledge and care in the daily discharge of his duties in the library and also to receive and act upon the suggestions and directions of the Library Committee in all their details and these qualifications are, in the opinion of your committee of far more importance than literary tastes or pursuits.[7]

Yet, notwithstanding the committee's complaints and the fact that Monck Mason was seventy years old and in declining health, it was thought convenient to ask him to continue for 'a short time' as librarian, and he actually stayed another three years. On 10 June 1851 John Bermingham Miller QC was appointed in his stead.[8]

In the years following the opening of the King's Inns Library its collection of books and pamphlets grew rapidly. On 10 November 1831 the benchers had ordered a catalogue to be printed as soon as the books were arranged, 'for the use of the profession'. The printed catalogue of 1801 listed 3,132 titles, while that subsequently printed in 1836 listed 10,998. By 1846, Acheson Lyle, a bencher of King's Inns and the Chief Remembrancer of Ireland, was able to tell members of parliament that the society's collection included 'almost all books' on international and constitutional law, the history of the law, or history in reference to law. He added that, 'the benchers are most anxious to increase the number, and whenever we hear that a valuable book can be found, we immediately send to endeavour to have it purchased'. That same year,

6 BMB, 1835–44, pp. 158–9, 220. Perhaps this 'Mr Langrishe' was a relative of the librarian's wife, Anne Langrishe.
7 BMB, 1844–49 p. 211; BMB, 1849–56, p. 87, where the benchers confirm this recommendation. In 1848, books stolen from the library were found on sale in the shop of a bookseller on Eden Quay (BMB, 1844–49, p. 229).
8 BMB, 1849–56, pp. 77, 87. A copy of Monck Mason's *Testimony of St Patrick against the false pretensions of Rome to primitive antiquity in Ireland* (Dublin, 1846), which in December 1850 he signed at King's Inns for F. R. Stewart, is in the National Library of Ireland (ref. J. 28282).

at the behest of the benchers, a 'juridical catalogue' of law books belonging to the society was prepared by Henry Connor and published. However, the benchers also possessed large numbers of non-law books and, on 17 June 1848, the Library Committee called for a new catalogue to be published, 'which is so much wanted because of the miscellaneous library every day becoming more extensive and valuable'. In 1849, Monck Mason estimated that the society possessed 30,938 volumes, 'besides about 400 separate pamphlets and about 150 manuscripts', and the collection was said to be second in size in Dublin only to that of Trinity College. By 1851 the benchers were once more remarking on the need for 'a full and correct catalogue to be in the library of all the books now and hereafter to be contained therein and with proper references to be annexed to such catalogue so that the said books may be conveniently had for the persons who may be entitled to have access to them'. In 1852, the space for books in the main library and gallery was 'now nearly occupied' and the use of the basement for storage was being considered. In April 1856, the benchers estimated that they owned about 42,000 volumes. They noted

that of these about 9,000 are law books and that the large remainder amounting to about 33,000 are of a miscellaneous character consisting mainly of standard works in various departments of science and general literature, and several are in Greek, Latin, French, German, Spanish, Portuguese and Italian languages.[9]

The Library Committee complained about the way in which law books were mixed up with other types of book, but were even more concerned about the subject of cataloguing, 'upon the prime importance of which, indispensable in a large library, it would be superfluous to comment'. They pointed out the inadequacy of the existing catalogues, including that published by Connor, which contained no shelf references and which had not been kept up to date, and so was of 'very limited utility'. They thought that what was immediately required 'above all things' was a complete catalogue of the miscellaneous or non-law books, that portion of the library

9 BMB, 1830–35, p. 45; BMB, 1835–44, p. 159; BMB, 1844–49, p. 215; BMB, 1849–56, pp. 76, 102, 215, 219; *Select committee on legal education*, p. 172; Connor, *Catalogue of King's Inns*; *Return on public libraries*, p. 22, where Monck Mason says that average attendance since 1843 had been about 42 persons daily; ibid., q. 2524 (Eugene Curry).

being in a 'discreditable condition'. They recalled certain earlier expressions of concern by the benchers about the deficiency of the society's catalogues, and lamented the fact that so little had been done to remedy the situation. This had resulted in, amongst other things, an accumulation of duplicate copies 'of works which ought to be disposed of by sale', and of which they estimated there to be about 2,000.[10]

Turning to the need to appoint a new librarian in place of the deceased John Miller, it was considered crucially important that,

In addition to the essential qualifications of vigour and activity of mind and body, an efficient librarian should possess a practical knowledge of the state of the book trade and of the character and value of the leading works in the departments of literature, ancient and modern English and foreign, which should be found in a complete library such as that of the King's Inns ought to be. The librarian should be able to point out the deficiencies which from time to time require to be supplied in these several departments and to advise the Library Committee as to the purchases to be made: so that the funds of which the society are trustees may be expended in the most efficient and economical manner.[11]

The benchers decided to advertise the position and to seek someone who had been trained in the skills necessary for 'the arrangement, control and management of a great library' and who possessed practical experience therein. On 13 June 1856, out of 88 persons from Ireland, Britain and beyond, who had applied for the job, the benchers chose James Haig. Haig had worked for 22 years as an assistant librarian at the Faculty of Advocates in Edinburgh. Two years after his appointment in Dublin, the benchers permitted him to publish two hundred copies of a list of the society's incunables that had been printed in England. It is ironic that, having gone to such trouble to select him, the benchers subsequently felt obliged, in 1862, to sack Haig because of complaints that he had 'been seen to enter the library in a state of intoxication' on a number of occasions. Later, they agreed to give him a reference testifying to his 'efficiency as our librarian and to the general industry, zeal and skill exhibited by him ...'[12]

10 BMB, 1849–56, pp. 219–25 for Library Committee, 'The present state of the library' (24 April 1856).
11 Ibid.
12 BMB, 1849–56, pp. 234–6; BMB, 1856–69, pp. 123–4 (23 April 1862); Librarian: rules for selection, 1856 (King's Inns MS); Library Committee

Under Haig and his successors, the collection of books continued to grow until the library was bursting at the seams, and in 1891 the then librarian, James MacIvor, informed the benchers that 'we have at present no room in the library for any more books'. He reported that it contained 'something under 60,000 volumes'. He said that approximately 4,500 books were 'now improperly stored in the library' and added, in parenthesis, an observation about the society's collection which expressed bluntly a point of view undoubtedly shared over the years by some members of the profession: 'a large proportion of these are of course *useless* books!' [his emphasis]. The benchers were informed that, 'During the last few years presses and shelves have been erected in every available spot and the library is almost entirely full from garret to basement, the books in some departments being packed rather than shelved'. This was considered both awkward for readers and the cause of injury to books. So the society decided to build the present library annex, which was commenced in June 1891 and completed by May of the following year. It was designed by James Franklin Fuller and built by a firm owned by the Beckett family, whose most famous scion in the twentieth century would be Samuel Beckett, winner of the Nobel prize for literature. Fuller also designed an interesting circular building of nine bays in four stories, for construction as a book store in the garden behind the library, but this was never executed.[13]

The location of King's Inns Library was considered inconvenient by legal practitioners, being a walk of fifteen or twenty minutes from the Four Courts, and it was most busy in the hour before dinner.

minute book (King's Inns MS, hereafter LCMB), 1861–73, pp. 18–19, 31–2; Haig, *List of books*; The English word 'incunable/s' is from a Latin plural, '*incunabula*', which literally means 'swaddling clothes', but which came to be used figuratively for childhood and then for the earliest stages in the development of anything. It is, today, particularly associated with books produced in the infancy of the art of printing (*OED*, 1901).

13 Memo of Agreement between the society and James and William Beckett, May 1891 (King's Inns MS); LCMB, 1890–1909 (unpaginated), 12 Jan. 1891, 26 Oct. 1891, 31 Oct 1892; BMB, 1885–1901, p. 170 (12 Jan. 1891), where it appears that the benchers favoured building an annex over converting the adjacent house on Henrietta Street (no. 11) into an extension; ibid., p. 185 (22 April 1891); King's Inns has two sketches of Fuller's proposed circular structure. After it became possible to enter the gallery from within the new annex, the old staircase that gave access to the gallery was taken down. This had continued the stairs that still run from outside the under-treasurer's office down to the basement. A ghostly trace of their former upper stretch is the sealed door in an external wall, to the right of the main entrance into the reading room

It is a reminder of the once compact size of Dublin that, in 1846, one bencher said that the distance from the courts to King's Inns Library was 'probably, as far as many residences of the barristers'. Increasingly, for their professional needs, barristers and judges made use of the Law Library at the Four Courts. In 1818 this was 'a very small thing indeed', confined to an octagonal room about fifteen feet across. However, by 1846 it had moved and was described by Acheson Lyle, himself a bencher, as being 'now a very handsome library, and a remarkably good one' which 'contains every work connected with the law in all its branches that can be got'. In 1897, a new Law Library was completed at the Four Courts, in which year the General Council of the Bar was constituted.[14]

Notwithstanding the fact that by 1846 King's Inns and the Law Library were each acquiring a copy of almost every new law book, the benchers did not favour a suggestion that they move their collection to the Four Courts. As Acheson Lyle explained to a committee of the House of Commons,

The subject was brought forward by Chief Justice Doherty; in consequence of seeing the splendid library [of the Faculty of Advocates] at Edinburgh, he once or twice has drawn the attention of the benchers to moving it, without making any formal proposition upon the subject; and it has been discussed; and the reason that has been assigned for not doing so, chiefly has been that there is an admirable library, containing every book almost used in the law, immediately at the Court, and that there was no necessity for bringing a second; and that if this, which is a miscellaneous library, was brought there, it might tend rather to distract the barristers' attention from the business than to fix it.[15]

For their part, in 1866, the attorneys and solicitors departed from King's Inns and developed their own library in the Solicitors' Building behind the Four Courts.

During the last decades of the nineteenth century the architectural quality and social standing of Henrietta Street declined. Until then, lawyers and law students had frequently rented rooms in houses close by King's Inns Library. Most of those houses had

14 BMB, 1804–19, f. 103; Wright, *Dublin*, p. 291; *Select committee on legal education*, pp. 171–2; *Report on public libraries*, q. 2884; Hogan, *Legal profession*, pp. 55–6. In 1846, Lyle also noted that King's Inns had spent 'a very considerable sum of money' in fitting up the new Law Library, for which the government had provided rooms at the Four Courts.
15 *Select committee on legal education*, p. 171 (Lyle). John Doherty was chief justice of the Common Pleas, 1830–1850.

come to be owned by the remarkable Tristram Kennedy, founder of the Dublin Law Institute and a major figure of influence on the development of legal education in Britain and Ireland. In 1878, Kennedy proposed that the society of King's Inns buy his and all of the other properties on Henrietta Street and, also, erect a gateway near the bottom of the hill to enclose those houses within the inns itself. Unfortunately, the benchers let pass the opportunity to create a distinct legal quarter for Dublin. Following his death in 1885, Kennedy's estate was broken up. By 1900, only three of the houses on Henrietta Street were not in tenements, and not one lawyer remained in residence. However, in 1865, the benchers had bought from Kennedy the house next to their library, and, until 1984, insisted that successive librarians live in it during their periods of employment.[16]

16 Kenny, *Tristram Kennedy*, pp. 218–35; Tristram Kennedy papers: assignment of house, 1865 (King's Inns MS); BMB, 1856–69, pp. 134, 145; BMB, 1885–1901, p.467; BMB, 1928–39, pp. 331, 340; BMB, 1939–56, pp. 152–3; Standing Committee minute book, 1960–75, pp. 234, 253. Kennedy gave King's Inns the portraits of Alexander Crookshank and Joseph Napier, which hang in the library's vestibule. The former was his uncle, and the latter a part-time lecturer at his Dublin Law Institute.

CHAPTER FOUR

Copyright and other privileges, 1801–1963

IN 1801, NOTWITHSTANDING the fact that there was then no proper library building at King's Inns, the society was included with Trinity College Dublin as one of two Irish beneficiaries of the Copyright Act passed that year. The Scottish Faculty of Advocates, as well as eight other Scottish and English libraries (but not those of the London inns of court), had enjoyed a similar privilege since 1709. Under the provisions of the 1801 Act, and specifically 'for the use of the library', the benchers of King's Inns were, thereafter, entitled to the delivery of a free copy of every new book and reprint published in the United Kingdom. Charles Abbot, chief secretary for Ireland, was instrumental in obtaining this privilege, but his intervention appears to have been at the personal instigation of Bartholomew Duhigg. Publishers resented the obligation on them to give away free copies and campaigned to restrict it. In 1814, a further Copyright Act required the eleven relevant libraries specifically to make a demand in writing if they wanted any particular books. The eleven institutions determined to protect their privileges from further erosion and, in 1816, Monck Mason of King's Inns represented the two benefiting Irish libraries at a meeting at Sion College, London, called to discuss the matter.[1]

In 1818, Warburton, Whitelaw and Walsh remarked that the room then being used by the benchers as a temporary library 'will soon be overloaded with books of all sorts', and expressed the opinion that King's Inns ought to confine itself to receiving books about law and history and that books on other subjects should be sent to libraries such as Marsh's and that of the Dublin Society,

---

1 St Clair and Craik, *The Advocates' Library*, pp. 26–7; *Stat. Parl. U.K.*, 41 Geo III (1801), c.107; *Stat. Parl. U.K.*, 54 Geo III (1814), c.156; Abbot (ed.), *Diary and correspondence of Charles Abbot, Lord Colchester*, i, 273; Kenny, 'Counsellor Duhigg', 313–4; Kinane, 'Legal deposit', 122–3. I have rejected as unlikely a suggestion that Fitzgibbon was responsible for winning the copyright privilege for King's Inns (Kenny, *King's Inns*, p. 246, n. 16).

'which have no benefit from the act'. Their opinion was ignored. However, the society experienced certain difficulties in getting hold of works to which it was entitled. In 1830, having somewhat neglected the problem until their new library on Henrietta Street was nearing completion, the benchers asked Francis Blackburne for a legal opinion on their position. He advised that they could not successfully sue under the Copyright Act because King's Inns was not a body corporate for such purposes. In 1834, they engaged the same agent that Trinity College Dublin employed, and paid him £60 to acquire books to which they were entitled.[2]

Publishers found the demand for free books oppressive and lobbied successfully for a further amendment to the law. So, under the Copyright Act 1836, King's Inns and five of the ten other libraries mentioned in earlier Acts lost their rights to books. However, they were allowed instead 'such an annual sum as may be equal in value to and a compensation for any loss which such library may sustain'. That sum was to be 'ascertained according to the value of the books which may have been actually received' and, on that basis since 1836, King's Inns has continued to receive a payment of, or equivalent to, £433. 6s. 8d. annually in compensation for the loss of its copyright privilege.[3]

In the light of subsequent developments, one notable feature of that grant of compensation is that it was conditional. Section 3 of the same Act of 1836 stipulated that the proprietors or managers of each of the qualifying libraries,

shall and they are hereby required to apply the annual compensation hereby authorised to be made in the purchase of books of literature, science and the arts, for the use of and to be kept and preserved in such library.

By accepting compensation under the terms of the Act of 1836, the benchers in effect acknowledged publicly that their library was not simply a law library, and indicated that they intended to continue to purchase works relating to literature, science and the arts.

2 Warburton, Whitelaw and Walsh, *Dublin*, p. 1019; 'Copyright Act: case for the opinion of Mr Francis Blackburne, 1830' (King's Inns MS); BMB, 1830–35, pp. 11, 136; *Select committee on legal education*, 1846, p.170.
3 *Stat. Parl. U.K.*, 6 & 7 Will IV (1836), c.110. Compensation was out of the government's consolidated fund. No institution was to be paid compensation in any year until sufficient proof was adduced that the preceding grant had been spent on the purposes specified in the Act.

This was unsurprising in that their catalogue of 1801 shows that, at the very outset, the books which the society had acquired in 1788 from the library of Christopher Robinson did not pertain exclusively to law. In 1856, as we saw above, the benchers quite explicitly asserted that theirs 'ought to be' what they called 'a complete library', namely one replete with works of literature. Between 1836 and 1911 the benchers were obliged to acquire their law stock from funds other than those received in compensation. However, in 1911, a new statutory provision permitted the compensation to be spent simply 'in the purchase of books for the use of and to be preserved in the library', thus removing the necessity for such books to be works of literature, science and the arts. Books bought with the compensation fund had still be 'preserved' in the library and could not be sold.[4]

Some people thought that the receipt of public funding imposed an obligation on King's Inns to admit the general public to its library, but the society disagreed. Its own librarian, Stephen Dickson, had indeed referred to 'the society's public library' at a time when the benchers had not yet even benefited from the passage of the Copyright Act 1801, but he appears to have used the word 'public' in an archaic sense in which it was employed by universities to refer only to eligible members of their own particular communities. Those persons actually permitted to read in the King's Inns Library were judges, barristers, attorneys, solicitors, students for the bar and (from 1848) proctors in the ecclesiastical and admiralty courts. When, in 1849, Monck Mason confirmed to a committee of the House of Commons that this was so ('The library is not open to the public generally'), its members were decidedly unimpressed. Eugene Curry, the Irish antiquarian, told the same committee, which was then investigating ways in which to extend public access to libraries in large towns, that 'it is felt to be a hardship in Dublin that it [King's Inns Library] is not open to the public'. He conceded that 'very often' persons not otherwise eligible to enter are 'allowed to consult a particular book or tract in it'. The committee reported that, in its view, the libraries of the Royal Dublin Society, of the Royal Irish Academy and of 'the Queen's Inns' (as King's Inns was occasionally known during the reigns of female sovereigns), 'all

4 Copyright Act 1911 (*Acts parl. U.K.*, 1 & 2 Geo V, c. 46, s.34). From 1843 onwards, the society has extant accounts of books purchased with the Treasury grant (King's Inns MSS M3 and M10).

receiving grants of public money, owe to the public the requital of free admission and of access in the evening'. However, the benchers did not change their policy. In contrast, the Faculty of Advocates in Edinburgh was less exclusive and the solicitor-general for Scotland told members of parliament that, 'I cannot imagine that the privilege [copyright] was intended to be given simply for use of a body of private barristers. Though the library is the property of the Advocates, practically it is the property of the public, for there is no library in Great Britain where the access given to the public generally is more liberal than in the Advocates' Library'. Robert Travers, assistant-librarian at Trinity College Dublin, engaged Monck Mason in acrimonious correspondence on the subject of public access at King's Inns. In 1859, when James Haig was librarian, Edward Edwards attacked the benchers for allegedly maintaining their library in a spirit of 'bigoted exclusion', and complained that it was administered by men who were 'wont to reply to courteous enquiries by official insolence'. Edwards's complaints were dismissed as being without foundation by W.F. Littledale, himself an attorney and critic of the benchers' management of King's Inns. In modern times, researchers and scholars have generally been granted permission to consult the society's books and manuscripts.[5]

Although, until 1866, Irish attorneys were obliged to belong to King's Inns, and although students for the bar were permitted access to King's Inns Library, the benchers were paternalistically dismissive of a request from the former to allow their apprentices the privilege of the latter. Apprentices had never been permitted to use the library. The benchers replied that, during the hours when the library was open, every apprentice ought to be employed in learning the technical and other details of his master's business:

But even assuming that some apprentices would have leisure during those hours, and disposition also, for legal study, it is to be remembered that the King's Inns library is not confined to law books – that on the contrary it now contains a great collection of miscellaneous literature, embracing not only works upon the highest subjects of human knowledge, but also numerous

5 BMB, 1792–1803, f. 171 (Feb. 1801); BMB, 1844–49, p. 103; BMB, 1849–56, p. 103; *Return on public libraries*. p. 22; *Select committee on public libraries*, p. x and p. 93; ibid., evidence, qq. 2524–2532; Casteleyn, *Literacy and libraries in Ireland*, p. 170; Edwards, *Memoirs of libraries*, ii, 68; Littledale, *King's Inns*, p. 45; King's Inns grant, etc., 1957–59 (National Archives) at the memorandum for government, 26 November 1958, p. 6; *OED* (1909) for uses of the word 'public'.

publications of an humble range which, however important and useful and instructive, are infinitely more attractive and engaging than any law book can possibly be made; and we see no sufficient grounds for concluding if the King's Inns were thrown open to apprentices that young men from sixteen to twenty or one-and-twenty would devote their limited leisure to legal study in preference to lighter and more agreeable reading. We are informed that actual experience of the classes of books most read in the King's Inns library would lead to the opposite inference.[6]

It is too shocking to contemplate what might have been the consequences for Ireland's legal profession had solicitors' apprentices been then admitted to the library of King's Inns and allowed to read some of its more 'attractive and engaging' books.

In 1922, as Ireland was being politically divided, King's Inns sent to Belfast 'many valuable' law books from the society's collection, including the penultimate editions of legal text-books in its possession. These were for use by the bar of Northern Ireland, in what was then intended to be 'a branch library of the King's Inns'.[7] That same year, there was a vivid illustration of the benefits of having more than one substantial law library in Dublin when, following the destruction of the Four Courts during the Civil War and the temporary use of King's Inns for the sittings of some courts, King's Inns Library was 'placed until further notice at the disposal of the Bar as a place of daily assembly in the same manner and under the same conditions (so far as possible) as the Law Library, Four Courts, has been hitherto used ...' Extra tables and chairs were placed along the gallery, although the Library Committee 'did not think it desirable that Barristers Bags should be brought into the library reading room'. Books could be borrowed for use before a judge, provided that the barrister borrowing them first gave a signed undertaking to return them immediately after use.[8]

The benchers of the new Irish Free State continued to be faced with the problem of making ends meet, and their fine library was

---

6 BMB, 1849–56, pp. 214–5. The benchers went on to point out that King's Inns had paid for the erection and furnishing of the Solicitors' Building at the Four Courts, and that this contained a library for solicitors to which, in 1846, the benchers had donated £500, as well as providing duplicate copies of certain 'practically useful' books. They noted that students for the Bar paid an admission fee to King's Inns, which apprentices did not. See BMB, 1844–49, p. 60 and pp. 92–4 for a list of the 45 duplicate titles.

7 BMB, 1917–28, pp. 154, 161, 168; LCMB, 1920–54, at 14 Nov. 1921; Northern Ireland Bar: transfer of books (King's Inns MS).

8 LCMB, 1920–54, at 21 April and 1 May 1922.

a significant drain on their resources. Its collection went on expanding after the completion of the annexe, but less money than necessary was spent on its maintenance and repair. Following the creation of an independent state, the Department of Finance in Dublin accepted the responsibility of paying King's Inns its fixed annual compensation for the loss of copyright privileges.[9] In 1945, the benchers' statutory obligation to spend the compensation fund on acquiring and, to a lesser extent, repairing books was altered by a short Act that allowed the expenditure of up to one half of the amount on binding. It was estimated that between 8,000 and 10,000 of the volumes in the library needed to be rebound, and the government was persuaded to grant £3,000 towards that purpose.[10] What the 1945 Act did not do was to repeal the provision that prevented King's Inns from disposing of any book that had been bought with the compensation fund. Of course, other books, which had not been delivered under the copyright privileges or which had not been purchased from compensation monies, might be sold. However, the society's method of accounting over the years made it unfeasible to determine which books had been acquired under the Acts or from the compensation fund and which had not. Thus, the society was effectively prevented from selling any of its books. Later, in a report for his fellow benchers, Judge John Kenny would refer to this problem:

As the annual sum had been lodged each year to the credit of the Society's general account and as the cost of the books purchased had been paid out of the general account, it would be almost impossible to identify the books which could be sold.[11]

In 1963, at the request of the benchers, the law was to be amended to give the society of King's Inns a clear power to sell any books. The circumstances of that change will be considered in the next chapter. Meanwhile, it is worth noting here that another statute which was also passed in 1945 was to have unpleasant, if

9 Ibid., at 29 Oct. 1923 and 14 Jan. 1924; Free State Grant to King's Inns Library (King's Inns MS).
10 King's Inns Library Act, 1945; King's Inns grant, 1945 (National Archives); *Dáil Éireann deb.*, vol. 97, cols. 1729–32 (27 June 1945). The Copyright Act 1911 was continued by the Industrial and Commercial Property (Protection) Act, 1927, s.174 (1). Before 1945, it was customary for the society to spend about £40 of the annual compensation fund on binding for the purposes of preservation.
11 BMB, 1957–64, p. 226 (11 Jan. 1962).

unanticipated, consequences for the benchers when they attempted
to avail of the benefits of that later amendment. The Documents and
Pictures (Regulation of Export) Act (no. 29) provided in section 3
that,

It shall not be lawful for any person to export any article to which the Act
applies unless such person is the holder of an export licence authorising the
export of the article and the licence is delivered at the time of export to the
proper officer of customs and excise.

The articles to which the Act was stated to apply included, under
section 2, 'any document (other than a document wholly in print)
which is over one hundred years old', and this definition might
include a book with manuscript notes or hand-coloured prints.
However, the Act was not as sweeping as at first sight it appeared,
insofar as section 4 obliged the relevant minister to grant a licence
when requested to do so. The minister was empowered to require
a particular applicant to afford the minister facilities for making
photocopies of the article prior to its export.

The benchers' financial problems were exacerbated by the fact
that the fixed amount of compensation under the Copyright Acts
was diminishing in relative value as years passed. Thus, from 1956
to 1959, for example, the annual cost of running the library was
approximately £2,500 (ordinary maintenance, salaries and the
purchase and binding of books). Against this was offset the annual
government grant of £433. 6s. 8d. payable pursuant to the terms
of the repeal of the Copyright Act 1801.[12] The society was also
spending money on administration, on certain educational courses
and on the provision of dining facilities. In the mid-twentieth
century, King's Inns was drifting ever more into debt and the outlook
for the society was bleak. Its principal sources of income were the
fees of students and benchers, and fees paid to the society for
admitting persons to the degree of barrister. Although fees were
increased, they remained inadequate for the needs of the society.

In the circumstances, it was decided to approach the government for a much larger grant than the £3,000 that the society had
earlier received towards binding books. Chief Justice Conor A.
Maguire contacted the attorney-general to request a meeting to

---

12 Factual statement in regard to the sale of certain books, by George
Murnaghan and Raymond O'Neill, Feb. 1973 (King's Inns MS, hereafter
FS), paragraphs 17–19.

discuss the society's financial difficulties with the Taoiseach, who was then John A. Costello, himself a bencher. In November 1956, Maguire sent the attorney-general a memorandum which pointed out that, in the library, 'some of the decorations have not been renewed since 1827 ... The interior generally conveys an atmosphere of depression. It should be bright and attractive, reasonably so, to secure the attention of students and readers and the barristers who must go there to consult authoritative books and reports not available elsewhere in Ireland'.[13]

The benchers intended to ask that a sum be made available to King's Inns from certain monies known as the 'funds of suitors'. These were unclaimed amounts that, for various reasons, had been paid into the courts over many years, and the full amount of which was unlikely ever to be claimed. The funds had previously, but rarely, been drawn upon by governments. On those occasions they had usually been spent for purposes connected with the legal system. At the end of the eighteenth century, they helped to pay for the new Four Courts. In 1832, a Nisi Prius court and, in 1834, the Public Record Office were constructed with their assistance. In 1894, the barristers had benefited professionally from them when a new Law Library was built at the Four Courts. Only twice were they used for a purpose unconnected with the law. That was in 1908 and 1911, when they funded 'housing of the working class'. On every occasion when some of the funds were spent, it had been necessary for the government to pass special legislation, and the benchers faced the task of convincing ministers that this was not only worth doing for the first time since the foundation of the state but also worth doing for the benefit of King's Inns.

They did not get their requested meeting until 31 July 1957, by which time the government had changed and Eamon de Valera was taoiseach. Present with de Valera were Minister for Finance James Ryan, Minister for Justice Oscar Traynor and Attorney-General Aindreas Ó Caoimh. De Valera had decided that the latter 'might be invited to attend provided his position as a bencher did not cause him any embarrassment'. Evidently, it did not.[14] Prior

13 'The King's Inns and the King's Inns Library', in King's Inns grant, etc., 1957–59 (National Archives). The memorandum was written by Judge Martin Maguire.
14 King's Inns grant, etc., 1957–59 (National Archives), for a hand-written note on a copy of a typed letter to the secretary of the Department of Justice, 26 July 1957.

to this meeting, Thomas Coyne, secretary of the Department of Justice, had presented a withering memorandum to his minister. Coyne believed that, in seeking just £20,000, the benchers had seriously underestimated their own requirements and he proposed that the government either recognise that the society of King's Inns needed more money than had been sought or relieve the benchers, entirely, 'of any responsibility for running the library':

I have no doubt at all that the benchers would be glad to be shut of the library, which is something of a white elephant. Its location is so inconvenient that it is very little frequented even by lawyers ...

Coyne thought that it was visited by no more than half a dozen people a day except during lecture terms: 'This being so, it might be suggested that the State should take over the library which contains some valuable works, but I hardly think that this arrangement is feasible at the present time, or that the Department of Finance would be likely to agree to it.'[15]

In fact, the benchers had already decided that their first estimate of their needs was too low, and at their meeting with the taoiseach the chief justice pointed out that they were now looking for £50,000. Maguire recalled that the fees of students had been twice increased and the benchers' subscription doubled. The taoiseach expressed concern that if money was granted to one vocational body, in the manner envisaged, then others might look for similar grants. A memorandum of the meeting states that,

To an inquiry by the Minister for Finance as to the possibility of securing a contribution from the profession towards the expenses of the King's Inns there was no satisfactory answer. But the drift of the discussion was to the effect that the services rendered to practitioners were limited to the provision of Commons (dinners) for which barristers had to pay, and access to the library, which was inconveniently located, and that these services were not of such practical value to the profession that any substantial contribution could be expected from it.[16]

Nevertheless, the government was persuaded to help the society. Ministers were guided by an official cabinet memorandum which pointed out, with reference to King's Inns, that 'unless it receives financial assistance it cannot keep the library open'. Indeed, by the

15 Ibid., for Coyne's memorandum, 31 July 1957.
16 Ibid., for memorandum of meeting, 31 July 1957, unsigned.

Act that was subsequently passed, the benchers were granted £70,000. That was 250 per cent more than they had originally sought, and 40 per cent more than they requested at their meeting with the taoiseach. Yet, even that amount turned out to be not enough for the society's needs, and the benchers began to turn their attention to how they might have the copyright laws amended to enable them to sell some of their books.[17]

17 Ibid., for memorandum for government, 26 November 1958, p. 4; Funds of Suitors Act, 1959, which also allowed for a grant to be made to the Abbey Theatre. During this period, Coyne and his department appear to have been generally antipathetic to the bench. One author writes of the 'rather sneering' tone of their response to representations by the judges in respect of both the establishment of new courts and the judges' use of constitutional arguments concerning their own salaries and pension rights (Ruane, 'The independence of the Irish Supreme Court', pp. 130–6).

CHAPTER FIVE

Plans for selling, 1960–1963

IN 1944, THE BENCHERS entrusted their books to the care of the society's first female librarian, Bridget Walsh (later Mrs McMenamin). Evidently, they did not subsequently invoke that term in her contract which obliged her, in the event of her marriage, to resign if requested to do so. She faced the recurring problem of maintaining an adequate catalogue of the collection, and the absence of a satisfactory catalogue made it more difficult to plan for the future. Thus, in 1957, she reported that 'the records of the holdings of the library are totally inadequate and for the specific purposes of stock-taking, non-existent'. McMenamin pointed out that the catalogues of authors were large folio volumes, 'hand-written in various styles and so over-crowded that strict alphabetical sequence is not possible', and that there was no subject catalogue. She recommended the arranging and cataloguing of the society's collection of about 10,000 pamphlets of the seventeenth to the nineteenth centuries. She added that the library shelves were over-crowded and that the selection and preparation of books for binding needed to be undertaken by a competent person. In her report of 1957, McMenamin added an observation which may indicate that some of the benchers were already thinking of selling part of the collection. She wrote that, 'a special effort needs to be made to assess the value of the many interesting books in the library'.[1]

The possibility that a sale of some kind was being contemplated is strengthened by the fact that, in May of the following year, Chief Justice Conor A. Maguire wrote to certain librarians in Dublin and drew their attention to some 'interesting books on medical subjects', owned by King's Inns and listed on an attached page. Some of those to whom he wrote interpreted his letter as an invitation to them to purchase the volumes, which was hardly

---

1 BMB, 1939–56, pp. 152–3; Report attached to typed extract from LCMB, dated 13 Nov. 1957 (in Library correspondence files (King's Inns MS)). Walsh had been assistant librarian since 1938. Her own assistant between 1945 and 1957 was T.U. Sadlier, who later jointly edited *King's Inns admissions*.

surprising given that prices were shown opposite each of the nine titles. The chief justice felt it necessary to write again, soon afterwards, to explain that 'the figure opposite each book was merely a note taken by our librarian from the list of current book prices. There was no intention to offer the books for sale. It was merely intended to make available in your library a list of books which might be of interest to research students'. It seems unlikely that such a list would have been prepared and priced unless someone at King's Inns was already, in 1958, considering the possibility of selling books.[2]

About this time Richard Hayes, director of the National Library, became particularly interested in some of the holdings of the benchers and, in October 1958, wrote to Conor Maguire,

My dear Chief Justice,

I understand that you are chairman of the Committee which directs the King's Inns Library.

There are a large number of manuscripts and rare pamphlets in that Library of great historical importance. It is essential that these sources should be catalogued and made available for research. It would probably cost about £500 to get the work done. It would be most useful to all students of Irish history if you could persuade the Government to make such a sum available in next year's estimates.

The work could best be done, I imagine, by a young graduate in history, who was also trained in cataloguing, either as part time work or as permanent employment for nine or twelve months. The National Library would be glad to advise on the technical side of the work and if necessary provide instruction on the cataloguing of historical source material.

If you can bring this off, it will be of great value to historians.

With all good wishes,
Yours sincerely,

(Sgd.) R.J. Hayes Director.[3]

Hayes (1902–76) was a gifted scholar who, in 1940, had become director of the National Library. He organised the finding

---

2 Chief justice to the librarians of Trinity College Dublin, University College Dublin, Marsh's Library, Central Catholic Library, Irish Central Library for Students and the Royal College of Surgeons, 20 May and 5 June 1958, with replies. He also wrote to the Royal College of Physicians. These and all other letters, unless where otherwise stated below, are from Library correspondence files, 1957–2001 (King's Inns MSS).
3 Hayes to Maguire, 20 Oct. 1958.

and copying on microfilm of documents of Irish interest scattered throughout the world, and he acquired for the National Library some great collections of manuscripts and photographs. These achievements and interests would make the terms of his later recommendation to the benchers on the sale of their books, which will be considered below, all the more remarkable. During his lifetime he compiled a number of complex, national bibliographical guides, which have proven invaluable to generations of Irish writers. At the time that he wrote to King's Inns in 1958, he was already heavily engaged in organising his monumental catalogues of Irish manuscripts and periodicals.[4]

Hayes's proposal for a catalogue of the manuscripts and pamphlets at King's Inns was greeted with enthusiasm by the chief justice and by the Library Committee. However, at a meeting of the bench, 'after considerable discussion it was agreed on a show of hands, not to ask the government for this additional sum'. The chief justice explained to Hayes that, already, 'at this moment the government are considering an application by the benchers for the sum of £50,000', and the benchers felt that it would not be justifiable to apply for a further special grant of the kind suggested. As it transpired, under the Funds of Suitors Act 1959, the government actually allowed £70,000 to King's Inns in order for the society to recoup or defray expenditure incurred in renovating its buildings and for the general purposes of the society or the maintenance of the library. Of this amount, £20,000 was immediately applied in reducing the society's overdraft, which at that time stood at almost £26,000. However, the benchers also agreed that some of the money might be used to undertake certain urgent restoration and management work in their library. In January 1960, a sub-committee chaired by the chief justice decided that this work ought to include cataloguing and indexing, as well as the proper arrangement of their many pamphlets and the 'ascertainment of valuable books and provision for their protection'.[5]

---

4 Boylan, *Dict. of Ir. Biography*, pp. 170–1; Henchy, *National Library*, pp. 17–19.
5 Maguire to Hayes, 21 Oct. and 2 Dec. 1958; LCMB, 1954–81, pp. 48–9 (10 Nov. 1958); FS, paragraphs 7–9, 11; BMB, 1957–64, pp. 89–91 (11 Nov. 1958); Memo of meeting of sub-committee, 28 Jan. 1960 (King's Inns MS). A short feature on King's Inns in the *Illustrated London News* (25 April 1959) included a sketch of the interior of King's Inns Library, which the author described as being 'famous for its two second folios of Shakespeare'.

Hayes pursued this possibility of progress at King's Inns Library and did so in a manner that was very striking. At a meeting of the benchers on 25 April 1960, the chief justice reported that 'recently' he had had a talk with the director of the National Library 'regarding the cataloguing of our rare pamphlets' and that 'the director was most anxious to help and suggested that a member of his staff, who is very experienced in this work, be employed'. The chief justice had gathered from Hayes that the work would take 'quite a considerable time' and had invited the latter to submit his views and suggestions in writing. On 1 June 1960 Hayes sent his memorandum to the benchers and, in it, strayed far beyond the matter of cataloguing. He suggested most significantly, among other things, that 'there should be no hesitation' about selling off 'certain scientific works of high sale value' in order to raise money for more law books, and that such sales might be made to libraries abroad. He thought that the benchers should concentrate their collection 'to a greater extent on works in the fields of law, political science and economics', rather than attempt to remain up to date as a general reference library:

I have examined the collections in the King's Inns Library with a view to ascertaining what steps are necessary to make the more valuable parts of these collections available to those likely to be interested in them. They cannot, of course, be regarded as available until they are fully catalogued and their contents known in detail. They have not been used to any extent in the past and will not be in the future until this work is done. Three of these special collections within the general collection are of outstanding historical interest and importance.

The general collection of books forms a very fine library and I was struck by the very large number of expensive books of general interest in very good bindings which adorn its shelves. It is obvious that the collection over a long period of years has been chosen with taste and discrimination and that the aim has been to add works of permanent value and interest. At the same time one cannot help feeling that outside the members of King's Inns, law students and a few others, the learned public and visiting scholars are unlikely to use it. Its rather inaccessible position in the city is a contributing factor to this. There is, moreover, the further point that one naturally assumes that the King's Inns Library is essentially a 'law library'. In fact it is not. It is a general library like the National Library or Trinity College Library on a much smaller scale.

For financial reasons and for want of space for growth I feel that in the future it should concentrate to a greater extent on works in the fields of law, political science and economics rather than in an attempt to remain up to date as a general reference library. I would also suggest that in cases where it happens to contain certain scientific works of high sale value there should be no hesitation in disposing of some of these to provide funds for the addition of works of a legal character. If it is not possible to sell works of this kind, the difficulty might be overcome by arranging an exchange through a big London bookseller of some scientific works for legal works. It should be taken into account, in this connection, that by retaining on its shelves very rare scientific works which will never be consulted, the King's Inns Library is keeping out of scientific circulation works which are badly needed by scientific libraries destroyed during the war or scientific libraries newly founded and unable to find anywhere rare scientific works published during the 19th century. This is a disservice to the world of learning.

There are three large special collections in the library which, as already mentioned, are of great importance and which are not inappropriate to a law library. Their contents can become a notable contribution to historical knowledge. These collections are (1) The collection of pamphlets; (2) The collection of Irish appeals to the House of Lords; (3) The legal and historical manuscripts.

1) The collection of pamphlets contains about 7,000 items. It is true that many of these will be found elsewhere in large Irish libraries such as the National Library, Trinity College Library and the Haliday collection of the Royal Irish Academy. It can be assumed, however, that in a pamphlet collection of this size there must be many items not accessible elsewhere and to find these there is no alternative except to catalogue them all, and when doing so to check them against the contents of at least one other large collection such as that of the National Library.

2) The collection of Irish appeals to the House of Lords in 97 large volumes, is one of the richest veins for unique Irish historical information which I have come across for many years. There is a cursory hand-list of it which is quite useless for historical research. There are numerous references in these appeals to records which were lost in the destruction of the Public Record Office in 1922. It requires to be catalogued in special detail to bring to notice these hidden treasures and this collection should be a priority in any cataloguing scheme for the Library. There are about 4,000 appeals in the collection. I can best emphasise the value of this collection by saying that I do not believe one could find anywhere else in Ireland (even as many as?) 400 of those 4,000 documents.

3) The manuscript collection contains about 200 volumes. Without cataloguing these it is not possible to form an estimate of their value and interest. They seem to be mainly of a legal and historical kind. If there are even half a dozen items of special interest among these volumes it would justify the expense of cataloguing them.

The cataloguing of these three collections would cost a substantial sum of money but this should be regarded as capital expenditure and it would be, of course, far cheaper to pay an outside expert to do this work within a limited period than to recruit any additional staff for the Library. The person selected to do the work must, of course, be one experienced and fully trained in the cataloguing of historical research material. It would not be possible to find a competent person who could give his full time to the work.[6]

Hayes offered to recommend as a cataloguer 'a trained librarian from one of the learned libraries in Dublin' who would be available in that person's spare time. He himself was willing to supervise the work, which he estimated would cost in total £980. He noted that a contractual arrangement had been made a few years earlier for the cataloguing of the large Irish medical library bequeathed to the Royal College of Physicians by Dr T.P.C. Kirkpatrick, and recalled that, 'The rate of payment and the number of items to be catalogued per hour was worked out jointly by the representatives of the Wellcome Foundation of London and me'. On 20 June 1960 his report on King's Inns was sent to the Library Committee, which adopted it in principle. Yet, almost a full year passed before the benchers, 'after much discussion' and 'by [a] large majority', decided that 'a beginning should be made with the cataloguing of the House of Lords appeals', and agreed to provide funds for that purpose. Bound together in these appeal volumes are both printed and manuscript documents. By 27 August 1962, an index of 1,000 cards was typed under the supervision of Hayes. Each card is filed at King's Inns under the name of the appellant to the House of Lords, but gives only a bare indication of the nature of the case. As regards the two other collections in which Hayes was particularly interested, the catalogue of the society's manuscripts is still incomplete, although much progress has been made, especially in relation to records of King's Inns itself or papers in the Irish language. There is still no discrete listing of the library's pamphlet collection.[7]

Later, the benchers were to go back to Hayes for an opinion on aspects of their sale of library stock in 1972. His advice then, as shall be seen, was somewhat shocking insofar as he appeared to give them unqualified support for their course of action. However,

6 BMB, 1957–64, pp. 162–3 (25 April 1960); LCMB, p. 72 (20 June 1960); King's Inns files for full copy of the memo, signed 31 May 1960; Hayes to Maguire, 1 June 1960 and reply of the following day.
7 BMB, pp. 207–8 (9 May 1961); LCMB, pp. 72–3 (20 June 1960), pp. 87–8 (12 June 1961); Standing Committee minutes (King's Inns MS, hereafter SCM), 1960–75, p. 56. Individual pamphlets may be found in the library's general catalogue and many are now included also in the English Short-Title Catalogue (ESTC), an Anglo-American initiative.

it may be noted at this point that, while he suggested in 1960 that scientific works might be sold, Hayes had also expressed the opinion that the society's extensive collection of pamphlets were 'not inappropriate to a law library'. These pamphlets were by no means entirely devoted to legal matters. He acknowledged in his report of that year that 'the collection over a long period of years has been chosen with taste and discrimination and that the aim has been to add works of permanent value and interest'.

The benchers continued to be concerned about their finances and decided, amongst other measures taken, to ask the Library Committee to prepare a general plan for their library. Members were worried about the risk of fire and theft, and the question of adequate insurance for their collection was also raised. Some benchers recognised the desirability of having a proper catalogue. For her part, the librarian kept an eye on the prices being paid for books of which the King's Inns had copies. A 'special list of books' was prepared, the content and nature of which is unclear, and this was furnished for inspection to a representative of the Huntington Library and Art Gallery in San Marino, California. Over the years the Huntington has acquired many valuable manuscripts and other works from Europe. At one point its then chairman, Homer Crotty, appears to have been spoken to by Chief Justice Maguire about the collection at King's Inns. On 24 May 1961 Crotty wrote on behalf of his librarian, Robert Dougan, a letter of introduction to Maguire in which he said that,

Due to the wide experience Mr Dougan has had with books I felt he could be of assistance to you on the question as to what should be done with those books in the King's Inns for which there seems to be no present need. You may have in mind the auction in the last two years of the surplus books by the Signet Library in Edinburgh.

Crotty added that if there were any books which the King's Inns would like to sell at a mutually agreeable price, then 'I am sure we will all be pleased', and he and his wife sent their warm personal regards to the chief justice and his spouse.[8]

The letter from California was forwarded to the librarian of King's Inns by the chief justice, who asked that McMenamin 'would have a copy of the special list of books available for Mr

8 Dougan to Maguire, 24 May 1961. For the Signet Library sale, see below pp. 50, 146.

Dougan when he calls' and who stated that Dougan 'would also like to see the last book (German) which you got for the library'. In the same year as the chairman of the Huntington wrote to Maguire, books from the Cashel Diocesan Library were sold to the Folger Shakespeare Library in Washington D.C. as a means to establish a trust fund for the maintenance of that Tipperary repository.[9]

McMenamin was well aware that at least some of the society's volumes were very valuable. In 1960, the librarian had reported to the committee that a copy of the *Report of the scientific results of the voyage of H.M.S. Challenger during the years 1873–76,* published for the Royal Society in fifty volumes, had been sold recently at Sotheby's in London for £850. This information was of interest because the society itself possessed a copy of the Challenger report containing about 300 maps and charts and about 2,800 plates, those of any birds being coloured. A fortnight later, she noted that a collection of the publications of the Hakluyt Society had been sold in England for £2,500 and the Library Committee was exultant: 'English bookseller [Dawson's of Pall Mall] recently offered £800 for our copy of this work! Our set has extra volumes.' The librarian was instantly authorised to place a standing order for Sotheby's catalogues. One year later, McMenamin reported that Maximilian's *Travels in the interior of North America,* a copy of which was in the library, had been sold at Sotheby's for £1,600. It was also recorded that the Nuremberg chronicles had fetched £1,600 in Munich. In 1972, Sotheby's would sell the society's copy of *Challenger* for £1,300, of Maximilian for £6,800 and of the *Nuremberg chronicles* (1493) for £2,100.[10]

It is clear that informal consideration was being given at this period to the disposal of some of the society's collection, which was scarcely surprising given the earlier recommendations by Richard Hayes which were considered above. In 1961, Judge John Kenny prepared for the Library Committee a draft report on the option of selling books from its library. Its presentation on 13 November 1961 gave rise to 'a long discussion' about the possible

9 Private secretary of chief justice to McMenamin, 26 June 1961; Osborough, 'On selling cathedral libraries', 74.
10 LCMB, 1954–81, p. 62 (16 Nov. 1959), p. 63 (11 Jan. 1960), p. 65 (25 Jan. 1960), pp. 81–2 (23 Jan. 1961). On 20 Nov. 1972 the society's 251 Hakluyt volumes (1847–1970) were sold to one T. Thorp for £800 (Sotheby's 'Price list', lot 226). In 1992, Sotheby's sold a coloured copy of the *Nuremberg chronicles* (1493) for US$264,000.

sale of books, including valuable works as well as those of Irish interest. Following a number of meetings, the members of the Library Committee were unable to reach agreement on what precisely should be done, but were unanimous in deciding to issue an interim report to the full bench on 'a matter of some urgency'. This 'matter of some urgency' was the need to amend the law to allow King's Inns to dispose of its books should the society wish to do so, and the matter was considered all the more urgent because heads of legislation had been prepared for a new Copyright Bill which was expected to be brought forward in the near future. The members of the Library Committee informed the full bench that they had 'not yet decided whether they will recommend a policy of selling some of the books of the library but they are of opinion that they should have power to sell the books whatever policy is decided upon'. The interim report recommended that the Minister for Industry and Commerce be asked to include in the pending Copyright Bill a proposed section giving the benchers the right to sell books in the library and to apply the proceeds in paying salaries and fees for the preparation of a catalogue, in paying salaries for a larger library staff, and for the maintenance and repair of the library buildings and for the purchase of other books and, also, for the power to exchange books. The benchers considered and adopted the report with just one amendment. Where the Library Committee envisaged applying the proceeds of any sale solely on law books, the full bench deleted the word 'law'.[11]

When, in February 1962, the Library Committee again discussed the possibility of selling some of its books, Judge George Murnaghan roundly criticised Kenny's original draft. The minutes record that,

Mr Justice Murnaghan said that the Report did not go far enough, that the library was not a public library but a private library for the members of King's Inns. He said that many books were being purchased which were not used and that it was a misuse of the funds to purchase books of general interest when there was not enough money to purchase worthwhile legal books.

There is the question of security; non-legal books are most valuable and cannot be insured. Only basis for insurance is that we keep them as an investment; if they are an investment, then must come a time when it is

11 'Interim Report of the Library Committee', pp. 1–4, inserted in envelope bound between p. 226 and p. 227 of BMB, 1957–64; FS, paragraph 15 erroneously includes the word 'law' before 'books', thus ignoring the effect of the amendment.

prudent to realise those investments and now is the time to realise [them] to put library on good working basis and this means complete overhaul.[12]

The Fianna Fáil government of the day agreed to a provision being inserted in the Copyright Bill of 1962 to enable the benchers to sell part of their collection. It was clearly not a contentious proposal, and during the debate in Dáil Éireann only two deputies spoke about the matter. Jack Lynch, who as Minister for Industry and Commerce introduced the Copyright Bill, said that, 'The benchers think that there are some books in the library which could usefully be disposed of, and the proceeds applied in binding or cataloguing books of more interest to the users of the library'. For his part, Liam Cosgrave, leader of Fine Gael, was also enthusiastic about the prospect. Responding to Lynch, Cosgrave remarked that,

It is desirable to make the amendment which is suggested in section 56. I have no doubt the benchers of the King's Inns have a number of books which are of no continued use to the people who use the King's Inns Library. Consequently, the power to sell or exchange these books is desirable in order to enable them to devote the money secured from such sale to the purpose either of acquiring additional books or binding or cataloguing existing books there.[13]

Thus, the purpose for which the law was being changed was represented by both Lynch and Cosgrave as being specifically that of acquiring other books or repairing and cataloguing those which the society already owned. However, the Copyright Act 1963 was not itself so restrictive. It simply provided in section 58 that,

Notwithstanding anything contained in the King's Inns Library Act, 1945, or the enactments referred to therein or the Copyright Act, 1801, or the Copyright Act, 1836, the Benchers of the Honourable Society of King's Inns may sell or exchange any of the books of the King's Inns Library, Dublin, whether acquired before or after the commencement of this section.

One wonders if Jack Lynch later thought that he had been misled as a minister when the benchers subsequently placed books for sale at Sotheby's, in order to raise cash for general purposes. Then, as we shall see, they invited him as taoiseach to allocate

12 LCMB, 1954–81, pp. 97–8 (5 Feb. 1962).
13 *Dáil Éireann deb.*, vol. 198, cols. 243–6 (28 Nov. 1962).

funds to purchase the volumes for Ireland. At that later date one newspaper editor would ruefully recall Minister Lynch's reference in the Dáil in 1962 to books 'which could usefully be disposed of', commenting that this phrase had 'an anodyne character' and wondering if deputies might have been more concerned had the minister said 'which could be disposed of for a large sum'.[14]

14 *Irish Times*, 6 Nov. 1972.

CHAPTER SIX

Sotheby's promise, 1969

THE SOCIETY'S POWERS under section 58 of the Copyright Act 1963 would not be first exercised until the controversial auctions of 1972. Meanwhile, the benchers spent considerable sums on 'special repairs, renovation and decorations' at King's Inns – almost £30,000 in 1963 ('mainly on the library'), £11,625 in 1964 and £10,888 in 1965. In June 1966, they boldly asked the government for another grant from the funds of suitors, explaining that the previous grant had proven inadequate because of an increase in building costs and because of a further outbreak of dry rot in the dining-hall. The benchers quite dramatically informed the taoiseach that,

To enable the Society to carry out its educational and other functions and to maintain its buildings which have a world wide reputation, it is essential that the capital funds of the Society should be recouped as otherwise it will be impossible to carry on even if students' fees were raised to an altogether inordinate level.

Ministers were then planning to spend some of the funds of suitors on the Abbey Theatre and the Cork Opera House, and officials were already concerned that the public might think there were worthier ways of using the money. The benchers clearly hoped to benefit from the funds of suitors for a second time in seven years, but a briefing note prepared at the department of justice indicates that there was a considerable degree of antipathy towards their society among some civil servants. The writer did not mince his words:

The benchers say that if their capital funds are not made good they will be unable to carry out the educational and other functions of the Society, and to maintain the Society's buildings. The plain fact of the matter is that the educational activities of the Society are little more than a joke. As to the other functions, the country could well do without them. Indeed, the late Chief Justice Kennedy thought that the Society should have been abolished when the Free State came into being.

The author of this memorandum, a copy of which the Minister for Justice, Brian Lenihan, sent to the taoiseach, Séan Lemass, also referred to the earlier suggestion by the secretary of his department who, in 1957, had raised the possibility of the state running King's Inns Library. He embellished that idea by suggesting now that the National Library was 'ideally constituted' to make such a take-over, although he failed to explain how an institution which itself was overcrowded and underfunded might meet the many challenges involved in managing another collection at Henrietta Street. In the event, the National Library did not get involved and the benchers did not get any of the funds of suitors. Liam Cosgrave argued their case in the Dáil, but the Act that was passed made no provision for King's Inns. Between 1966 and 1968 the benchers spent not a penny on building purposes, but in 1969 did lay out £5,392. Although some of their earlier grant had been invested as a capital fund and provided a rising annual income for the library, the library continued to operate at a debit during the same period, this being on average £1,631.[1]

However, the society's financial difficulties might never have become the cause of controversy about selling books had an arsonist had his way. At about 4.30 a.m., on 11 August 1968, a fire was started at King's Inns Library. It had been 'a planned, malicious act and was quite obviously not the work of children', reported George Murnaghan to his fellow benchers. A nun, living in the convent across the street from the library, saw smoke and raised the alarm. Dublin Fire Brigade was then on strike, so army personnel arrived to fight the blaze. Gardai found five petrol containers, one for five gallons. Petrol had been spilled on top of tables and on the floor and an attempt had been made to set alight heaps of books. Maura Neylon, the society's future librarian, was at that time acting as librarian for a few days. She later described the scene:

On my arrival the fire was extinguished. The area affected was the reading room and the adjoining annexes. There was a strong smell of smoke and petrol in these areas and in addition there were stains of petrol on the books on the table and on the side of the reading room adjoining the annexes. In Annexe 3 on the left hand side as one enters the shelves and most of the books had been destroyed or damaged by the fire itself or by the water during the process of extinguishing the fire. In Annexe 2 and 4 the damage, although considerable, was less extensive. The water from the fire hoses had

1 FS, paragraphs 10, 17, 18, 42; King's Inns grant, 1966 (National Archives).

penetrated into Annexe 1 and the basement underneath and had caused considerable damage there. I subsequently assisted in the compilation of a list of the destroyed and damaged books.[2]

It was pure luck that the benchers' entire collection of books, pamphlets and manuscripts, along with the building that housed them, had escaped the reputed fate of the great library of Alexandria. Far from being entirely consumed by fire, in fact, King's Inns Library had suffered relatively little harm, and its most valuable volumes were unscathed. It was mainly law books that had been burnt by fire or soaked by water, and it was possible to replace many of these because they happened not be rare. Eventually, the benchers were to be awarded £29,246 in malicious damages by the Circuit Criminal Court, its presiding judge, Peter O'Malley, describing this as 'a frightening figure'. However, it represented a loss that was far less frightening than what might have been. The near disaster raised in the minds of the benchers the question of whether or not their insurance cover was adequate. Without an itemised assessment of their collection it was difficult to know what level of insurance might be enough for the replacement of those books of which duplicates could be bought. In 1962, Richard Hayes was said to have advised King's Inns that 'it was not good business to insure books that could not be replaced'. He felt that any money paid for such cover could be more usefully employed in buying new books, 'especially law books'.[3]

In July 1969, the Standing Committee noted the retirement of Mrs McMenamin, librarian of King's Inns since 1945, and fell to considering the matter of remuneration for her successor as well as for any other library staff. The ensuing discussion reveals that Judge Murnaghan had already been in contact with Sotheby's and that some judges were in favour of disposing of part of their collection:

2 BMB, 1964–75, p. 144 (7 Oct. 1968); Statement re fire in library, August 1968 by Mary Neylon, 7 Jan. 1971 (King's Inns Library files), *Evening Herald,* 12 August 1968. The convent occupies a house built by Luke Gardiner as his Dublin mansion, and later home to Tristram Kennedy and his Dublin Law Institute.
3 SCM, 1960–75, p. 56 (27 Aug. 1962). Report of malicious damages case (unidentified, undated press cutting), with report by Neylon, 1978 (Library: arson files (King's Inns MSS)). Scholars now suspect that the Alexandrian library may never have been completely destroyed by fire (Harris, *History of libraries*, pp. 42–7).

Mr Justice Kenny: If increased salaries are to be paid this must be met by (a) increasing fees or (b) selling some of our books. Many books he thought could be sold without great loss to the library, especially such books as are of little value or interest to Irish readers. He believed that a list of 60 books could be prepared for sale which would realise something in the order of £100,000.

Mr Justice Murnaghan: There cannot be a conclusive discussion on the matter until a list of the books is prepared. He had an offer from Sotheby's to prepare such list free of charge and he was now prepared to take advantage of this offer.

Murnaghan's proposal was agreed, to the subsequent annoyance of the Library Committee which had not been consulted. Nevertheless, no such list of books in the library was prepared prior to the benchers concluding that part of their library should be sold.[4]

Shortly after this meeting, Lord John Kerr of Sotheby's wrote to George Murnaghan to say that he had been asked by a 'Mr Pritzel' to contact the judge 'because I understand that a sale of at least part of King's Inns Library is being contemplated'. He told Murnaghan, 'I would of course be very pleased to do what I can to help but I wonder whether in the first instance you could give me some idea of the scope and nature of the library'. Murnaghan replied that,

Some time ago I spoke to Mr John Hunt, about the possibility that King's Inns Library would sell at least some of its non-legal books and he very kindly said that he would contact Messrs. Sotheby & Co. and arrange that somebody would come over, look at the books and advise the Library Committee thereon without any commitment on the part of the Library.

As you are probably aware King's Inns Library had once the privilege under The Copyright Act of being entitled to receive a copy of every work published in the United Kingdom. This right I regret to say was commuted for a yearly cash payment many years ago. However, before being commuted many non-legal books came into the Library under the said right.

There is at present a move to rationalise the position of the Library which has no up-to-date catalogue, and which is primarily a legal library.

If it should happen that you would have a representative in Dublin in the near future perhaps he would contact me and I would be glad to show him the particular books which might be sold. This would probably be more satisfactory, and certainly easier from my point of view, than if I were to prepare a list of the books themselves. My home address is ...[5]

4 SCM, 1960–75, pp. 240–1 (9 July 1969), 242 (29 July 1969), 250 (9 Dec. 1969); FS, paragraph 20.
5 Kerr to Murnaghan, 23 July 1969; Murnaghan to Kerr, 29 July 1969.

Sotheby's responded enthusiastically to the suggestion by Judge Murnaghan. A representative of the London auction house, Hellmut Feisenberger, soon travelled to Dublin and, as shall be seen, made a quick inspection of some books of general and special interest at King's Inns. It was to be the first of three crucial visits by him. Born at Magdeburg, Germany, in 1909, Feisenberger was the son of a judge of the Supreme Court in Leipzig and had himself studied law in Berlin. Although brought up a Christian, his father was Jewish and Hellmut fled Germany in 1933. He abandoned law to pursue a living in the book trade, where he became a specialist in early scientific and medical books. In 1960 he moved to Sotheby's from Dawson's of Pall Mall where he had been chief cataloguer of rare books. He became an associate director of Sotheby's, retiring in 1975 but remaining a consultant. He died on 27 August 1999. According to a highly complimentary obituary in *The Times* of London, Feisenberger had joined Sotheby's at a time when the company was expanding rapidly and he 'had plenty of ways in which to demonstrate his skills, as his sale catalogues and valuations vividly illustrate'. He was said to be one of 'a distinguished group of Europeans who widened and deepened both the scholarship and outlook of the English book trade':

Feisenberger was more than a bookseller. He had a keen respect for scholarship in its many forms, and, like his wife, was widely read. The sadly unavoidable sale of the library which they formed made those interests vividly clear, for it contained not only the acknowledged classics but many less celebrated books which are nevertheless of significance. There were also good collections of books on bibliography, art and architecture.[6]

In October 1969, Feisenberger wrote to Murnaghan enclosing a report for the benchers 'on the books which you showed me' when in Dublin. He wrote, 'I hope this is what you wanted and that it will help to persuade your colleagues to take the appropriate action. If, as I hope, you will decide on a sale, I should of course be only too pleased to come back again and go into the matter in greater detail'. He added, on a personal note, 'I had a most enjoyable visit and I thank you and Mrs Murnaghan again for your kind hospitality'.[7] In his report for the benchers, Feisenberger offered 'to organise a memorable series of sales on your behalf':

6 *The Times*, 30 Sept. 1999.
7 Feisenberger to Murnaghan, 22 Oct. 1969, with attached report for the society.

I have made a very rapid first inspection of the non-legal books in your library and have been asked by The Hon. Mr. Justice Murnaghan to report on these and make some recommendations as to their future treatment.

This is a very large collection of many thousands of volumes including early printed books, English literature and history, French, Italian and German history, theology, English topography, Americana, Atlases, geography and other subjects, also a very large and valuable collection of about 1,000 pamphlets bound in volumes.

In 1960, Richard Hayes had reported, as seen above, that 'the collection of pamphlets contains about 7,000 items' and it was apparently his estimate rather than that of Feisenberger which in 1976 Sotheby's itself would rely upon when again involved in assessing the collection for King's Inns. Whether the figure of '1,000' was simply a typographical error by Feisenberger, or was a reflection of what he himself described as the 'very rapid' nature of his first inspection, is unknown. His report continued,

The function of your library is, of course, a legal one and this report arises out of a plan you are discussing for the possible sale of these non-legal books. I would most strongly support this suggestion for the following reasons:—

These books represent a very considerable capital asset, at a very rough estimate indeed, somewhere between £100,000 and £200,000 at least. But it is an asset that wants looking after. Firstly: although the condition of the books is good on the whole and some bindings have been repaired, most of the bindings are rather shabby and many lack their spines. All this should be repaired to avoid further deterioration and would involve a considerable expenditure. Secondly: if the books are being kept, a proper catalogue of such an important collection should certainly be compiled and printed, again requiring some expenditure.

The function of your library is a purely legal one. The other books are, I understand, never used at all, and indeed without a printed catalogue their existence remains unknown. The sections I inspected are not even of any particular Irish interest.

In these days the demand for rare and antiquarian books of this kind from institutions and individuals all over the world is enormous and, with the opening up of new centres of learning all the time, is growing. It seems to me, therefore, that anyone in the possession of such material that is not being used should consider making it available for the purposes of scholarship at the place where it is most wanted. Naturally, with any great Institution such as yours, the feeling for its history, its old possessions, and traditions is justifiably strong. On the other hand I feel there is also a duty involved here in making the very best use of these considerable assets in your possession.

If you decided to sell, you would in the first place obtain a very considerable capital sum which would enable you to maintain and develop your library as one of the best legal ones in the English-speaking world –

apart from any other purposes you might want to use it for in maintaining your Institution. If you entrusted your collection to us for sale, we would be able to issue a series of important catalogues which would remain as a monument to your non-legal library. In a public auction and with the resources at our disposal you would be certain of world-wide publicity and the keenest competition resulting in the highest possible prices. Secondly, by this means you would assure that eventually the books would go where they are most needed; no one pays the present high prices for material unless he really wants it.

Many great Institutions have in recent years sold material in our rooms which was surplus to their requirements not only to raise money but also as the most rational method to get scholarly and antiquarian books to those places in the world that want them most. In particular I would mention a case almost identical with yours. The Writers to the Signet in Edinburgh, comparable in importance in the legal system of Scotland to yours, sold their non-legal books in a series of six sales in 1959–1960 for a total of £160,000. The sales were a great success and gave full satisfaction both to the sellers and to the buyers all over the world. In addition to these and more recently, the Boston Medical Library, the Newberry Library in Chicago, the Folger Shakespeare Library in Washington and the Royal Medical Society in Edinburgh have used the facilities of our rooms to rationalise their holdings or to raise money to enable them to buy books more congruous to their functions.

In view of all these considerations I would most strongly recommend that you should dispose of all those books in the library which have no particular connection either with the law or with Ireland. And if you took this decision, this firm would do its utmost to assist you in every possible way and to organise a memorable series of sales on your behalf.[8]

In January 1970, Maura Neylon was appointed librarian of King's Inns, having previously acted on occasion in place of McMenamin. Neylon (who also used 'Mary' as her first name) was coming into the job at a difficult time, and the benchers' subsequent decision to sell certain books that other Dublin libraries did not have on their shelves would place her in an awkward position. Less than four years earlier, she had co-authored a short work on Irish public libraries, in which Ellen Power, the librarian of University College Dublin, had been warmly thanked by the authors 'for her invaluable advice and assistance in the preparation of the work'.[9] Soon, Neylon would

---

8 Ibid. Sotheby's organised the Signet Library sales to which Feisenberger refers. However, contrary to the impression which gained credence after its sale of 14,000 books and 9,000 pamphlets, the Signet retained a general collection, especially of Scottish books. It felt constrained to sell books because of financial difficulties (Ballantyne, *Signet Library*, pp. 60–1, 152, 178–81).
9 Neylon and Henchy, *Public libraries in Ireland*, preface.

see Power's expression of interest in certain books, which her university could not afford but which it would like to have, ignored by the benchers.

Five weeks after Neylon's appointment, the benchers' Standing Committee 'formally' asked the Library Committee for its views 'on the sale of certain non-legal books' as had been recommended in the Sotheby's report of 21 October 1969. In due course, the Library Committee replied that Sotheby's ought to 'be requested to report on the scientific and theological items in the library and to get an estimate of the selling price with a view to their sale'. Standing Committee in turn agreed to recommend this course of action to the benchers, but 'with the addition of the word geographical after the word theological'. It decided further that Sotheby's 'be asked not simply for a report', but also for 'a list and valuation of the books in these categories which they consider might be sold'. On 6 April 1970 the benchers, upon a proposal by the president of the High Court seconded by Judge Kenny, accepted these recommendations 'by a substantial majority'. On a show of hands, they rejected an alternative motion. This, proposed by Judge Séan Butler and seconded by a senior counsel, Tom O'Higgins, had suggested more cautiously 'that Messrs Sotheby's be asked for an approximate estimate of the cost of preparing a valuation of the books in these categories'. Butler and O'Higgins recognised that the task of preparing an accurate list and valuation would be time-consuming. As it transpired, no such cost was to arise because a full listing and detailed valuation of all of the society's scientific, theological and geographical books was never actually made. During this period also, when the benchers were deciding whether or not to ask Sotheby's for a report on their collection, Feisenberger declined to come to Dublin to inspect the books of King's Inns which had been damaged in the fire of 1968 and in relation to which the society claimed compensation from public funds under the malicious injuries code. Instead, Sotheby's agreed to give its valuation from a list provided by the benchers, charging the nominal fee of £10 rather than the normal one per cent, and so saving the society £243.[10]

In 1970, expenditure by the society on repairs, renovation and decorations rose sharply and, indeed, almost doubled. Having

10 LCMB, 1954–81, pp. 175–6, 182 (6 Feb. 1970); BMB, pp. 188–9 (6 April 1970); Letter of under-treasurer to librarian (23 June 1971); Feisenberger to Neylon, 16 Feb. 1970 and 5 March 1970. Sotheby's valuation for arson damage to books was £25,300.

spent nothing in 1966–68, following the government's refusal to grant more money from the funds of suitors, the society had parted with £5,392 for repairs and decoration in 1969 but spent £9,740 in 1970 and £22,126 in 1971. According to George Murnaghan and Raymond O'Neill, 'the expenditure in 1970 and 1971 related mainly to kitchen renovations but included considerable demolition work in the Park'. Given the financial difficulties which the society faced, it was a bold move to spend so much on catering facilities. This was especially so when more money than ever was needed for the library, where the debit rose sharply from £2,510 to £3,503 in 1970 and then almost doubled to £6,804 in 1971, this being 'largely attributable to the purchase of a series of foreign law reports not previously kept in the library'. The gross total cost of ordinary maintenance of the library during the sixteen years 1956–71 was £58,000 approximately and the net cost (after allowing for the annual copyright compensation and investment income from the government grant of 1959), was £35,000 approximately. By June 1971 the society's overdraft had risen to £47,000, approximately.[11]

11 FS, paragraphs 17, 18, 19, 41.

CHAPTER SEVEN

'Nothing of Irish interest'?

GIVEN THE DECISION of the benchers to ask Sotheby's to proceed to list and evaluate part of their collection, following Feisenberger's first visit, it is surprising that a year passed before the representative of that auction house was in a position to report to them again, and even more surprising that he was permitted to do so verbally. In April 1971, Feisenberger wrote to Murnaghan informing him of the former's forthcoming arrival in Dublin. On 21 June 1971 Feisenberger joined a meeting of the Library Committee attended by the chief justice and others. There he discussed the proposed sale of scientific, theological and geographical items. He emphasised to members of the committee the necessity of selling books, 'in order to provide funds for the administration of the library and the restoration and cataloguing of books, and said that the books proposed for sale would be a diminishing asset, if retained'. The Library Committee was impressed by this presentation: 'It was agreed to recommend to the benchers the sale of the books selected by Dr Feisenberger. *Nothing of Irish interest to be sold.*'[1] The term 'Irish interest', adopted and underlined by the Library Committee, was not defined but it appears to have been understood to mean works by Irish authors or works in the title of which there was a reference to Ireland. It would also be taken to include at least some books published in Ireland. The phrase 'nothing of Irish interest to be sold' was to prove contentious during the ensuing auctions.

No sooner had the Library Committee made its decision than a note of caution was struck. At a subsequent meeting of the Benchers, on 30 June 1971, it was decided unanimously that 'the books selected by Dr Feisenberger', of which there was no full list, should be sold only after preliminary consultations with the government and various library authorities. There was 'a considerable

---

1 Feisenberger to Murnaghan, 1 April 1971; FS, paragraph 24; LCMB, 21 June 1971.

discussion covering such ground as: the necessity for the sale; the number to be sold; the desirability of affording Irish libraries and learned bodies an opportunity of purchasing; the form of letter to be sent to the Taoiseach [Jack Lynch] and other bodies informing them of the proposed sale etc.' The benchers agreed that copies of the letter being dispatched to the taoiseach would be sent to the National Library, Trinity College Dublin, University College Dublin, University College Cork, University College Galway, Queen's University Belfast and the University of Ulster at Coleraine, as well as to the Minister for Industry and Commerce.[2]

Chief Justice Cearbhall Ó Dálaigh, who would subsequently serve as president of Ireland between 1974 and 1976, then wrote on behalf of the benchers,

A Thaoisigh Uasail,

The amount spent on repairs and renewals to King's Inns and King's Inns Library greatly exceeded the funds made available in 1959 from the Funds of Suitors, and the Benchers have, by reason of this, incurred a very heavy overdraft. As you are aware, the Benchers have an important function as an educational institution, catering for the education of students desiring to enter into practice at the Bar, and they maintain what is undoubtedly the most comprehensive law library in Ireland.

Additional funds are now required to pay off the overdraft, and to put King's Inns on a proper financial footing, to enable the Benchers to improve the educational facilities, and to improve the Library and have the books in it properly catalogued.

Included in the Library are many works of a non-legal character, some of them of very great value. Many of these books could not be replaced, if they should be destroyed, and the insurance of such a collection is not practicable. Under the Copyright Act, 1963, power was given to the Benchers to sell books in the Library. They now propose to dispose of some of the non-legal works in order to raise funds for the purposes mentioned.

As an initial step they intend to sell through Messrs Sotheby & Co. those books in the Library which come under the classification of scientific, religious and geographical, *save such as may have any reference to Ireland.*

It is proposed to notify the National Library and the university libraries in Ireland of this intention, and to furnish to them a list of the more notable volumes contained in the said classifications. The benchers consider that they should also notify the Government of their intention, in case the Government should be interested in having any particular volume or volume retained in the country and not sent for public auction. A copy of the list which is being sent to the libraries mentioned above is enclosed for the information of the government.

2 BMB, pp. 220–1 (30 June 1971).

The benchers' arrangements with Messrs Sotheby's & Co. are such that it is essential to know at an early date whether the Government has any special wishes in the matter.[3]

When Sotheby's catalogues were eventually published the following year they included far more books than were on the short list that was now circulated to the taoiseach and various librarians. The catalogues would also give a much fuller and more accurate description of each work on the short list, although a small number of titles, especially of the oldest works, are still difficult to identify clearly from the later auction catalogues. References on the short list to valuable maps are particularly inadequate, with the words 'Various Maps and Atlases' apparently including among other treasures a single lot of 605 engraved maps which Sotheby's would later describe as 'a magnificent collection', and which sold on 20 November 1972 for £17,000 (lot 183). A total of more than 1,445 lots were later sold, some containing multiple titles, where this first list had just 255 titles. The vast majority of books on the preliminary list and in the subsequent auction were volumes which lowly funded Irish libraries were unlikely to consider buying at that time in preference to other works which they needed or coveted and which were of more direct interest to Irish readers.[4]

However, some books with Irish connections appeared on the short list now circulated by the benchers. Their inclusion seems to have been deemed acceptable because their titles contained no explicit 'reference to Ireland', in the words of the letter from Ó Dálaigh to Lynch. This suggests either that books were selected in haste, or that the benchers as a body favoured a narrower test of exclusion than that of 'Irish interest' recommended by their library committee. So, for example, a book by William Stokes, 'regius professor of physic' at Trinity College Dublin, was on the short list (*Diseases of the heart and the aorta*). The title page of Stokes's book identifies his position at the university and the fact

---

3 Ó Dálaigh to Lynch, 2 July 1971; King's Inns books, 1972 (University College Dublin MSS).

4 Paradoxically, entries on the list for Nicholson's *Atlas*, Brown's *New General Atlas* and Vancouver's *Chart of Holland* do not appear to be specifically repeated in the catalogues. Where in the catalogues, too, are the listed '*Egypt: C.G. Rawlinson.* Berlin. n.d. (*c.*1890)', '*Encyclopaedia of the arts, science and literature, 1819–20.* 5 vols.' and '*Journal of Roman Studies*'? What is the 'Book of coloured engravings: oblong folio'? The list included eight of the nine medical books which, as seen above, some librarians had understood to be offered for sale in 1958.

that the volume was published in Dublin in 1854. The society itself possesses a study of Stokes by his own son. Yet, they attempted to sell his book, as well as works by other Irish authors and books published in Ireland.

One may quibble that the short list then circulated by the benchers did not include *all* books with an Irish connection intended for sale by Sotheby's. It is also the case that the 256 titles on the list sent to the libraries did not include *all* of 'the more notable volumes' or even all of 'the more important works' as the chief justice in his covering letters had informed the taoiseach and the universities. However, there is no doubt that the list circulated in July 1971 included many of the most important works and was generally indicative of what was on offer. As this did not stir the government to respond by providing special funds in order for libraries to acquire some of the titles which they were unable to afford from their existing budgets, the circulation of a fuller list of volumes for sale might not have made any significant difference to the outcome of the whole process. It is impossible to know if the publication of full details of all of the approximately 7,000 volumes which were going for sale would have shocked the public or stirred politicians into action when the shorter but significant list did not do so.

On 6 July 1971 the taoiseach's private secretary replied formally to the letter from the chief justice which had invited intervention: 'The Taoiseach notes that a copy of the list has been sent to the National Library and will arrange that the Library authorities will advise the benchers if the Government would be interested in having any particular volume or volumes retained in the country.' It may be noted, at this point, that the National Library of Scotland had purchased from the Scottish legal profession, at Sotheby's valuation, more than 2,000 books that the Signet Library decided to sell in 1960. However, in 1971, Patrick Henchy, the director of the National Library of Ireland, advised the chief justice that his institution was not in a position to acquire any of the King's Inns books, being short of both space and staff. He also wrote at this time to the Department of Education, which was responsible for funding his library and which had asked him to comment on Ó Dálaigh's letter to Lynch. Henchy was more interested in making a general point about the loss of Irish manuscripts and books from the country than in keeping the King's Inns collection in Ireland:

I feel that the benchers wish to save themselves from a possible criticism that they are exporting books that should remain here. But these books are not of Irish interest. Our main interest is in books (and manuscripts) of Irish interest and as a first priority we seek sufficient funds to purchase these. It would be unreasonable for the Government to spend a huge sum in purchasing these books while ignoring the escape of valuable Irish items.[5]

His assertion that the books were 'not of Irish interest' ought to be read in the context of his managing a library with very little money, and of his feeling obliged to give priority to books and manuscripts of the most direct relevance to Irish researchers. As we shall see, when the National Library soon afterwards got more space and more staff, Henchy then proposed that his institution should receive some of the books from King's Inns intended for sale at Sotheby's. He was then to describe the society's collection as being 'of a high cultural and scholarly order'.

Certainly, a number of librarians would have liked to have taken possession of some or all of the books on sale but could not afford them. On 19 July 1971, Peter Brown, librarian of Trinity College Dublin, wrote to the chief justice and informed him that of 261 books on the short list that had been circulated to libraries there were just 103 in Trinity. Describing himself as being 'dismayed' by the benchers' proposed sale, Brown stated that, 'It will sadden many people to see such books leaving the country when more than half of them are almost certainly the only copies in Ireland. But I am in no position to think of obtaining them for Trinity; I spend in all less than £2,000 a year on older books'. He wrote,

Even in the context of the wealth of books in Oxford I must admit that I was severely critical of those colleges that contemplated relieving their financial position by selling from the older collections in their libraries. It seemed to me that they would lose much of great worth for what would prove to be only temporary financial advantage; and once such books have gone they will never be replaced. Of course, I know nothing of the position of the King's Inns but I have to say that I am opposed to the selling of such books outside the country, not because of any particular volume but because of the reduction in the total wealth of books in Dublin, and indeed there is not such a richness of books that we can afford any reduction.

5 FS, paragraph 26; BMB, 1964–75, p. 228 (29 July 1971); Ballantyne, *Signet Library*, pp. 179–81; Henchy to the Secretary, Dept. of Education (National Library of Ireland MS, ref. C.O. 673, 22 July 1971); Henchy, *National Library*, pp. 21–4.

He told the chief justice that only a few months earlier he had attempted to purchase within Ireland a collection of Irish legal books, 'many of them being older books that I needed to fill gaps in the Trinity collection', but that he had been unsuccessful and feared the books were gone abroad. 'Even though they were not the sole copies in the country I regard this as a severe loss and as showing some lack of awareness on the part of the sellers', wrote Brown.

From University College Dublin on 27 July there came another reply to the chief justice which could not have been more explicit. Ellen Power, the librarian, wrote that,

Since University College Dublin Library was established consequent on the 1908 Act, an opportunity to acquire early books as they were published did not arise. The books listed would, therefore, form a welcome addition to the Library. However, we are not, I fear, in a position to acquire them in competition with Messrs. Sotheby.

Of the *incunabula* (books printed before 1501) listed, the *Nuremberg Chronicle* (page 1), printed and published by Anton Koberger, is an interesting example of the output of a 15th century publishing house and of a house which operated throughout Europe, almost on E.E.C. scale. It is frequently mentioned in our classes in the School of Librarianship. It would be good to have this copy for students' inspection and appraisal.

Power added that certain volumes connected with medicine 'would be greatly appreciated in our Medical Library, especially those published in Ireland'. She included these in a list of 28 'other items which we should like', along with the *Nuremberg chronicles*. One of them was by William Stokes, the professor at Trinity College Dublin. Another was a rare edition of a work by Hippocrates, edited by a renowned herbalist, Leonhard Fuchs, and published in Basle in 1537. The copy in King's Inns Library was bound in one volume with a rare version of a classical Latin work, published in Basle in 1526. The latter was edited by one of the greatest scholars of the early humanist movement in northern Europe, Beatus Rhenanus, who was a personal friend of Erasmus and who also edited the first edition of the collected works of Erasmus. The humanist library of Beatus Rhenanus himself is one of the oldest surviving collections in Europe, and is carefully preserved at Sélestat, south of Strasbourg in France.[6]

6 Power to Ó Dálaigh, 27 July 1971 (UCD MS); *Hippocratis medicorum omnium principis Epidemion liber sextus, a Leonardo Fuchsio medico latinitate donatus*, etc.

If Power thought that the benchers would give University College Dublin all of the lots that she had mentioned in her letter, then she was sadly mistaken. Twenty-three were sold to bidders at Sotheby's, and five were withdrawn. The highest price fetched by any of them was £2,100 for the *Nuremberg chronicles* (lot 218, 24 April 1972). The volume containing the editions by Fuchs and Rhenanus went for £120 (lot 371, 14 November 1972). Given that Power's wishful list was based only on eight pages of titles circulated to the libraries, one wonders how many more books she might have included had she known what would appear subsequently in the far more extensive auction catalogues.[7]

In the light of replies from Power and others to the chief justice's letter, the benchers met again on 29 July 1971 and accepted a proposal from Judge Butler that the taoiseach be approached once more and 'told that the benchers deplored the reasons which compelled them to dispose of part of the King's Inns Library and did not if possible want the books to leave the country'.[8]

Accordingly, Cearbhall Ó Dálaigh wrote a second time to Jack Lynch. He told the taoiseach that in addition to the director of the National Library, 'to whom you forwarded my previous letter', the librarians of colleges of the National University of Ireland and of Trinity College Dublin had been informed of the proposed sale and furnished with a list of books:

I enclose copies of the replies received from the librarians of University College Dublin and Trinity College. It appears from these letters that a large number of the volumes being sold are of particular academic and cultural interest. The librarian of Trinity College has pointed out that in the case of many of the volumes no other copy exists in Ireland and that if once allowed to leave the country they would most certainly be irreplaceable. I also enclose a copy of the reply received from the librarian of University College Galway which expresses concern at the prospect of the sale. It seems that he has also

---

(Basle, 1537); Beatus Rhenanus, *In C. Plinium. Repurgatur in hoc libro praefatio Pliniana a multis mendis et ipsis naturalis historiae ... castigantur* (Basle, 1526). In her letter, Power adopted the abbreviated titles of books from the short list circulated by the benchers. Its unsatisfactory nature is illustrated by the fact that this Fuchs edition of Hippocrates is described, therein, simply as *'Hippocratis Medicorum Omnium Principis. 1537'*.

7 For full details of the works that Power particularly desired for the library of University College Dublin, and for their subsequent fate, see Appendix One below.

8 BMB, 1964–75, p. 228 (29 July 1971).

written to you. Neither the National Library nor any of these other institutions is in a position to acquire any of the books on the open market. The Benchers have asked me to inform you that they regret the necessity of selling these books. The decision to sell was dictated primarily by the need to secure a capital sum sufficient to maintain the Library as a first class modern legal library, which they regard as their principal concern; and also to maintain the fabric and institutions [*sic*] of the Inns without the alternative necessity of raising students' fees. The decision was also influenced by two further matters: first, the books are inadequately catalogued and as a result are unknown or not readily available to scholars and others who may require to consult them and, secondly, their rarity and value makes them almost impossible to insure or to replace if damaged or lost.

The Benchers are in general sympathy with the views expressed in the librarians' letters. They would gladly co-operate with any proposal to retain either the entire collection or individual volumes in Ireland and to have them adequately catalogued and made available. In particular they would either sell or make available to any institution at the reserve price fixed by Messrs Sotheby's or otherwise agreed upon. The Benchers are, however, in imperative need of the capital sum which the value of the books represents. Because of the amount involved it would appear that they can only be retained in the country if the Government might consider it appropriate to have the collection retained by having recourse to the dormant court funds.

In reference to the specific objection made by the librarian of U.C.G. to the decision by the Benchers to sell the books, I say that the Library only enjoyed copyright facilities from 1800 to 1841 [*sic*] and that by far the greater part of the books being sold and almost all the valuable ones were not acquired under that privilege.

Instructions for the sale were given to M/S Sotheby's some time ago and arrangements for the sale are progressing. Consequently if the Government wishes to consider any action the decision is a matter of urgency.[9]

The librarian of University College Galway, Christopher Townley, continued to express concern about the sale and clearly felt that the benchers ought not to dispose of any book that they had acquired by virtue of any Act of parliament. His point about copyright privilege was stronger than the chief justice cared to acknowledge in his second letter to Lynch. This was so because the statute of 1836 which repealed the copyright privileges of King's Inns also instituted the payment from public monies of annual compensation for that loss and required that such compensation be spent in a particular fashion, as was demonstrated above.

9 Ó Dálaigh to Lynch, 6 August 1971. The date '1841' appears to be an error for 1836, when King's Inns lost its entitlement under the 1801 Act.

In practice the benchers were not certain from which of their sources of income they subsequently acquired particular titles.

According to George Murnaghan and Raymond O'Neill, no reply to Ó Dálaigh's second letter was received from the taoiseach. In fairness, it must be said that Jack Lynch had a lot on his mind that month. On 9 August 1971, just three days after the letter was written, internment without trial was reintroduced in Northern Ireland and widespread violence erupted.[10]

10 FS, paragraph 27.

CHAPTER EIGHT

The removal van

IN LATE AUGUST 1971, Feisenberger wrote to King's Inns to say that he would be in Dublin 'in or about 20 September, when the van will be there to collect the books'. During that week of his third and final visit to King's Inns any books which Feisenberger selected were all packed into a van and driven off to London. He and the society's librarian then enjoyed a cordial working relationship. According to Murnaghan and O'Neill, 'At that time, the librarian made a list of what appeared to her to be the more important of the books sent for sale, but it was not possible for her to make a comprehensive list or description thereof.' There exists at King's Inns Library an unsigned, typed list of just 200 titles which is five pages long, and which ends with the following note, apparently by Neylon:

Dr Feisenberger spent three days in the library and selected over 3,000 books. The above is a list compiled during his first day and a half here. In the following day and a half he selected works mainly from the scientific section and some serials.[1]

Feisenberger took the view that the catalogues prepared in London would be a sufficient record of the books removed from the society's library. It is clear that, as the van from Sotheby's drove down Henrietta Street laden with some 7,000 volumes comprising almost three thousand titles, nobody at King's Inns knew exactly which books had gone from the society's library. Not even Sotheby's had a list. What is unclear is how Feisenberger determined which works had 'any reference to Ireland' and, therefore, ought to be excluded from the sales as the chief justice had promised the taoiseach. His test appears to have been whether or not a book was specifically 'about' Ireland. That it might have an Irish author or publisher, or otherwise be of Irish interest, was not in itself necessarily sufficient to have it excluded from auction.

1 Feisenberger to Neylon, 24 Aug. 1971; FS, paragraph 28. The list is on the Library correspondence files, 1957–2001 (King's Inns MS).

The fact that the books being taken away were not stamped as having been withdrawn by King's Inns underlines the remarkable degree of trust involved in such an arrangement. It meant that, except for a couple of hundred works which were inadequately listed before they were removed, any loss or theft of the society's volumes would go completely unnoticed. There is, and was then, no way of checking if the auction catalogues circulated by Sotheby's shortly before the sales actually include all of the books removed from King's Inns Library. In his letter of July 1969 to John Kerr of Sotheby's, broaching the possibility of a sale, George Murnaghan had written that he would find it 'easier' if a representative of the auction house could call and inspect 'particular books' rather than he himself 'prepare a list', and it was on this entirely informal basis that the selection was ultimately made. Feisenberger appears to have dismissed a suggestion that he catalogue the books while selecting them from the shelves, as 'quite impractical and a job which we could not possibly or fairly be asked to undertake'. He pointed out that the sale catalogues would show which books Sotheby's had selected.[2] There is no reason, whatsoever, for believing that any of the benchers' books went astray or were damaged while in the care of Sotheby's, and no inference may be drawn from this account that Sotheby's ever acted other than entirely properly in connection with the King's Inns sales. It would be years later, and in a different context, that the ethics of distinguished London auction houses came under scrutiny following a number of incidents. However, it might still have been preferable if the movement of books to England had been undertaken more methodically by the benchers. There was no way for them to check that the books put on sale were in the same condition as they had been when they left King's Inns. So when Feisenberger later told Murnaghan that 'in quite a number of the books, plates and maps had obviously been torn out', it must be assumed that this damage was done before they were packed into the van and left Dublin.[3]

Early in October 1971 Feisenberger wrote to Murnaghan stating that everything had arrived safely in London and would very

---

2 Murnaghan to Kerr, 29 July 1969; Feisenberger to Murnaghan, 23 May 1972.
3 BMB, 1964–75, p. 258 (4 May 1972); Watson, *Sotheby's*, pp. 211–21; Ian Dunlop, 'Not the sort of image they want to sell', in *Independent on Sunday* (27 Feb. 2000), p. 19; Penelope Dening, 'Sotheby's and Christie's may yet end in dock for price-fixing', in *Ir. Times* (26 Feb. 2000). For a general history of Sotheby's, see also Lacey, *Sotheby's*.

shortly be unpacked and organised for the first sale. But his main purpose in writing was to alert the judge to a certain development:

I think I ought to tell you that somehow or other the Irish press has already got hold of some information about your sale. Our Press Office was asked about it yesterday by the *Irish Independent*. We all thought it better to give them a little information rather than say nothing at all because – knowing what the press is like – they would search into it even more if we said nothing. We therefore gave them some very vague information, saying that the books had arrived here but had not yet been properly examined and that in any case the sale would not take place until next year. But we did emphasize that no Irish material of any kind is included and that it consists of some books on Geography, Philosophy and Medicine. Our Press Office is very skilful in handling these matters and we thought that by doing it this way the press would probably calm down. However, I thought it better to inform you of our action in case they come back to you.[4]

Sotheby's had mistakenly informed the *Irish Independent* that no Irish material of any kind was included in the forthcoming auction. Moreover, their Press Office appears to have miscalculated the strength of feeling in Ireland relating to the planned sales. It was not only journalists who were interested in it. By December the Department of Justice was quietly considering the possibility of making money available, perhaps again from the funds of suitors, so that the National Library might acquire the benchers' books. The director of the National Library, Patrick Henchy, was now in a position to be interested when his bosses at the Department of Education again wrote to him about the King's Inns sale. He replied,

I feel that if the money required for the purchase of the books in question can be found by having recourse to a source other than the exchequer (as suggested in the Department of Justice letter), then I would welcome the idea. If one can judge the entire collection from the selected list supplied it would appear that it is of a high cultural and scholarly order. There are, occasionally, such books and collections of books that the National Library would wish to acquire for the nation, but, because of the limitations placed upon us, we cannot contemplate their purchase. The solution suggested for keeping the collection in Ireland appears to be an ideal one.

In conjunction with Trinity College Library it has been our policy to endeavour to build up the collection of the particular library where the greater strength lies. Accordingly, it is desirable that the books acquired by Legal Deposit (1801–1841) should, as required, go to Trinity College

4 Feisenberger to Murnaghan, 6 Oct. 1971.

Library. This would also allay the criticism of those who hold that the auctioning of these in London breaks a public trust.

The position of the National Library has, happily, changed since the matter was first raised. The Minister for Education has promised additional accommodation and staff in the near future. We will now be able to expand as a National Library should, and we will be in a position to accept, catalogue, maintain and make available to our readers collections, or parts of collections, such as those which have been sent to Sotheby's by the benchers. As the National Library is the state library and has not a restricted readership like the libraries of the universities it seems reasonable to suggest that those, other than the lots received under Legal Deposit which could be deposited in Trinity College Library, would be acquired by the National Library. We already possess a copy of the *Nuremberg Chronicle*, and I would suggest that this, with any other such duplicates, be deposited in University College [Dublin?] Library.

As our primary concern continues to be with the acquisition of Irish items, I would like to know if the benchers have any plans for the eventual disposal of their Irish material, including the Swift Collection.[5]

Barristers too wished to know more. One week before Christmas, at the annual general meeting of the Bar, they appointed a committee to discover 'when and on what grounds' the benchers had decided to sell books and whether the latter had authority to make that decision. More significantly, the barristers also wanted to know 'who selected the books to be sold, and whether there is a complete list of books sent to Sotheby's', as well as 'who authorised the physical transfer of the books from the King's Inns Library to Sotheby's'. That the terms of the resolution establishing the committee was too intemperate for some barristers is suggested by the fact that, three days before Christmas, the annual general meeting resumed and King's Inns was then assured that both the proposer and seconder of the motion 'expressly stated that they were in no way critical of, or antipathetic to, the benchers in this matter, and that they felt they spoke for the whole Bar in this respect'.[6]

5 Henchy to the Secretary, Dept. of Education, 17 Dec. 1971 (National Library MS). Although King's Inns possesses two books that appear to have belonged to Swift, and others by him, it has no designated 'Swift Collection'. Kennedy, 'Great Irish libraries', refers to certain 'extensive correspondence' between Swift scholars and the library of King's Inns. See also p. 143 below. For '1841' see p. 60, n. 9 above.
6 G. D. Coyle, secretary, General Council of the Bar of Ireland, to F.A. Magee, under-treasurer, King's Inns, 17 and 22 Dec. 1971. Although Mary Robinson was unable to attend the first meeting of the Bar, 'owing to a meeting of the legal committee of which I am a member in Brussels', she sent a long list of questions that ought to be asked about the sale (Robinson family papers).

When the barristers' enquiries were considered by the benchers, in January 1972, Murnaghan explained to his colleagues that 'Dr Feisenberger was to prepare a catalogue and he [Murnaghan] had hoped to get a copy before Christmas, but so far it had not reached him. He proposed to write to Dr Feisenberger for the catalogue or a list of the books removed'. It was agreed to give the Bar all particulars or information available, but the barristers found it necessary to write again in March seeking the details requested and stating that 'the Bar regards the matter as one of urgency'.[7]

Despite what are said to have been numerous requests from Murnaghan to Sotheby's for a copy or proof of the catalogue of the books for sale to be sent well in advance of the auction, no copy thereof was received in Dublin until about mid-April 1972, shortly before the auction. One assumes that Sotheby's followed its usual practice in relation to the preparation of a catalogue. The failure of the benchers themselves to make a full and accurate list of what they had subsequently let go to Sotheby's was simply highlighted by any necessary or unusual delay in the preparation of a final professional catalogue. It had been a winter of industrial unrest in Britain and, in early March 1972, Feisenberger wrote to Murnaghan at his home address that, 'We have been working under very great difficulties owing to the electricity blackouts and the present go-slow of the printers'. He had a particular proposal in connection with the catalogue, but this fell on deaf ears and nothing came of it:

It is also very important in my opinion, that we have a short note at the beginning, explaining and justifying the sale. Would you care to draft this for me, otherwise I shall try and compose something and submit it to your approval. In this connection it would also be a good idea if I could possibly have a few notes on the history of the library, if you have any. Perhaps one could make a reference to the period during which you were a copyright library, if you have the exact dates. One could make all this into a little preface which I think would greatly help to prevent any discussion or attack on the sale. If I could have your views on all this I should be very grateful.

If you are still interested to come to London as I hope you do, we should be delighted to have you as our guest. Shall I provisionally book you a room from April 24 for two or three nights?[8]

No such preface as that suggested by Feisenberger was to grace the catalogues of King's Inns books which Sotheby's published. It

7 BMB, 1964–75, p. 241 (11 Jan. 1971); Coyle to Magee, 4 March 1972.
8 FS, paragraph 29; Feisenberger to Murnaghan, 8 March 1972.

may be assumed that Murnaghan did not agree with the assessment that 'a little preface' which included 'a short note ... explaining and justifying the sale' would, in fact, 'greatly help to prevent any discussion or attack on the sale'. Indeed, this suggestion by Feisenberger indicates that he did not fully understand the possible cultural implications of such a sale of Irish books in London, implications which might only be highlighted by the publication of 'a few notes on the history of the library'. His reference to the Copyright Act implies that he assumed that many books had been acquired by the society of King's Inns simply because they were free and not because the society really wanted them. If so, this was an assumption by Feisenberger which is not borne out by a reading of the society's records. These show that benchers of earlier years had wished to create a broad collection. Moreover, the chief justice had already told the taoiseach that few of the books put up for sale had actually been acquired under the provisions of the copyright statute.

CHAPTER NINE

Questions in the Dáil

ANY EXPECTATION THAT the sale would pass off without public controversy was soon dashed. On 13 April 1972 An Taisce, the National Trust for Ireland, decided to investigate the possibilities of buying in or retaining in Ireland some of the rarer lots due to be auctioned. Various librarians were contacted and gave their support. A check in Trinity College Dublin revealed that Trinity had not got copies of 209 of the 829 King's Inns lots listed by Sotheby's in their April catalogues. The librarians of University College Dublin and University College Galway also reported that these 209 lots were not in their holdings. Shortages of time and of staff were said to have prevented a similar check in the National Library.[1]

On the morning of 15 April 1972 a letter from Thomas P. O'Neill, then lecturer in history at University College Galway, appeared in the *Irish Independent* and left no reader in doubt of the strength of feeling which was about to make a heated controversy of the forthcoming sale by King's Inns. In his letter, O'Neill remarked sarcastically, 'Now that Conservation Year has passed away quietly we can get on with the disposal of our heritage.' He objected firstly to the proposed sale of twenty incunables, 'some with early manuscript annotations and one incorporating a thirteenth century manuscript fragment'. He also protested at the proposed sale of various sixteenth and seventeenth map collections, as well as five particular books. These were the only recorded European copy of a work by Cardinal Richelieu; a rare Waterford imprint of 1555 ('spurious, I know, but nevertheless of great interest'); a first edition of Fynes Moryson's *Itinerary* (1617), 'including his account of Lord Mountjoy's campaign of 1601–3'; 'a rare newsletter of the Popish

---

1 Nicholas Robinson, 'Resumé of An Taisce's involvement in the sale of books from the King's Inns Library' (18 May 1971) (An Taisce MSS), p. 1, which states that the 'group involved' at this time on behalf of An Taisce consisted of John Temple Lang, Nicholas Robinson, N. A. Jameson, M. O'N. Walshe, Mary ('Paul') Pollard and T.P. O'Neill, and that these had received 'expert assistance' from N. Figgis, Bruce Arnold, W. Dillon and J.F. Newman & Son.

Plot, 1679–1682'; and, finally, as O'Neill noted, 'the first book to suggest tenant purchase as a solution to the Irish land question (the only other copy I know in Ireland is in T.C.D.)'. Two of these books were subsequently withdrawn and returned to King's Inns, two were purchased at the sale by An Taisce and one was sold off at auction.[2] O'Neill further objected to the sale of books 'by Irish travellers and explorers (e.g. Tyndall, McClure, McClintock, etc.)'.[3] He also drew attention generally to other 'rare travel books with accounts of convict settlements in Australia which have considerable Irish interest', but did not identify these.[4]

On the same day that it published O'Neill's letter the *Irish Independent* also carried an article and an editorial about the sale. In this article Bruce Arnold wrote that the books listed by O'Neill 'and more than one hundred others in the auction are unique copies as far as Ireland is concerned and their disposal on the open international market effectively prevents their acquisition by any Irish library, because of shortage of funds'. Arnold, an historian of art

2 The first two were lot 202 (Richelieu, *A Christian instruction*, Paris, 1662) and lot 163 (John Olde, *Acquital or purgation of ... Edward VI ...*). These were to be bought by An Taisce at the sale on 24 April, for £62 and £380 respectively, and are now in the library of University College Galway. The third, by Morrison (lot 620), was withdrawn for return to King's Inns. The fourth was, according to a note on the King's Inns files, *The weekly pacquet of advice from Rome on the history of Popery ... to each being added the Popish Courant, vol. 1 to 3. 1679–82* (lot 256). This was sold at auction to Pottesman for £10. According to this same note, the fifth was F. von Raumer, *England in 1835: a series of letters written to friends in Germany ...* 3 vols., 1836 (among other titles in lot 423), which was withdrawn and returned to King's Inns.

3 This was apparently a reference to, among other titles, John Tyndall, *Hours of exercise in the Alps*, 1871 (one of four titles identified among nine titles in lot 809); (Captain) R. McClure, *The discovery of the north-west passage*, 1856, and (Captain) McClintock, *A narrative of the discovery of the fate of Sir John Franklin*, 1859 (two of six titles identified among nine in lot 810). On 26 April, lots 809 and 810 were sold to Gaston's Alpine Books, for £15 and £55 respectively (Sotheby's 'Price list').

4 On 25 April An Taisce bought, for £150, G. Barrington, *An account of a voyage to New South Wales*, 2 vols., 1810 (lot 294). On 26 April University College Galway bought, for £55, P. E. de Strzelecki, *Physical description of New South Wales*, 1845 (lot 731). That same day, the King's Inns withdrew, for return to its own library, David Collins, *An account of the English colony in New South Wales ... to which are added some particulars of New Zealand*, 1808 (lot 377). Twenty other books relating to Australia, including Roderick Flanagan, *History of New South Wales*, 1862, and [J. O'Hara], *History of New South Wales*, 1817, were subsequently listed, apparently by O'Neill, in a document that is on the King's Inns file, but these books were all sold off at the April auction.

and literature, raised very serious questions about the manner in which the sale itself was organised: 'The rare books expert from Sotheby's, Dr Feisenberger, was apparently given free access to the library. No catalogue of the books he chose was either asked for or given. They were simply crated and shipped to London. The only comprehensive list was the catalogue which was subsequently prepared there. There was, therefore, no independent valuation of the collection which is now to be auctioned.' Arnold expressed his concern that the sale might set a precedent for other institutional libraries in Ireland. In its editorial in the same issue the *Irish Independent* patiently explained why the benchers considered it necessary to sell the books, noting that, 'Overheads, clearly, are significant and the practical legal conclusion appears to have been that rather than have ancient volumes of value and of interest to the scholastic community quietly gathering dust in a little frequented library, much better to sell them abroad, if that is where the money is.' But, the editorial continued,

The significant omission in this line of argument is that, if applied to all our items of potential interest to collectors, this country would eventually be cleaned out of prized material. *Incunabula* do not have to be borrowed regularly in order to justify their place in a library: there is such a thing as our national heritage and the physical part of it, including books, is essential to it. This is a refined and long-term point of view but one would expect the Benchers of King's Inns, with, in fairness to them, the aid of the government, to give a lead in this field.

Later that day Tom O'Higgins, who was a Dáil deputy as well as a bencher, informed Conor McAnally of the *Evening Herald* that the books had been 'offered to libraries in the country, but I understand that it was not possible to preserve them because of their value'. It was stated by him that the library was not being widely used for non-legal purposes and that the very valuable books represented a fire and burglary risk. Speaking for the benchers, Raymond O'Neill, SC, was quoted elsewhere as saying that only three or four books of possible Irish interest appeared on the list of those sent to Sotheby's for auction and 'if they are of interest, they will be withdrawn'.[5]

5 *Ir. Independent* and *Ir. Press*, 15 Apr. 1972; *Ev. Herald*, 15 Apr. 1972; O'Higgins was a Fine Gael TD who, on behalf of that party, unsuccessfully contested the presidential elections of 1966 and 1973. Subsequently, he became chief justice (1974–85) and a judge of the European Court of Justice (1985–91).

However, T.P. O'Neill and others began to broaden the attack on the sale. O'Neill enquired if the benchers thought that the only things of value in the country worth keeping were all Irish. He pointed out that the Chester Beatty Library, an invaluable collection belonging to the state, was composed of almost all non-Irish material. He said that a council of experts in various fields should have been set up to scrutinise what was being exported by King's Inns. He accepted that the universities had been contacted about the books, but argued that it was unreasonable to expect that they could afford to buy more than one or two of them. Senator Mary Robinson was also voicing her concerns publicly. Then a barrister and Reid Professor of Law at Trinity College Dublin, which she represented in Seanad Éireann, the future president of Ireland deplored the sale and claimed that 'none of the money raised is to be used for improving the legal library or for the security and care of what is left'. Rumours that the books were being sold off principally to pay for the new kitchen, at a time when the cost of dining by law students, barristers and benchers was subsidised, were fanning the flames of protest. Each student was obliged to attend sixteen dinners each year as part of her or his progress towards the degree of barrister-at-law and each dinner cost only £1, notwithstanding the generous provision of alcohol. A spokesman for one organisation of UCD law students, The Phoenix Society, told the *Evening Herald* that, 'We think it is a disgrace but we are just powerless to do anything about it. We especially condemn it when the money is being used to pay for dining customs which are totally out of date. We have to put on barristers' cloaks, and at the top of the massive hall the benchers sit. They have butlers walking around dressed out of Dickens: it is all totally ridiculous.' In fact, the benchers' debts were far greater than the sum expended on their new kitchen and they also had future requirements to consider, some of which related to their library.[6]

By 17 April 1972 the King's Inns Library Committee had received a catalogue of the forthcoming April auction. They decided that just ten items would be withdrawn from sale: 'Four obviously had reference to Ireland.' The remaining six had been bound in Dublin although containing no reference to Ireland. However, the committee also authorised Murnaghan to withdraw any other works which seemed to be 'of Irish interest'.[7]

6 *Ev. Herald*, 15 April 1972.
7 FS, paragraph 31; BMB, p. 254 (4 May 1972).

The librarians of Trinity College Dublin, University College Dublin and University College Galway had become so alarmed that they decided to make a public protest about the forthcoming sale. On 18 April 1972 the *Irish Independent* reported receiving a letter from them in which they said that they were 'deeply concerned at the possible loss to the nation of the King's Inns books that are now announced for auction at Sotheby's':

The librarians say that the catalogue produced by Sotheby's 'reveals clearly the importance of these books and the majority are not to be found in the other libraries in the country'. They express the hope that means to save the collection 'will be forthcoming'.

That same day, various librarians checked what were described by An Taisce as 'all major and some smaller library holdings', with particular reference to those incunables which the benchers of King's Inns were selling. Nine of the lots were found to be unique to Ireland. An Taisce made a strategic decision to concentrate on saving the incunables before all else.[8]

On 19 April 1972, as controversy grew, the benchers convened specially to consider a request by Radio Telefís Éireann for the society's participation in a radio interview and to decide what, if any, steps should be taken regarding publicity given to the sale of books. There had been a phone call from Maxwell Sweeney, a radio producer, stating that T.P. O'Neill was going to be interviewed on RTE and affording the benchers an opportunity of taking part in the discussion. Chief Justice Ó Dálaigh suggested that it was time to decide 'whether (a) to have the Bench as a body draft a reply to the propaganda (b) appoint a spokesman (c) ignore the matter'. He added that he wanted it recorded that he was 'in favour of again writing to the Taoiseach, even at this late moment, asking him to reconsider his attitude to the sale of the books', and his proposal to this effect was seconded by John A. Costello, a senior counsel and former taoiseach. The chief justice pointed out that neither the National Library nor any of the other institutions contacted by the benchers was in a position to acquire any of the books on the open market. Nevertheless, his motion was defeated following a lengthy discussion. A further motion from Patrick Bourke, SC, that a statement be drafted to inform the public of the society's financial

8 Robinson, 'Resumé', p. 1 (An Taisce MS).

position and of the reason for selling books, was withdrawn and the benchers ultimately agreed to do nothing.[9]

By now, politicians were turning their attention to the controversy. On 20 April 1972, Deputies Haughey, Desmond and Thornley raised questions in the Dáil concerning the sale. Barry Desmond and David Thornley, both of the Labour Party, invited a statement on what they described as a 'matter of urgent public importance'. Charles J. Haughey, the former Minister for Justice who in 1970 had been acquitted of a charge of conspiracy to import arms illegally, asked if the Minister for Education, his Fianna Fáil party colleague, would provide funds for the National Library to acquire the rare books being sold by the benchers. Haughey himself was later to contribute £100 to An Taisce's special collection for the purchase of the King's Inns copy of 'the confessions' (*Confessiones*) of St Augustine of Hippo. Although the deputies' questions were directed at the Minister for Education they were dealt with by the minister's parliamentary secretary, or junior, Michael O'Kennedy. O'Kennedy, later to be a commissioner of the European Union, told the Dáil that King's Inns had 'given an undertaking that such books as may have reference to Ireland will not be included in the sale'. He added, 'This being so I am not satisfied that considerations of the national interest arise to an extent which would warrant the provision of the very considerable sums of money which would be involved in retaining through purchase the remaining books'. He informed the house that 'we have a list of all the books to be sold. From a perusal of the list it appears that what the Benchers have said is, in fact, the case. The books are more collectors' items than books of any special interest to Ireland ...' Clearly the minister had reached a conclusion different from that of the university librarians and of An Taisce. In stating that the books were not of any special interest to Ireland, he may well have relied upon the first memorandum of the director of the National Library to the Department of Education, dated 22 July 1971, and considered above, in which Patrick Henchy had identified his priorities and described the books at Sotheby's as being 'not of Irish interest'. However, O'Kennedy made no reference to the second memo-

9 BMB, pp. 250–2 (19 Apr. 1972). Ó Dálaigh had been appointed a bencher in 1946. The only bencher more senior than him was Costello, appointed a full twenty years earlier in 1926. Costello was taoiseach from 1948 to 1951, and again from 1954 to 1957.

randum from Henchy, dated 17 December 1971, and also considered above, which described the books for sale as being 'of a high cultural and scholarly order' and which welcomed the idea of acquiring them 'for the nation'.

Barry Desmond, who later became a government minister before being appointed to the European Court of Auditors, asked O'Kennedy how one might define historical library items which are not of Irish interest? 'Since when would a particular piece of religious, scientific or geographical literature not be of Irish interest … ?', he queried. O'Kennedy retorted by pointing out that no ministerial approval was required for the sale because 'these are all printed documents'. He added that, 'the priority would be for the National Library to acquire books which have a specific Irish interest. If the Deputy looks through the list he will find that nothing of specifically Irish interest … will be offered for sale, and if they are included in the catalogue by mistake they will be withdrawn'. Fine Gael's Tom O'Higgins then intervened. Himself a bencher and a future chief justice, he invited O'Kennedy to tell the Dáil if it was a fact that 'these books were offered to each library in the country and specifically to the Taoiseach as Head of the Government, and that every effort was made to interest possible purchasers inside the country before the books were sent to Sotheby's'. O'Kennedy answered simply that the taoiseach had been notified and that the books had been offered to the National Library. In an ambiguous intervention, possibly intended to be a sarcastic comment on the past absence from King's Inns Library of some of those who were now objecting to the sale, O'Higgins wanted to know if O'Kennedy was 'aware of the well-worn path down to the King's Inns of all these historians and very knowledgeable persons who have spent the last ten years examining these books?'

As the exchanges heated up the junior minister was accused of flippancy and the epithet 'Philistines' was hurled across the house at the government benches. Deputy Thornley demanded to know, 'Is the Parliamentary Secretary prepared to co-operate in a situation in which we continue to flog our national heritage to the Americans and English?' O'Kennedy became irritated by his interrogation and protested, 'I understand as well as Deputy Thornley and his fellow academics in the benches over there that an Irishman does not confine his interest to matters of Irish historical interest.' In a further jibe, which by the nature of its content suggests that he had before him merely the abbreviated list of titles sent to the libraries the previous summer and not a full listing or catalogue, O'Kennedy wanted to know if the deputy was really suggesting 'that we should regard as a priority the retention of books such as *Antiquities of Pola in Istria, Nuremberg Chronicle, Carnival of Rome, Views of Venice, Ancient Rome* or whatever else – '.[10]

Mr Desmond: Why not, if this is the heritage of this country?

Mr O'Kennedy: What the Deputy is suggesting is that we should have an embargo on the sale of all books.

Dr Thornley: Does the Parliamentary Secretary propose that the National Gallery should now sell its Renoirs, its Hogarths or its Gainsboroughs since they are not of Irish interest?

(Interruptions)

Dr O'Donovan TD rose to make a special plea on behalf of Fynes Moryson's *Itinerary* of 1617, to which O'Neill had already drawn attention in his letter to the newspapers. O'Kennedy promised to 'take a note of the particular book with which he is concerned and if it is included and is of special significance we can suggest that it be withdrawn'. The work was indeed included in the catalogue for 26 April (lot 620) but was then withdrawn and returned to Dublin. O'Kennedy informed Charles Haughey that it was felt that the collection would fetch 'something of the order of £200,000', especially given 'that so many of these books are collectors' items'. He confessed that he did not know how much the benchers needed 'for their immediate purposes' but told the house that the benchers

have indicated that the purpose of the sale is to pay off their overdraft arising out of repairs and renewals to the King's Inns and King's Inns Library, to put the King's Inns on a proper financial footing to enable the benchers to improve their educational facilities, and – I think this may be some

10 *Dáil Éireann deb.*, vol. 260, cols. 762–7 (20 April 1972). These five titles had appeared on the first page of the short list circulated by the benchers in the same form given in the Dáil by O'Kennedy. They are Thomas Allason, *Picturesque views of the antiquities of Pola in Istria, folio 1819* (lot 9, sold 24 April to Maggs, £48); Hartmann Schedel, *Liber chronicarum cum figuris et imaginibus ab initio mundi*, 1st ed., 1493, including 1809 woodcuts (lot 218, known as the 'Nuremberg *chronicle[s]*', sold 24 April to Maggs, £2,100); Bartolomeo Pinelli, *Five last days of the carnival of Rome*, 1830 (lot 538, sold 7 November to C. E. King, £7); Antonio Canaletto, *Prospectus magni canalis Venetiarum*, Venice, 1751 (lot 46, sold 24 April to K. Mohler, £700); Bonaventure d'Overbeke, *Les restes de l'ancienne Rome*, 1763 (lot 170, sold 24 April to B. Weinreb, £140).

compensation to the intellectuals in the Labour party who regard the rest of us as Philistines – to improve the library and to have the books in it properly catalogued.

The parliamentary exchanges ended with Haughey, the future taoiseach, making a plea that, 'in these times of reasonable budgetary affluence', money might be made available as it had been in 1967 to purchase for the National Museum of Ireland certain Irish items known as 'the Killymoon Hoard' that were for sale in London.

On the same day as the Dáil debated the sale, an Irishman at Jesus College Cambridge, Edward McParland, put pen to paper to plead with the benchers on behalf of one particular book. His letter shows clearly that, insofar as the government had reassured the Dáil that 'nothing of specifically Irish interest ... will be offered for sale, and if they are included in the catalogue by mistake they will be withdrawn', the house had been misinformed. The book to which he refers was in fact later to be sold to Nebenzahl for £130. McParland, today a distinguished architectural historian and academic at Trinity College Dublin, then wrote:

As it is the intention of the Benchers to consider withdrawing from the Sotheby's sale books of Irish interest, I should like to draw their attention to lot 150 on the first day – James Murphy's *Arabian antiquities of Spain* [engraved title, 98 plates, folio, 1815]. Murphy was a Cork-born architect described in Mulvany's *Life of James Gandon* as having been employed on alterations to the Dublin Parliament House. He was a protégé of William Burton Conyngham of Slane, the leading patron of the arts (after Lord Charlemont) in Ireland in the late eighteenth century. Conyngham financed Murphy's travels to Spain and Portugal and the resulting engravings were of considerable importance in the history of the Gothic revival. *The Arabian Antiquities* influenced such Irish architects as William Vitruvius Morrison for instance in his decoration of Baronscourt. Murphy's are rare books of, I would cautiously judge, considerable Irish interest. I understand of course that this letter may arrive too late for anything to be done – for this I apologise. Yours, etc.[11]

11 SCM, 1960–75, p. 284 (30 Apr. 1971); McParland to King's Inns (20 April 1972). A year earlier McParland had received permission to inspect the minutes of King's Inns in connection with his research on Irish architecture of the late eighteenth and early nineteenth century. His *James Gandon: Vitruvius Hibernicus* is a major study of the architect that includes many references to King's Inns. At McParland et al., *Architecture of Richard Morrison and William Vitruvius Morrison*, p. 24, it is said that, 'The Moorish fret pattern taken from J. C. Murphy's *Arabian Antiquities of Spain* which the Morrisons used at Ballyfin reappears in the borders of the ceiling [at Baronscourt]'.

In fact, McParland was not too late to have his letter read. Its suggestion was passed on by the librarian to the benchers attending a meeting of the Standing Committee on the afternoon of 21 April. The librarian also included Murphy's *Arabian antiquities* on a separate list of sixteen 'items recommended for withdrawal'. Eight of the sixteen were bracketed by her as 'Irish authors' but only one of these was among five of the sixteen items actually withdrawn from auction. Indeed, two of that particular five were only withdrawn because An Taisce had decided to buy them at an agreed price, and two more were to be re-entered for sale in November, when An Taisce also agreed to buy them.[12]

Arabian antiquities also appeared on a list of 27 books (in 25 lots) published by the national newspapers on the morning of 21 April 1972 (see Appendix Three below). This list was appended to a letter signed by Séan Corkery, librarian at Maynooth College, and Mary Pollard, keeper of early printed books at Trinity College Dublin, amongst others. The authors were angry at the proposed sale by King's Inns, and at the fact that books of Irish interest had been removed from Henrietta Street to Sotheby's. They wrote that,

Of the books listed in their sale catalogue at least twenty-five are by any definition of Irish interest – either by Irish authors, relate to Irishmen, or were produced in this country. We append a list of these books. The benchers so far appear to have made no attempt to prevent their sale. We wonder why not in view of Mr Raymond O'Neill's statement that all Irish books would be withdrawn from the sale.

Of the 25 lots appended, thirteen were subsequently withdrawn from sale. Four of the remaining lots were bought by An Taisce, and the other eight were sold privately.

Also on the morning of 21 April, writing in the *Irish Times*, William Dillon objected to the sale of many of the items, and identified a factor that had irritated scholars and historians:

It is that the King's Inns only circulated a truncated list of the books that they intended to dispose of by public sale; another point of grievance was that many Irish libraries, scholars and bibliophiles have only very recently received the elaborate catalogue of the sale which commences on Monday next.

12 See Appendix Two for the librarian's annotated list.

Dillon singled out certain books for favourable attention (see Appendix Four below). Among these were both the *Nuremberg chronicles*, which on the previous day the government's spokesman had belittled in the Dáil but which the librarian at UCD had earlier indicated to be of great interest, and *Calabria*, a series of 66 hand-coloured engraved prints described by Sotheby's as 'remarkable and rare' and illustrating an Italian earthquake of 1783. The plates were nearly all signed by Schiantarelli, whom Dillon described as 'the distinguished European architect'. As already noted, the volume of the *Nuremberg chronicles* (lot 218) would be sold at auction on 24 April for £2,100. *Calabria* was withdrawn at auction on 24 April (lot 45), but subsequently re-entered on 7 November 1972 when it fetched £420 (lot 426). In all, Dillon referred specifically to fifteen lots, of which only one is known to have been withdrawn by King's Inns (lot 636). Five of the others were bought by An Taisce and eight were sold privately, while the fate of the fifteenth is uncertain. Dillon blamed the exodus of valuable works partly on 'bad Irish legislation in the form of the Copyright Act of 1963', which he said had 'undoubtedly encouraged the benchers of the King's Inns to sell their inheritance'. He conceded that,

Admittedly the King's Inns did circulate a brief list of some of the books which they were sending for sale. The miserable allocations by the Department of Education to the libraries of Ireland would not encourage the possibility of the libraries being able to purchase some of the unique books. Many Scottish county libraries probably have more finance for acquisitions than all the institutional libraries of Ireland.

CHAPTER TEN

First sales, April 1972

ON 20 AND 21 APRIL 1972, with the sales at Sotheby's imminent, King's Inns received three letters from An Taisce. Murnaghan reported that these were handed to him personally only at 5.00 p.m. on 21 April, just as the Standing Committee convened. In one letter An Taisce made an offer of £1,750 for six particular lots printed before 1501 (incunables) and this was accepted. The lots were withdrawn from auction and purchased by An Taisce for the National Library, Maynooth College and Trinity College Dublin, each of which had contributed £500 to a special fund. The balance was contributed by the Friends of the National Collections of Ireland (£200) and an anonymous donor living in Liverpool (£50). According to An Taisce, these lots and three other incunables were 'unique in the country'. Two of that three were also withdrawn from auction in April (lots 70 and 205), but were subsequently sold on 7 November at Sotheby's, being Augustinus Datus, *Elegantiolae*, Daventer, 1489 (lot 443, to T. Thorp, £140) and Werner Rolewinck, *Fasciculus temporum*, Cologne, c.1483 (lot 556, to F. Bondi, £100). Sotheby's were aware of the existence of only two other copies of *Elegantiolae*, one being in The Hague and one in Copenhagen. It had a large woodcut of a lecturer and pupils on its title page. The other work identified by An Taisce as being 'unique in the country' was Augustine's *Confessiones*. This, as we shall see, became the object of strained negotiations before being finally purchased by An Taisce.[1]

In one of its letters, An Taisce drew attention to statutory requirements relating to the exportation of documents and attached a list of 21 particular lots which, in its opinion, the benchers were not

---

1 John Temple Lang to Murnaghan, 20 and 21 April 1972 (An Taisce MS); SCM, 1960–75, p. 305 (21 April 1972); BMB, p. 254 (4 May 1972); *Ir. Independent*, 24 Feb. 1972 and *Ir. Times*, 27 Apr. 1972; Brendan O'Donoghue, Director, National Library of Ireland, to the author, 17 Aug. 2000; Penelope Woods, Librarian, Russell Library, NUI Maynooth, to the author, 21 Aug. 2000. For the six lots of incunables bought in April by An Taisce (lots 33, 76, 115, 126, 180 and 181), and for their current locations, see Appendix Nine below.

entitled at that point to sell outside Ireland. John Temple Lang wrote from An Taisce,

We have noticed and it has been confirmed by our antiquarian advisers, that a number of the lots included in the auction appear to be or contain documents, such as manuscripts or maps, which are not wholly in print and which therefore should not be exported without a licence under the Documents and Pictures (Regulation of Export) Act 1945. We understand that no such licence has been granted in respect of any of the lots, no doubt because the books taken by Sotheby's were not inspected on behalf of the benchers before they were taken away.[2]

So, out of 829 lots in the April sale, 21 appeared to An Taisce to be affected by the Act of 1945. Of these lots eleven contained annotations or written fragments and ten contained hand-coloured plates and were thus not 'wholly in print'.[3] For example, Olde's *Acquittal*, published in 1555, had numerous handwritten notations throughout and ought not to have been exported without a licence. The catalogues published by Sotheby's were inadequate for the purposes of monitoring possible breaches of the 1945 Act, in that they did not include reference to all such manuscript notes on the books being sold for King's Inns.

When he selected old volumes at King's Inns for transportation to Sotheby's in London, Hellmut Feisenberger may have overlooked the fact that a number were not wholly in print. It is not known if he was even aware of the terms of the Irish Documents and Pictures Act 1945, or of the fact that its provisions appear to have been contravened when he, on behalf of the benchers, had various books and maps loaded into a van in Dublin and driven off to England. Certainly, Michael O'Kennedy seems to have been ignorant of the facts, or of the law, when he spoke as parliamentary secretary in the Dáil and informed the House that no licence was required by the benchers.[4]

Concerning the statutory requirements, An Taisce had raised an important point in its letter to King's Inns. However, the benchers said that there was insufficient time available at the meeting of the Standing Committee to deal with the matter. Finding this to be 'an unsatisfactory response', An Taisce spent Saturday 22 April

---

2 *Ir. Times*, 24 Apr. 1972; An Taisce MSS. A copy of the list was sent by An Taisce to Michael O'Kennedy T.D., parliamentary secretary to the Minister for Education.
3 Nicholas Robinson to Carson, 4 May 1972 (An Taisce MS).
4 *Dáil Éireann deb.*, vol. 260, cols. 762–67 (20 April 1972).

1972 in a full day's briefing with solicitors and counsel, during which all legal implications of the sale were explored and affidavits for injunctions drafted. On the afternoon of Sunday 23 April, the day before the sales were due to commence, Chief Justice Ó Dálaigh telephoned Murnaghan, who later reported that,

> He told me that he had reason to believe that an application would be made that evening for an injunction to restrain the sale of the books alleged to have been exported without a licence. The Chief Justice further told me that he had spoken to a majority of the Standing Committee on the telephone and that they had agreed that the said books should be withdrawn from the sale. We had a very long conversation. Eventually I told the Chief Justice that I would examine each of the books on the list and withdraw any that I considered should have been covered by a licence. This did not satisfy the Chief Justice. I was eventually persuaded to agree to withdraw these books. I am bound to say that I was unaware of the provisions of the Act. In this I was not alone. The books were in London and no licence had been delivered to the proper office of C[ustoms] & E[xcise] at time of export.[5]

There is a legal maxim that 'ignorance of the law is no excuse' and An Taisce was now informed 'after long negotiations' that, 'In view of the question of the application of the Document and Picture (Regulation and Export) Act 1945 having been raised, the items on that list [from An Taisce], save those disposed of to An Taisce, will be withdrawn from the sale'.[6]

According to Aengus Fanning of the *Irish Independent*,

> The benchers had no alternative but to withdraw the books once it had been pointed out to them they had transgressed the law. But it is difficult to see how any legal proceedings could have resulted. The attorney-general who would have to initiate legal action is himself a bencher, as are the judges of the High Court and Supreme Court. In effect they would have to take action against themselves.

Fanning also noted that the benchers were 'self-electing', an observation which underlined the fact that the controversy was not only attracting attention to the sale of books but also creating publicity about the very nature of the society of King's Inns.[7]

---

5 Robinson, 'Resumé', p. 1 (An Taisce MS). The counsel were Mary Robinson, married to Nicholas, and Richard P. Johnson. The solicitors were John F. Buckley and Ciarán McAnally; BMB, pp. 255–6 (4 May 1972), and a draft of this same account in Murnaghan's hand in Library correspondence files (King's Inns MS).
6 *Ir. Times* and *Ir. Press*, 24 Apr. 1972; *Sunday Press*, 5 Nov. 1972.
7 *Ir. Independent*, 24 Apr. 1972. Fanning later became editor of the *Sunday Independent*; FS, paragraphs 33–4.

As well as discussing on 21 April 1972 the possible need to withdraw particular books from the forthcoming auction, pending a resolution of the issue of export licences, the benchers' Standing Committee also considered the appropriate test for deciding what if any other books to withdraw. Ought the test to be that they were 'of Irish interest' (which was the formulation earlier adopted by the Library Committee on 20 June 1970 and again on 17 April 1972) or that they had 'reference to Ireland'? Murnaghan subsequently told other benchers that the Standing Committee had agreed upon the latter ('reference to Ireland') because it was the form of words used in the letter of the chief justice to the taoiseach dated 2 July 1971, which was considered above. Yet, somewhat confusingly, Murnaghan also told his fellow benchers that the Standing Committee had at the same time given him the power to withdraw from the sale any items which seemed to him 'to be of Irish interest'.[8] The distinction was important because one could argue that many of the books were 'of Irish interest', whereas far fewer contained a 'reference to Ireland'. Judge Murnaghan, Minister O'Kennedy and others appear to have adopted the very narrow view that a reference to Ireland ought to be explicit in the book's title. At the last moment Murnaghan was to be persuaded to take a somewhat broader view, following strong representations from the chief justice. However, there were still some people who hoped that the sale might be stopped altogether. In a letter to a newspaper, Muriel McCarthy, the librarian, wrote that, instead of selling their books, the benchers ought to have appealed generally for financial help, and to have done so both to members of the legal profession and to 'all who have an interest in our heritage'. Their behaviour reminded her of some words of the fifteenth-century wag, Sebastian Brant:

First in this dance of fools I stand.
For though I've books on every hand,
I read them not, nor understand.[9]

Because the benchers had failed to satisfy protestors concerning the possible sale of books of Irish interest, Nicholas Robinson of

8 SCM, 1960–75, p. 305 (21 Apr. 1972), where it appears that at the next meeting of the Standing Committee, some weeks after the April sales were over, Murnaghan corrected the minutes as they had been originally drafted by replacing a reference to items of 'special Irish interest' with the words 'with reference to Ireland' before signing them; BMB, 1964–75, p. 254 (4 May 1972).
9 *Ir. Times*, 24 Apr. 1972.

An Taisce travelled to London to attend the auction at Sotheby's from 24 to 26 April. He is the husband of Mary Robinson, later president of Ireland but then a barrister and senator, who was herself also critical of the benchers' decision. With Nicholas Robinson went Mary Pollard, the librarian from Trinity College Dublin who had signed a letter of protest to the newspapers. Pollard was described by Dick Walsh of the *Irish Times* as 'a widely respected bibliographer'. Nicholas Robinson says today that Murnaghan largely blamed Pollard for creating the whole fuss, but at the time she herself gave much of the credit to Robinson, whom she described as 'an extremely energetic and determined young man straining at the leash'. In a letter to the librarian of the University of Birmingham she wrote that, 'Nothing could have been done without the help of a chap called Nick Robinson, who organised an An Taisce umbrella for us and in general acted as organiser of the attack.' In London, Pollard and Robinson had a full briefing on Sotheby's procedures from a sympathetic English dealer.[10]

On Sunday, the day before the sale was due to commence, Nicholas Robinson publicly expressed concern that 23 of the 25 lots listed by Corkery, Pollard and others in their earlier letter to the newspapers were still included in the sale (Augustine's *Confessiones* had been withdrawn pending further negotiations and Olde's 'Waterford' imprint had been sold to An Taisce). He announced that, 'We will be keeping a very close watch and I can promise that if any of these books are sold we will be kicking up quite a fuss.' Behind the scenes, the campaign clearly had some effect. Early on Monday morning, Murnaghan informed Sotheby's not only that six lots of incunables in the catalogue had been sold to An Taisce (as considered above), but also that he had been instructed to withdraw ten other lots as being of 'Irish interest', and that he was withdrawing a further eighteen because of the licence situation. He later informed the benchers that, 'Messrs Sotheby were to say the least of it, very displeased' and the auctioneers charged a commission on the books withdrawn. Yet, surprisingly and notwithstanding

10 *Ir. Times*, 25 Apr. 1972; Robinson, 'Resumé', p. 1 (An Taisce MS); Pollard to K.W. Humphries, 11 May 1972. She identified the other principal activists as T.P. O'Neill, Falkner Grierson and Neville Figgis. Mary Pollard, who is also known to acquaintances as 'Paul' Pollard, has recently made a major contribution to Irish bibliography with her *List of members of the Dublin Book Trade 1550–1800*. Nicholas Robinson is not related to Christopher Robinson, whose former library is the nucleus of the benchers' collection.

such tensions, Nicholas Robinson noted at the time that An Taisce was consulted by the benchers as to whether or not nine other books in the April sales were 'of sufficiently outstanding Irish importance to merit special consideration'. An Taisce replied that they were not of such 'outstanding' importance, although they were 'of substantial Irish interest', and the benchers sold them at auction.[11]

The eighteen books withdrawn 'because of the licence situation' were examined individually by Murnaghan:

Nine of these are all printed but maps or engraved plates have been hand-coloured. Two others are bound in pieces of irrelevant manuscript which I gather was not uncommon. The remaining lots have manuscript marginal notes or other writing, including two hand-drawn maps, which might technically bring them within the provisions of the Act. In so far as I could read, what was in manuscript was neither with reference to Ireland nor of Irish interest.[12]

That Monday morning the sale itself opened with a statement by Lord John Kerr, director of Sotheby's book section, who also acted as the auctioneer. He was reported to have announced that,

At the instruction of the benchers of the King's Inns, Dublin, a number of books have been withdrawn from the sale. Some of them are of marginal Irish interest and a few have already been acquired by the National Trust of Ireland. A few other books, not of any Irish interest, have been withdrawn because it has been claimed that they might infringe an export regulation of 1945.[13]

The Times of London reported on 25 April that

A last-minute attempt to save books sent for sale by the King's Inns Library, Dublin, for the Irish patrimony, upset dealers when they arrived at Sotheby's yesterday. The cream of the books included in the three-day sale have been withdrawn and most dealers learnt of this only when they reached the sale room. Some had come from America for the sale.

Another British observer described the event as 'something of an embarrassment', inaccurately blaming unspecified 'pressure from the Irish government' for 'leaving the unfortunate and guiltless

11 *Ir. Independent*, 21 and 24 Apr. 1972. For the 25 lots and their fate see Appendix Three, and for the books 'of substantial Irish interest' sold see Appendix Ten; BMB, 1964–75, p. 256 (4 May 1972).
12 FS; BMB, 1964–75, p. 257 (4 May 1972).
13 *Ir. Press*, 25 Apr. 1972. It was actually a statutory provision and not simply an 'export regulation' that their removal from Ireland was said to infringe.

auctioneers to face the irritated trade, the victim (it was said) of the contemporary frost in Anglo-Irish relations'. By now, Dick Walsh of the *Irish Times* was referring to the whole row as 'the battle of the books', and reporting an account by An Taisce of an exchange between Robinson and Murnaghan:

Yesterday [Monday] Mr Robinson told Mr Justice Murnaghan that books by Irish authors were of Irish interest, the spokesman for An Taisce said. Mr Justice Murnaghan, however, maintained that the benchers' undertaking that books of Irish interest would be withdrawn covered only books which referred to Ireland. According to the report, Mr Robinson replied that on this definition a painting by Jack B. Yeats which did not depict an Irish scene could not be held to be of Irish interest.[14]

Another newspaper reported that, 'The benchers' representative at the London sales, Mr Justice Murnaghan, claimed that their undertaking was only in respect of books which referred specifically to Ireland, irrespective of the nationality of their authors'. Mary Pollard told a reporter that alternative criteria for establishing 'Irish interest' might be 'based on Irish authorship, Irish subject matter and Ireland as a place of printing'. The publicity was agitating the chief justice who again phoned Murnaghan, this time at 7.30 a.m. on the second day of the sale. He also sent him a telegram.[15]

In all, during the three days of the April auctions, the benchers withdrew forty-three books (see Appendix Six below for these). While An Taisce welcomed the decision of the benchers to withdraw certain items, albeit in some cases for future sale, its chairman pointed out that there was still in the auction much material of relevance to Ireland which was not governed by the 1945 Act. In addition to the six incunables which An Taisce then acquired on behalf of Irish libraries, the National Trust for Ireland also purchased some other lots entered in the April auctions, including three of those which had been listed by Corkery and other protestors in their letter to the newspapers. When the April sales

14 *Ir. Times*, 25 Apr. 1972. The British observer was writing at 'News and Comment' on p. 397 of an unidentified contemporary publication (photocopy among Robinson family papers).
15 *Ir. Independent*, 25 Apr. 1972; *Ir. Press*, 25 Apr. 1972; BMB, 1964–75, p. 256 (4 May 1972). It is not known what was said on the telephone or in the telegram. Bruce Arnold wrote that Murnaghan was thought to be 'the driving force' behind the sales and noted 'an odd but illuminating coincidence', which was that the judge had a small library of his own and was 'proud enough of it to have had printed his own, especially designed bookplate' (*Ir. Independent*, 18 Nov. 1972).

ended, An Taisce issued a statement saying that it might be necessary to amend the 1945 Act to ensure that in future valuable books and objects of art were available to Irish purchasers before being sent abroad. The association noted presumptuously that it had been successful in ensuring that books 'which apparently should not legally have been exported and books which the benchers did not intend to sell, were brought back to Ireland'. The statement continued critically: 'It is a pity that the authorities and the libraries, who were informed by the benchers of their plans to sell the most important of these books, took no steps to ensure that they were kept in the country.'[16] In fact, many of the withdrawn lots were kept in London and sold at the next sales in November, licences having by then been issued under the 1946 Act.

An Taisce and others had been reduced to trying to rescue even a few volumes from the sale, using narrow and distasteful criteria. O'Neill described the position as 'a salvage operation minimising the worst results of a bad situation'. O'Neill appears to have been the compiler of a particular list of 59 titles of which a few were sold at auction to Taisce but of which most, including Murphy's *Arabian antiquities,* went to private purchasers.[17] The gross figure realised by the April auction, including private sales, was £64,327, yielding to the benchers after the deduction of Sotheby's commission a sum of £53,672. This was more than enough to match the sum of £31,866 which had been spent on repairs and decorations in 1970 and 1971, mainly on kitchen renovations, but was still far short of what the benchers believed that they needed to put their entire range of activities onto a sound footing. The *Irish Times* reported that, although only about three dozen of the 839 lots offered had been withdrawn by the benchers, 'one experienced observer thought this could well have cut the sale's aggregate by more than half'. Yet, Mary Pollard informed the librarian of the University of Birmingham that 'we achieved comparatively little in material terms'. Her annoyance was reflected in her adding, 'I hope we also made the benchers' names mud with Sotheby's and thoroughly fluttered the King's Inns dovecot.'[18]

16 *Ir. Times,* 27 Apr. 1972. See Appendix Nine below for the lots bought in April by Nicholas Robinson, as agent for An Taisce.
17 *Ir. Times,* 24 Apr. 1972; *Ir. Press,* 24 and 25 Apr. 1972; King's Inns Library sales files for O'Neill's list.
18 FS, paragraph 34; *Ir. Times,* 27 Apr. 1972; Pollard to Humphries, 11 May 1972.

It had been intended to hold the next sale of King's Inns books in July 1972, but Murnaghan now took it upon himself to authorise the auctioneers to postpone that sale until November: 'They did not consider July a good time, but were under the impression that we were anxious to have the sale completed as soon as possible.'[19]

On 2 May 1972 Feisenberger wrote to Murnaghan, at his home address. He observed that 'in spite of all our troubles we were delighted to have you here', and noted that Sotheby's had charged commission on all books either sold to 'the National Trust of Ireland' (An Taisce) or withdrawn. This, he asserted, had earlier been agreed with Murnaghan. When the benchers convened for a meeting on 4 May 1972, there were signs of strain due to the continuing controversy. The president of the high court, Aindreas Ó Caoimh, objected to the minutes being signed because in his view the previous meeting was not properly called. However, a large majority voted to sign them. The benchers then decided that Murnaghan and Raymond O'Neill should approach the Minister for Education 'to explain to him the society's problem in relation to the 1945 Act and the society's view that a licence thereunder was not necessary but to request him for such a licence should he consider that it was necessary'. They subsequently 'met with a sympathetic reception' from the minister, in respect of the books alleged to fall within the provisions of the law. Bruce Arnold later complained that these books were never submitted for inspection to Irish authorities 'and that only photostat copies of manuscript portions were supplied when these were requested'.[20]

Some of the benchers appear to have become increasingly concerned about the continuing absence of clear information about the books that had been removed from King's Inns Library and sent to Sotheby's but not yet sold. On 22 May 1972, their librarian wrote to the London auctioneers explaining that she had been directed by the Library Committee to ask for a list of the society's remaining books proposed for sale in November. This should be forwarded 'as soon as possible and before the sale catalogue is printed. Please send this list without delay'. At its meeting on 17 May, the Library Committee had also agreed to seek 'to negotiate terms of fee' for Richard Hayes to 'vet' the list whenever it arrived

---

19 BMB, 1964–75, pp. 257–8 (4 May 1972).
20 FS, paragraph 36; BMB, 1964–75, p. 253 (4 May 1972), p. 261 (31 May 1972) and p. 267 (2 Oct. 1972); *Ir. Independent*, 18 Oct. 1972.

from Sotheby's, both as to the Act of 1945 and as to 'books of Irish interest'.[21] Feisenberger responded to this letter by writing not to Neylon at King's Inns but to Murnaghan at his home address, stating that Neylon had also telephoned and left a message to say that she had not received all the books withdrawn in April:

I, of course, only returned the books printed in Ireland and kept the non-Irish and valuable books here as you requested. Unless you feel that there is *no* [his emphasis] hope that they can be offered in the future it would surely be pointless to send them back.

The Sotheby's representative dismissed the request for a list of the books still in his company's possession as 'quite impractical and a job which we could not possibly or fairly be asked to undertake'. He said that he remembered the question of a list being raised during his time in Dublin when he gave the same answer and pointed out that 'the sale catalogues show the books we have'. He added, 'I would be careful to send you the proofs of the catalogue before it is finally printed':

A number of the books have already been catalogued and I have also set aside a number of Irish items to be returned of which I may discover some more. The 'Irish' books withdrawn from the first sale were, of course, with one or two exceptions, English books some of which had been reprinted in Dublin. The only reason for my not removing them was that they obviously exist in Irish libraries as they had Dublin imprints and are not, on the whole, particularly rare.

Feisenberger went on to say that he had not answered Miss Neylon's letter 'for the time being'. In a separate letter to Murnaghan, dated four days earlier and also to his home, Feisenberger had noted that eighteen books had been returned by purchasers because the volumes contained defects 'which we had overlooked'. He intended to offer these again in November. He indicated that he did not wish to proceed with the catalogue until the matter of licences under the Act of 1945 was finalised.[22]

21 Neylon to Magee, under-treasurer of King's Inns, 22 May 1972.
22 Feisenberger to Murnaghan, 19 May and 23 May 1972.

CHAPTER ELEVEN

'Be blowed to your protests'

TO THE DISCOMFORT OF KING'S INNS, the sale of books was attracting ever more attention. The Library Committee at University College Galway wrote to Chief Justice Ó Dálaigh, 'placing [its] professional and academic advice at your disposal' and asking for a full list of what was next coming up for sale before this appeared in a printed catalogue. Ó Dálaigh told Miss Neylon that 'I personally consider that the request to examine a full list of books to be sold is very reasonable'.[1] In late May, the *Irish Times* published a satirical poem by Austin Clarke which cannot have pleased the benchers:

Song of the Empty Shelves
(In elegiac metre)

See how our lawyers shuffle in shabby gown and bob-tailed
Wig to plead before the Bench or brief themselves with long hopes:
Dreams of sumptuous dinners at the King's Inns
Mouthing in their minds. Surely they need a new enormous
Kitchen with the latest quick whisks, grinders, electric
Stoves, driers, dishwashers, stainless steel sinks!
Dog-earing advocates want bigger bones to bury.
Sotheby's will buy our unread tomes, knock 'em down:
Incunabula deprived of their historic
Worm-eaten dust, first-editions from their Gothic handpress,
Bible unbreeched, Blackstone, Coke ungartered.
Bid for the lot, my Boys. All go to pot.[2]

The librarian of King's Inns was becoming increasingly agitated by the whole dispute, which was creating new tensions. Neylon became frustrated when Sotheby's did not respond to her letters as quickly as she would have liked. Feisenberger grew irritated by

1 Christopher Townley to Ó Dálaigh, 4 May 1972; Ó Dálaigh to Neylon, 12 May 1972.
2 *Ir. Times*, 25 May 1972. On 1 June 1972 a letter from Clarke appeared in the *Irish Times*, pointing out that the words 'Wig to' had been omitted from the second line as published, and that the rest of the line was in error printed twice.

89

Neylon's tone and decided not to reply at all to certain correspondence from the King's Inns librarian. On 2 June 1972 he wrote
once more to Judge Murnaghan, at the latter's home address,

I am sorry to keep worrying you but I am bombarded with letters from Miss
Neylon – who has certainly changed colour since my visit to Dublin. I
enclose her latest effort. I am not answering any of these letters but I should
be grateful if you could let me have some news as to the future.

A note scribbled by the judge on this letter states, 'Wrote 13 June
asking for approx. date on which proofs w[oul]d be available'. In
fact, as we shall see, proofs were not to arrive until late September,
more than two months later. Meanwhile, the benchers received a
sobering reminder of the reasons why they needed to generate
greater income. In June 1972, they had a letter from the Bank of
Ireland relating to their overdraft.[3]

On 20 June 1972 the benchers 'authorised the engagement' of
Dr Richard Hayes to advise on the application of the 1945 Act to
the books to be included in the autumn sale by Sotheby's, and as
to whether any of those books were of Irish interest. By now,
Hayes was no longer director of the National Library but had
become keeper of the Chester Beatty Library, then housed on
Shrewsbury Road in Dublin. It was to that address that King's
Inns wrote, enclosing a list of the books withdrawn in April and
asking for an estimate of their value:

In particular we would like to know what valuation you would place on lot
15 – Augustinus *Confessiones* – one of the items withdrawn from the sale.
£3,000 was offered for this book at the sale and an American dealer
informed a member of the library committee that he was prepared to pay up
to £18,000 [corrected in hand on copy kept in King's Inns, from £10,000]
for it. I have a written offer of £7,000 from Maggs for lot 14 which was also
withdrawn [Collection of maps later sold for £17,000]. *Liber Chronicarum*
(item 218) was sold at the auction for £2,100.

Hayes was also asked for his advice on fire precautions.[4] Just one
week later, with no proofs yet available, Hayes wrote to Miss
Neylon: 'In reply to your letter, I regret to say that I am unable to
value the books you mention. My experience in the past has been
only with books of Irish interest and even with regard to these my

3 SCM, 1960–75, p. 309 (14 June 1972).
4 King's Inns to Hayes, 22 June 1972; FS, paragraph 37.

ideas of values would be completely out of date.' His next words must have come as music to the ears of some benchers:

> Sotheby's are, in my opinion, the only people competent to value miscellaneous books such as those on your list, as they have day to day experience of selling all kinds of rare books and know how prices have gone up in recent years. They also know in what condition each item is and this has an important bearing on the value.

But if this supported the benchers' choice of auctioneer, it was not the most striking of points in his letter. Critics of the sale, as well as those who respected Hayes for his work on the listing of Irish manuscripts, might have been shocked by what followed had they read it. Having made a few observations on the matter of fire precautions at King's Inns Library, he suddenly changed tack to conclude his letter bluntly as follows:

> I think you should sell off in Sotheby's most of the items of great rarity. After all the National Library *must* [his emphasis] give you an export licence if you give them the option of photographing the books which have manuscript notes.[5]

That Hayes was correct in his interpretation of the Act would later be confirmed by public comments made by a representative of An Taisce. Nicholas Robinson subsequently commented that the law was not designed to stop cultural treasures leaving the country, but was there to ensure that they could be photographed before they left, so that scholars could continue to study them. Photostats were, however, he said, inadequate from a scholar's point of view. One correspondent to the *Irish Times* put the matter more caustically:

> There will be those to maintain that I confuse the shadow with the substance. One can hear them say: 'The learning indeed is a marvellous thing, but sure the owld [*sic*] books are only the carts that carry it and the microfilm nowadays is a great man to preserve the word of wisdom.' If a doubt could be cast on the genealogy of the Book of Kells, the same voices, no doubt, would be heard suggesting that it should be copied and a fine few bob made from flogging the original in London or New York.[6]

5 Hayes to Neylon, 29 June 1972.
6 *Ir. Independent*, 8 Nov. 1972; *Ir. Times*, 23 Nov. 1972 (from James McGing of Dublin, who naively overlooked the added value of the Book of Kells as a tourist attraction. However, while his references to microfilm were made regardless of the quality of the reproduction, any scholar who has laboured to decipher such copies will, especially, sympathise with his viewpoint).

In July 1972, 'an exhibition of recently purchased antiquarian books' was mounted at the National Gallery of Ireland, in order to display the lots that An Taisce had purchased from the benchers. On 16 August 1972 the benchers formally and successfully applied for export licences for eighteen books withdrawn from sale in April, but now intended for auction in November. During the summer Miss Neylon found herself in London and visited Sotheby's. Feisenberger later assured her that 'it was a great pleasure to see you the other day' but there continued to be no sign of the proofs, anxiously awaited in Dublin. It was later reported to the benchers that,

Although the necessity of receiving copies or proofs of the catalogue for the Autumn auction was emphasised by Mr Justice Murnaghan to Dr Feisenberger in June 1972 and subsequently, a proof of the catalogue for the sale of King's Inns books to be included in the auction on 7th November 1972 was only received under covering letter dated 25th September 1972 with a request that it be returned approved or otherwise amended within 48 hours of Mr Justice Murnaghan's return to Dublin on October 2nd. The proofs of the catalogue of books to be included in the auctions on 13/14th November 1972 were received under covering letter dated 29th September 1972 with a request for an immediate reply.[7]

Nicholas Robinson had 'lengthy private discussions' with Judge John Kenny at about this time, but the sales proceeded. When the benchers next met, on 2 October, they agreed again to consult Richard Hayes for his opinion, this time as to what if any of the volumes should be removed from the catalogue before printing:

Despite the short time available, Dr Hayes kindly examined the proof catalogues and indicated a small number of items which he considered might be regarded as of Irish interest.

It is not known what works Hayes selected. His recommendations are said to have been communicated to Sotheby's on 4 October but, nevertheless, at least some of the items indicated by him on the proof catalogue for 7 November were included in the

7 Feisenberger to Neylon, 30 Aug. 1972; FS, paragraph 38; BMB, p. 267 (2 Oct. 1972). The eighteen books for which the benchers obtained licences were, as earlier numbered in the April sales catalogue, lots 14, 15, 34, 45, 60, 64, 70, 82, 85, 101, 165, 167, 171, 189, 205, 266, 439, 595 (Appendix Seven below for details of these books). On 7 Nov. 1972, the benchers received a licence also for lot 206 in the sale of 20 Nov., being Isaac Tirion's *Atlas* (*Dáil Éireann deb.*, vol. 264, cols. 1,425–8 (13 Dec. 1972)).

final printed catalogue for that date, and only later withdrawn from sale. Those indicated by Hayes for 13 and 14 November were said to have been kept out of the final catalogue. There are no entries for lots 277–9, 336 and 363 in the catalogue for 13 and 14 November. A list of books that were received back by the benchers from Sotheby's gives as returned to King's Inns the following titles which do not appear in any of the catalogues: A.R. Boyle, *De specificorum*; Robert Boyle, *New experimentation*; Robert Boyle, *Works*, 6 vols. (perhaps the three lots absent from the catalogue for 13 and 14 November between 276/Bowditch and 280/Bradley); Donovan, *Essay on galvinism* (perhaps that absent between 335/ Edward Donovan and 337/A. Drapiez); S. Haughton, *Principles of animal mechanics* (that absent between 362/Haslam and 364/ Hawkins?). Also given as returned are 'W. Stokes, *Treatise on fever*'; '[?D]. Green, *Life of Mahomet*'; '[?R. Bradley], *Discourses/ Growth of plants*'; '[??Nickerly or Mc??], *Gravity, etc.*'. It is remarkable that Hayes himself does not appear to have listed any of the titles that were thought by An Taisce to be worth saving from the sales of 13 and 14 November 1972.[8]

Among the changes made to the proof catalogues was one that excited the suspicion of Bruce Arnold. Writing in October 1972, he suggested that,

A small detail will indicate the sensitivity that is felt generally about the sale. Lot 430, for sale on November 7, includes a book by 'Palmer', which is indicated thus in the catalogue: 'Palmer (T.), *Flores Doctorem* [etc.].' In the proof for the catalogue this appeared thus: 'Palmer (T.) Hibernicus, *Flores Doctorem* [etc.].' The word 'Hibernicus' indicates that Palmer T. is, in fact, Thomas of Palmerstown, outside Dublin, a late 16th century Irish scholar and his book, published in Cologne in 1606, always has the word 'Hibernicus' on the title page. Yet it has been deleted in the catalogue as printed. Why?

He noted that the forthcoming autumn sales were not going to be held on days exclusively devoted to the books of King's Inns, but that books from other sources would be sold on the same days. He thought that this might reflect a reticence 'about giving too much prominence to the controversial decision by the benchers to go ahead with further sales following the row over the April auction'.[9]

8 FS, paragraph 38; BMB, 1964–75, p. 267 (2 Oct. 1972); List of returns from Sotheby's, dated 28 Feb. 1973 (Library correspondence files (King's Inns MS)).
9 *Ir. Independent*, 18 Oct. 1972. The list of returns at King's Inns includes 'Thomas Hybernicus, *Flores*, [etc.]'.

On 30 October 1972 the benchers considered a request from the Bar Council for a copy of the catalogue of books due to be sold in November. Murnaghan informed his colleagues that he had not yet received the final catalogue, but promised that if none came by the following day then he would furnish the Bar with a copy of the original proofs. Deciding to ignore a request from the *Sunday Press* for a statement on the controversy, the benchers next considered a letter to Murnaghan from Patrick Shaffrey, the honorary secretary of An Taisce, in which he expressed regret that An Taisce had not received the proof catalogues for 7, 13 and 14 November before those reached the trade. Shaffrey stated that the proofs had now been examined by a number of Irish bookmen and, on that basis, he included two lists of books that should be withdrawn from sale, the first on the grounds of 'Irish interest' (39 titles in 35 lots) and the second 'as a major cultural loss to the country as a whole' (7 lots, including the first edition of Augustine's *Confessiones*). These lists may be read in Appendix Eight below. He added that, 'we would lay a great deal more emphasis on this second category'. In response, the benchers empowered Murnaghan to seek the opinion of Richard Hayes on these books. At this same meeting, they also considered a request from An Taisce for an opportunity to purchase certain items prior to auction, 'at the prices estimated by Sotheby's, as arranged in April and in accordance with the Chief Justice's suggestion to the Taoiseach'. Shaffrey reminded the benchers of An Taisce's offer to buy Augustine's *Confessiones* for £2,500. In a separate letter to Chief Justice Ó Dálaigh at his home, Shaffrey wrote that he understood that the benchers had received a substantial offer for *Confessiones* from an unnamed American university and admitted that An Taisce was aware that 'the possible auction price being discussed by international dealers at Sotheby's was in the £8,000–£10,000 region'. He added that, 'We appreciate that the financial difficulties incurred by the society have been caused by the commitment to preserve a building which is itself an important part of our heritage. However, the importance of this edition, one of the rarest printed books extant, cannot be overemphasised'. Chief Justice Ronan Keane recalls visiting King's Inns Library during this period of controversy and being invited by Christopher Micks, SC, one of the benchers, to inspect Sotheby's catalogues or proof catalogues. Keane, then a practising barrister, observed that the society's copy of Augustine's *Confessiones* was of the greatest rarity and drew the librarian's attention to the fact that the benchers' copy had been rebound by George Bellew of Dublin. He told her that this information provided her with reasonable grounds for arguing that it ought to be kept in Ireland. Keane noted that other works by Augustine, being a second edition of *The city of God* (published in London in 1620) and a collection of his whole works (published in Paris in 1836–38 and identified by UCD as a collection that it would like to have) were also being sold by the society.[10]

At their meeting on 30 October, the benchers did eventually decide that their *Confessiones* should not leave Ireland and agreed, at the suggestion of Judge Brian Walsh, that they themselves would hold onto the book in the event of An Taisce not being persuaded to buy it. Murnaghan had earlier told the benchers, on 4 May 1972, that he had rejected An Taisce's offer of £2,500 for *Confessiones* and that he had informed Nicholas Robinson of An Taisce there was already an offer of £3,000 for it and that Sotheby's 'expected that it would make £5,000'. Now, however, the benchers agreed to ask Sotheby's to fix a reserve price for *Confessiones* and resolved that the volume be offered to An Taisce at that price: 'and further that if this offer was not accepted by An Taisce, the book should be bought in by the Benchers'. However, An Taisce was kept in the dark about the decision to return *Confessiones* to Ireland no matter what might be bid by third parties, and a memorandum by Nicholas Robinson of a meeting which he had with Chief Justice Ó Dálaigh the next day at the latter's chambers refers simply to Ó Dálaigh mentioning a 'reserve' of £4,000. Moreover, in a letter to An Taisce, Murnaghan flatly dismissed out of hand the possibility of not selling any book on the second of the two lists submitted by the National Trust, which list included Augustine's *Confessiones*:

The first of the two lists which you sent to me has been submitted to the Benchers' adviser [Hayes]. As you are aware, the Benchers, fully aware of everything which their decision involved, decided to sell the books contained in the second list, and they see no reason now to alter their decision.

The second An Taisce list consisted of *Confessiones* and six other very valuable items, of which the sale abroad would constitute, in the opinion of An Taisce, 'a major cultural loss to the country as a

10 BMB, 1964–75, p. 271 (30 Oct. 1972); FS, paragraph 39; Shaffrey to King's Inns, 23 Oct. 1972; Shaffrey to Ó Dálaigh, 28 Sept. 1972 (An Taisce MS); Keane, interviewed by author, June 2001.

whole'. Ultimately, five of the seven items were to be sold (including *Confessiones* to An Taisce) and two withdrawn (lots 422 and 484, Bradshaw and Kingsborough). As it happens, both of the lots withdrawn were also on the first list of 39 titles of Irish interest sent to Hayes. About Augustine's *Confessiones* Murnaghan added in his letter to An Taisce that,

As An Taisce are interested in this item I tell you, in <u>confidence</u> [his under-lining], that the reserve price on this item is £4,000. If you should tell me that you are prepared to pay this sum for this item on or before Saturday next the 4th November, then this item will be sold to you at this price.

Murnaghan's was a remarkable letter in that he insinuated that unless An Taisce coughed up £4,000 then *Confessiones* would be sold privately at auction. Certainly the benchers preferred to sell their valuable book to An Taisce rather than keep it at King's Inns. However, it is a matter of opinion how reasonable it was for Ó Dálaigh and Murnaghan to refer specifically to a 'reserve price' when a decision had already been taken not to sell the book to any buyer outside Ireland, even if a private bidder was preferred to pay above that 'reserve price'. Instead, as we have seen, the benchers had decided to 'buy it in' in the event of An Taisce failing to come up with £4,000. Unaware of the alternative agreed by the benchers, An Taisce finally paid £4,000 for Augustine's *Confessiones*. Among contributions received by An Taisce specifically towards the cost of acquiring the book was £100 from Charles J. Haughey, whom Bruce Arnold described at the time as 'a man who believes in backing his cultural concern about what happens in this country with his own money'. Having acquired the work, An Taisce immediately issued a statement pointing out that only thirty-four libraries throughout the world were known to have copies of this first edition, published in Strasbourg not later than 1470. When a copy had been exhibited by the British Museum it was described as 'the first great autobiography … its strength of thought and confession of weakness have been a constant support to Christians'. Augustine of Hippo (354–430) very significantly influenced the attitude of the medieval and later Christian churches towards sexual behaviour and pioneered a new form of autobiography. Since the British auction records were first published, only two first editions of *Confessiones* had been recorded as having been sold by auction, one in 1902 and one in 1951. An Taisce noted that,

'The King's Inns copy is of particular Irish interest as it was subsequently bound by George Bellew of Dublin, one of the leading Irish bookbinders of the early nineteenth century. There is no other copy is Ireland', and it is 'one of the country's greatest treasures':

For these reasons, together with our general conviction that such irreplaceable cultural treasures must be retained in this country, which boasts such an ancient tradition of learning, An Taisce considered it vital to retain this work in Ireland. After lengthy negotiations, the benchers decided on 31 October to make it available to An Taisce if £4,000 could be raised prior to auction ... a price widely acknowledged to be far below the expected market price. Both the benchers and An Taisce have been advised that at open auction this book would probably reach a figure considerably in excess of £10,000.[11]

Later that week a letter appeared in the *Irish Times* from Muriel McCarthy, the librarian, who asked if the benchers would now read Augustine's *Confessiones* 'or is it a case, as W.B. Yeats said, of "bald heads forgetful of their sins"?' Even more scathing of the benchers were certain verses composed by that other librarian, Mary ('Paul') Pollard. On 5 November 1972, she ran off on her own printing press 100 copies of an anonymous ballad, which she had composed and which she now circulated to lawyers and other relevant parties:

Excerpts from lines on
The International Book Year in Ireland
and the patriotic gesture of
the B-nch-rs of the Honorable Society of K-ng's Inns
in dispersing their Library in London, 1972

So the bold Justice Flog'em's in business again
And he's wheeling his barrow through London
We have to be fair in this general book year
And they shouldn't read English in Dublin

11 FS, paragraphs 38,39; BMB, p. 256 (4 May 1972); BMB, pp. 269–70 (30 Oct. 1972); Memo of N. Robinson, 31 Oct. 1972 (Robinson family papers), in which O Dálaigh is recorded as promising that the benchers would act upon the opinion of Richard Hayes; Murnaghan to Shaffrey, 31 Oct. 1972 (An Taisce MS); *Ir. Times*, 6 Nov. 1972; *Ir. Independent*, 11 Nov. 1972. One wonders if it was Bellew who was responsible for cropping the pages in such a way as to truncate some of the marginal manuscript notes on this copy of the work, subsequently donated by An Taisce to University College Galway.

The B-nchers played safe and consulted Authority,
'Is there any ould books here the natives could read?
But please to remember that Mullingar's history
Is all that would interest the likes of these.'

So God got his briefing but slipped up on scholarship
And O what a field day all S-th-by's had,
With the Law all unlicensed and swearing legality,
The people displeased and the bookmen all mad.

As for all you plain people, just cease your complaining-
What's a few mouldy books when the B-nchers can eat?
When our noble justiciars can gobble up Caxtons
And belch in contentment, their bellies replete?

O all you plain people we're digesting our library,
We can't ask you to read and won't ask you to dine;
What's your trifle of culture and heritage of learning
When this learned Society can savour its wine?

With the T—s—ch defending be blowed to your protests,
Early donors are dead and quite out of our way;
As we empty our bumpers our minds they are easy
Fate cannot harm us for we'll dine today.[12]

Just one day later, on 6 November 1972, a letter appeared in the *Irish Press* signed by the author of these verses and two other protestors. They pointed out that when permission to sell books from the library was granted to King's Inns by the Copyright Act 1963, the then Minister for Industry and Commerce, Mr Jack Lynch, had stated in the Dáil that, 'The benchers think that there are some books in the library which could usefully be disposed of and the proceeds applied in binding or cataloguing books of more interest to users of the library.' The writers asked, 'Is it unreasonable that the people of Ireland, having given permission through their representatives for these sales to take place, should expect that the assurance given in 1962 will be implemented?' They described the benchers' sale of books as an 'ill-conceived dispersal':

---

12 These verses also appeared in the *Ir. Times*, 7 Nov. 1972. In *Hibernia* (16 Nov. 1972) Andrew Pollak described Pollard's broadsheets as 'beautifully printed' and noted that, 'The only good thing to come out of the mischievous sale of our national heritage by the less-than-honourable legal gentlemen of the King's Inns seems to be a renaissance in the lost art of satirical broadsheet writing'.

One of the excuses put forward for the sale has been that the absence of any proper catalogue made the library of little use to scholars. Now that the benchers have stripped the library of many of its treasures can we expect that a proper programme of cataloguing what books remain will be undertaken? We presume that when the benchers took the decision to realise these large sums of money they must have had some practical proposals for expending them on the library, according to the intent of the Copyright Act of 1963.[13]

One wonders what the authors of the letter might have written had they foreseen that only today, almost thirty years after the controversial sales, is work due to begin on 'a proper programme of cataloguing what books remain'.

The History Society and Law Society of Trinity College Dublin entered the fray and accused the benchers of having failed in their moral obligation to the community, 'as custodians of such a valuable part of our heritage'. These societies also criticised the state for failing to help to preserve the collection. The Irish Federation of University Teachers protested too.[14] A letter to the *Irish Independent* included among its signatories the historians J.C. Beckett and R.D.C. Black. Its content was scathing:

The fact that bodies such as An Taisce may have been given an opportunity to select some of the work of Irish interest before the sale will do little to mitigate the loss to Ireland, which arises essentially from the random dispersal of an irreplaceable collection. The interest of Irish scholars is not confined to books 'of Irish interest', and the interest of overseas scholars in coming to Ireland is bound to be diminished when they learn that the heritage of rare books which is part of the country's culture is not cared for or preserved intact.

The authors pointed out that the contents of the important *Catalogue of pamphlets on economic subjects published between 1750 and 1900 and now housed in Irish libraries*, edited by Black himself and published in 1969 by the Queen's University of Belfast, had been rendered unreliable by King's Inns selling so many of its volumes. They called for all of the books in the sales to be returned to Ireland.[15]

13 *Ir. Press*, 6 Nov. 1972. Other signatories were Noel Jameson, and M. O'N. Walshe.
14 *Ir. Independent*, 7 Nov. 1972; *Ir. Times* letter, 8 Nov. 1972.
15 *Ir. Independent*, 7 Nov. 1972.

CHAPTER TWELVE

Second sales, November 1973

On behalf of An Taisce, Nicholas Robinson flew to London for the Sotheby's sale of 7 November 1972. On the night before the auction he told the *Irish Press* that he would not know until the auction actually began 'whether the King's Inns benchers have heeded our pleas'. Also in the city was T.P. O'Neill, who sent a note to Lord John Kerr of Sotheby's questioning the legality of the sale. In the note, he asked if a licence under the 1945 Act had been obtained for the export from Ireland of all lots which contained manuscript annotations, original photographs or colouring by hand. Moreover, referring to a second relevant statutory requirement, he asked also if a licence under the Act had been delivered at the time of export to the proper office of Customs and Excise. On the following day he reported that Kerr had told him that Sotheby's had been assured by Murnaghan that the sale was covered by licences. 'He gave no assurance whether the licence was delivered to the Irish authorities at the time of export,' said O'Neill. The latter also appealed to the government to meet pound for pound the money gathered by An Taisce to buy books at the sales but his appeal fell on deaf ears. The Minister for Education would later inform the Dáil that, 'I am not satisfied, as I said on a previous occasion, that considerations of the national interest would arise to an extent which would warrant a contribution from the State towards the expenditure which An Taisce incurred in the matter.'[1]

---

1 *Dáil Éireann deb.*, vol. 264, col. 1,426 (13 December 1972); *Sunday Press*, 5 Nov. 1972; *Ir. Independent, Ir. Press* and *Ir. Times*, 8 Nov. 1972. *Ir. Press*, 7 Nov. 1972 refers to a number of books of Irish interest sold, 'including a facsimile of the manuscript of St Paul's Epistle, with old Irish annotations, and a volume by one of the Grimm brothers; [and] John, "The Apocalypse of St John", published by the Dublin University Press'. Perhaps the first and third of these items are comprised in lot 505 which includes Chr. Fr. Matthaeus, *XIII epistolarum Pauli Codex Graecus ... nunc Bibl. Electoralis Dresdensis ... editus*, Meissen, 1818, and John Gwynn, *The Apocalypse of St John in a Syriac version hitherto unknown ... in the library of the Earl of Crawford*, s.l., 1829. Lot 505 was sold to Howes Bookshop for £10.

The sale of 7 November was described subsequently by Nicholas Robinson as 'a listless affair' when compared to those of April. He was advised that the prices obtained at auction were 'extremely low'. During the sale T.P. O'Neill was tempted to stand up and make a protest. However, he said later, 'I thought action like that might demean Irish people. It is clearly a matter for the benchers. The whole taste of the benchers seems to be culinary rather than cultural.' At the auction he himself bought three lots. Lots 485 and 486, sold together to him for £3, were *Codex Theodori Bezae Cantabrigiensis Evangelia et Apostolorum* ... ed. Thomas Kipling (2 vols., Cambridge, 1793) and *The Alcoran* [Quran] *of Mahomet, translated out of Arabick into French by the Sieur du Ryer and newly Englished* (1688). He also bought lot 567, Sigonius, Carolus. *Historiarum de Occidentali Imperio* (Basle, 1579), which is now in the library of University College Galway. It has manuscript notes on the flyleaf, and the autograph of one Henry Ware inside the cover. It is also signed 'R.H. Nash 1794', this being presumably the Rev. Richard Herbert Nash of Moyle House, Co. Tyrone, whose son Richard West Nash was a barrister. According to a note made in 1972 by Nicholas Robinson, Richard H. Nash's name was also on at least one other book in the auction (lot 524 or 525 of 7 November).[2]

Robinson returned to Dublin on the night of 7 November 1972 but was unable to bring back Augustine's *Confessiones*. Ironically, having been removed from Ireland without difficulty, this book had to be left in London for the time being because an export licence was required for its removal by An Taisce from Britain. Robinson expressed An Taisce's pleasure that some books had been withdrawn by the benchers from that day's sale, in particular Kingsborough's *Antiquities of Mexico*. He said that these books might be sold privately by King's Inns on condition that they remain in Ireland. Both he and O'Neill called for an extension of the 1945 Act. Robinson commented that the law did little more than provide for the copying of documents before they left Ireland. Photostats were, he said, inadequate from a scholar's point of view. That same night An Taisce issued a statement to say that they were still 'urgently' collecting money to purchase works at the next sales due later in

2 Contemporary memo by Nicholas Robinson, and note on his catalogue (Robinson family papers); *Ir. Press* and *Ir. Times*, 8 Nov. 1972.

November and that they were 'continuing their efforts to have books of Irish interest withdrawn'.[3]

On 9 November 1972 the continuing sales were raised in the Dáil by Liam Cosgrave TD, leader of Fine Gael. A barrister himself and author of a short historical article on the history of King's Inns, he asked if the minister was aware of concern about the sales and if he would initiate discussions with the benchers to acquire books of historical interest so that they could be retained for the nation. Cosgrave had been the sole opposition speaker when in 1962, as discussed above, Irish copyright law was changed by Dáil Éireann especially to allow King's Inns to sell books and he had then supported that change. He was now reminded by the Minister for Education of the fact that the benchers were at liberty to dispose of books from their library. The Minister was not satisfied that any useful purpose would be served at present by entering into discussions with the benchers in the matter. He said that the terms of the 1945 Act were being reviewed to see if amending legislation might be either necessary or desirable. He indicated that at the forthcoming sale of books the National Library proposed to seek to acquire one item which was not already in its possession.[4] That same day John O'Donovan wrote to the newspapers from his home in Dalkey to draw attention to the consequences of the benchers not having had their books stamped as 'withdrawn' prior to their sale by Sotheby's. It was now impossible to distinguish what had been sold from what might have been stolen. He described how a friend had offered to sell him a rare sixteenth century volume for a three figure sum: 'On the back of the title page was a rubber stamp announcing "King's Inns Library". I could find no cancellation mark, official or otherwise. In other words, there is nothing in this valuable volume to show that it has not been pilfered ...' Subsequently, An Taisce also made a complaint about the absence of cancellation stamps.[5]

On 12 November 1972 T.P. O'Neill returned to London to be present on the following two days at Sotheby's auction of medical and scientific works belonging to King's Inns. He was hoping to record any evidence of the former ownership of books being sold by King's Inns so that the influence of any such works on Irish writers, scientists and medical practitioners might be assessed. A

3 *Ir. Independent*, 8 Nov. 1972.
4 *Dáil Éireann deb.*, vol. 263, cols. 1,363–4; Cosgrave, 'King's Inns', 45–52.
5 *Ir. Press*, 13 Nov. 1972; *Ir. Independent*, 15 Nov. 1972.

statement from An Taisce, which O'Neill represented at the auction, said that An Taisce, 'again notes with regret the sale of books originally donated to the King's Inns Library. One book due to be sold in the present auction is inscribed "Presented by John Smith Furlong to the library of the King's Inns"'.[6]

O'Neill listed for the *Irish Times* at least nine lots 'of specific Irish interest in the sale' of 13 and 14 November, as well as four examples of other 'valuable and rare items relating to the history of science and medicine'. In the end seven of that first nine were among lots withdrawn by the benchers for return to King's Inns. Another, Kirwan's *Geological essays*, was bought by O'Neill himself for University College Galway. The reports of the British Association, which contained material of direct Irish interest, were sold privately. So too were all four of O'Neill's examples of non-Irish 'valuable and rare items relating to the history of science and medicine'. An Taisce did purchase, on behalf of University College Galway, Isaac Papin's *La vanité des sciences* (in lot 472 of 14 November), in relation to which no export licence had been issued, but which O'Neill noted had 'many pages of manuscript annotations of the late 17th century including information on Sir William Temple, the well-known Dublin Castle official of that period'. He regretted that 'many' works could not be bought by An Taisce at the auction prices.[7]

At a meeting of the benchers on 13 November 1972, John A. Costello suggested 'with some reluctance' that a case for the sale of the books should be made publicly but 'in a non-controversial manner'. Costello, who was both the senior bencher and a former taoiseach, recognised that the affair was a disaster for the public relations of King's Inns and added that, 'it was shameful to have the society maligned by those who were not aware of the nature of the benchers' case'. It was agreed that, as a matter of urgency, Judge George Murnaghan, with Judge Brian Walsh and Raymond

---

6 *Ir. Times*, 13 and 14 Nov. 1972. 'Furlong, John Smith. 1st s[on]. of William, Aungier St., Dublin, attorney, and Constance Smith': admitted to the degree of barrister-at-law, King's Inns, Jan. 1804 (*King's Inns admissions*, p. 180). According to a note by O'Neill (Robinson papers), that book was [(Rembertus) Dodoens], *Stirpium historiae pemptaedes sex, varie* ... Antwerp, 1616. Complete with many woodcuts, it was sold to one Mrs Wagner for £75 (lot 332 of 14 November).
7 Contemporary note by O'Neill (Robinson family papers); *Ir. Times*, 13 and 14 Nov. 1972; *Ir. Independent*, 15 Nov. 1972. For the books listed at this time by T.P. O'Neill, see Appendix Five.

O'Neill, SC, should prepare a factual statement setting out the background to the decision to sell books. However, the statement was to be circulated only to benchers and was not completed until after Christmas, by which stage the main sales were over. It is not known if Walsh ever participated in its preparation but he did not sign it.[8]

The next auction of King's Inns books was scheduled for 20 November 1972. As it approached, William Dillon wrote a second article on the controversy. He drew attention to the fact that there had been re-entered in the catalogue for this auction some very valuable items which had been withdrawn by the benchers from earlier sales pending consideration of the absence of an export licence. These included hundreds of hand-coloured maps:

It is understood that licences have now been issued retrospectively for this atlas and other books, which appeared to have been exported by the benchers contrary to the regulations of the State. Several questions still hang over the King's Inns disposal of their valuable non-legal books. Were many of them not given in trust for the use of members and students? May there not yet be breach-of-trust actions brought on the trustees? Is ignorance of an Irish Act of Parliament (Documents and Pictures Act, 1945), and apparent ignorant breaching of the regulations, to be rewarded by instant retrospective State permission to export what has already been exported?

Dillon reported that one of the books sold had included a rare book-plate of Daniel O'Connell, 'who may well have left the volume to the Irish library for ever. Surely such books should be disposed of only if the King's Inns was going into liquidation?'. Dillon may have been referring to Benyowsky's *Memoirs and travels*, published in Dublin in 1790 and sold to An Taisce at the April auctions for £28. This was subsequently deposited by An Taisce in University College Galway and bears an O'Connell book-plate. He called for the regulations on licensing to be toughened, not least because 'at present there is almost automatic rubber-stamp permission' to export books and he was highly critical of the government and of 'the intransigent attitude' of King's Inns:

The one and only real reason given is the need of money for improvements. Has the Honourable Society never heard of an emergency appeal and of the possibility of bargaining with the Minister of Finance to make a special contribution equal to an amount raised by public subscription?[9]

8 BMB, 1964–75, p. 273 (13 Nov. 1972); FS, *passim*.
9 *Ir. Times*, undated cutting, between 13 and 18 Nov. 1972. On 20 November Nicholas Robinson travelled to London to attend at Sotheby's, again for An Taisce.

Five lots sold on 20 November included maps that had been either drawn or published by John Rocque[s]. Richard Hayes pointed out to the benchers that 'Rocque was not an Irishman but, I believe, lived in Dublin for some time. He published a well-known map of Dublin. It seems to me unreasonable to regard maps by him of other countries as "of Irish interest".' Judge John Kenny told Nicholas Robinson that the proof catalogues for 13, 14 and 20 November had been checked by 'the highest authority in Ireland [presumably Hayes] and all books of Irish interest are excluded'. However, during the various November sales only two of the seven lots that had been identified by An Taisce as constituting 'a major cultural loss to the country as a whole' were withdrawn from sale. A third, Augustine's *Confessiones*, was let go to An Taisce at a special price of £4,000, while the four remaining major titles were sold at open auction in London. Of 39 other items in 35 lots in the November sales that An Taisce described as being 'of distinct Irish interest', the benchers appear to have withdrawn 25, sold thirteen privately and sold one to An Taisce itself.[10] The benchers also sold at auction the other and less valuable works by Augustine that were in the catalogue.[11]

The November sales realised a net total, after commission, of £60,943.77. It was asserted by Sotheby's that the prices realised, particularly at the sale on 7 November, were depreciated by the critical attitude and actions adopted in the press and elsewhere in relation to the sales of King's Inns books.[12]

10 J. Kenny to Robinson, 13 Oct. and 17 Oct. 1972, the second letter including a copy of advice by Hayes (Robinson family papers); *Ir. Independent* and *Ir. Press*, 22 Nov. 1972; Appendix Eight below, for all books which An Taisce wanted saved for Ireland as a priority.

11 On 7 November, Augustine's *The city of God*, translated by John Healey (2nd ed. of a work first published in 1610, London, 1620, lot 405) was sold to T. Thorp for £50; and *Opera Omnia* (11 vols. in 15, Paris, 1836–38, lot 406), in which University College Dublin had expressed an interest, went to Howes Bookshop for £45. For all books withdrawn in November by King's Inns, see Appendix Six and Appendix Seven below.

12 A note by Maura Neylon, 6 June 1973, indicated that certain books 'as they were unsold, are now returned' and awaited collection at Dublin docks. This shipment included 40 unidentified 'books of Irish interest', fifty-four volumes of papal bulls and a descriptive and illustrated catalogue of the Great Exhibition in five volumes, 1851, together with the catalogue of the Dublin international exhibition of 1865. But these last two (lot 468 of 7 Nov.) are also on another King's Inns list as returned 28 Feb. 1973!

Immediately following the auction of 20 November, Nicholas Robinson returned to Dublin bearing Augustine's *Confessiones*, in relation to which by then the British Department of Trade and Industry had issued an export licence. It was decided to have the book examined by a bibliographical expert and to have any necessary repairs or restoration carried out. An Taisce issued a statement saying that,

While books of this calibre require a licence from the British authorities to be returned it was apparently possible to export thousands of books from the King's Inns Library without any investigation as to their contents, or importance. In the few cases about which representations were made, licences were retrospectively issued without any detailed examination of the works sent for sale.

An Taisce was worried about what the benchers might yet do with other books in their collection and appealed to the King's Inns to 'give the nation some guarantee as to the future administration or disposal of the remainder of their library'.[13] Once more, T.P. O'Neill argued that the benchers had a particular responsibility in respect of bequests to their library.[14] He also asked in exasperation how one could explain 'the selling of a book like that by the Polish Count Strzelecki':

This man spent some years setting up soup kitchens to feed the Irish poor during the great famine. He almost died of fever caught at the time. Now the benchers sell his book to set up more elegant kitchens for themselves. Stainless steel cannot dazzle us against such cultural poverty.

O'Neill summed up the sense of abiding anger among critics of the benchers and worried about what might yet happen:

They have raped their library of 5,000 precious volumes in a manner which could not have been more calculated to damage the Irish heritage. No attempt

13 *Ir. Independent* and *Ir. Press*, 22 Nov, 1972.
14 *Ir. Times*, 22 Nov. 1972. O'Neill wrote that many books at King's Inns had come from the library of Edward Vaughan Hyde Kenealy, a noted barrister of the nineteenth century who had been a student in King's Inns and Gray's Inn, as well as at Trinity College Dublin, and who bequeathed certain volumes to the two Irish institutions. O'Neill added that, 'The books are now scattered far from his native land and so too are the books of many others' (T.C.D. MS Mun/Lib/12/32a for extract from Kenealy's will. See also *Irish Book Lover*, xi, nos. 1–2, Aug.–Sept. 1919, 3–6).

was made to find out whether other copies of the books to be sold existed in Ireland. The books themselves were not examined for manuscript annotations. No account was taken of the moral responsibility of the benchers to donors. The deposit of books under copyright acts was made into a personal asset rather than a public trust. The provisions of the Documents and Pictures (Regulation of Export) Act appear to have been largely ignored in the sale. A headline has been set in this matter which means that the Act is no longer operative. So much for the benchers.

Next he attacked the government, alleging that,

On two occasions the Dáil was misinformed as to the facts of the case. In April the Parliamentary Secretary to the Minister for Education said that the books were not of Irish interest despite the fact that the catalogue available at that time contained many books by Irishmen. The Minister for Education more recently said that the National Library of Ireland was bidding for a book at the auction. In fact it does not appear to have done so. Indeed, the government has, so far as one can judge, done absolutely nothing in this affair.

He noted that, in April, the Dáil had been told that the benchers expected to get £200,000 from auctioning their books but that so far they had raised only slightly more than £132,000, after seven days of sales, and even that sum must be reduced by the 15 per cent commission payable to Sotheby's. He asked, 'Are we to have a further succession of days at Sotheby's during 1973 on the same lines as those with which the benchers honoured the International Book Year of 1972?'[15] In fact, only a very small number of books belonging to King's Inns were put on sale during 1973, and they appear mainly to have been volumes that had been sold in 1972 but that were then returned by buyers, presumably because of some undisclosed defects. There was to be no repetition on the scale of those auctions that occurred in 1972.

The question remained of what was to be done with the books which An Taisce's representatives bought at Sotheby's. Six lots, all incunables, had been acquired specifically for the National Library, Trinity College Dublin and St Patrick's College, Maynooth. The distribution of these items (given in Appendix Nine below) was finally determined by drawing lots, following a certain amount of wrangling within and between the three institutions. One of the volumes that went to Maynooth, a Latin Bible published in 1487

15 T.P. O'Neill, 'International Book Sale Year?' in *Ir. Press*, 23 Nov. 1972. Strzelecki's *Physical description of New South Wales*, published in 1845 (lot 731 of April) was bought by An Taisce for £55, on behalf of University College Galway.

at Basle, contained an inscription to which the benchers might have paid more attention before embarking on their unfortunate sales. It was penned in Latin by one Johannes Haeke, a Master of Arts and Licentiate of Medicine, who probably acquired that particular copy of the Bible shortly after it was published. He later presented it to a convent at Roermond, near Maastricht in the Netherlands. He prayed, 'most fervently that nobody under colour of any pretext or through presumption may presume to alienate this book or to give it away or lend it to anybody'. It is not known how the sisters at Roermond were parted from their Bible, but the benchers relieved An Taisce of £140 for the privilege of donating it to the Russell Library of St Patrick's College, Maynooth.

Augustine's *Confessiones* was donated to University College Galway. All but a couple of the remaining items bought by An Taisce were also placed in that Galway library, which had agreed to pay £1,200 towards the purchase of Augustine's work. In doing so, University College Galway contributed more than twice as much as any other donor to the funds used by An Taisce to buy books in London. Earlier, it had been suggested by one journalist that 'the bulk of the rare books bought by An Taisce ... will probably be housed in the library at Trinity College [Dublin]. This by way of something of a reward to Trinity for its many favours to the National Trust'. However, Nicholas Robinson expressed the opinion to An Taisce that,

To my mind an ideal institution would be University College, Galway, who gave much support to An Taisce in its efforts. Galway's new library will be opened to students at the beginning of January and will be largely unstocked. If, by giving a modest lead, An Taisce were able to promote further donations, it would give the Trust extremely good publicity as a regional project.

In January 1973, the donation to University College Galway of *Confessiones* became the leading story on the front page of the *Connacht Tribune* when the book was presented at a special function sponsored by the Galway branch of An Taisce in the Aula Maxima. Particularly noted was 'the fine state of preservation' of the *Confessiones*. Also on display that day were some other London purchases. In all, 47 books which formerly belonged in King's Inns are now in University College Galway (see Appendix Nine below for these). Their presence there serves as a reminder of the role which the late T.P. O'Neill, and others who were associated with the west of Ireland, played in 1972 in 'the battle of the books'. It may be noted that, uniquely among local authority institutions, Mayo County Library gave a donation to An Taisce towards saving Augustine's *Confessiones*. Its contribution was £100, an amount which matched that given by Charles J. Haughey.[16]

In 1995, the National University of Ireland awarded honorary doctorates to Mary and Nicholas Robinson, the former being by then president of Ireland. In a formal address on that occasion, at University College Galway, Dr Colm Ó hEocha noted that,

As Honorary Secretary of An Taisce he [Nicholas] was very helpful to this College in acquiring for our James Hardiman Library an extensive collection of books which had been in the King's Inns Library in Dublin, including a valuable volume on [*sic*] St. Augustine. Emeritus Professor Tom O'Neill and the then Librarian, Christopher Townley, organised these acquisitions for the College; Nick Robinson oversaw their transfer in 1973 ...[17]

16 *Ev. Press*, 19 July 1972; N. Robinson to An Taisce, 4 Sept. 1972 (Robinson family papers); *Connacht Tribune*, 12 Jan. 1973; The library, University College Galway, to N. Robinson, 22 Feb. 1973.
17 'Text of the introductory address, June 26, 1995' (University College Galway MS), p. 2.

CHAPTER THIRTEEN

So, what was actually sold?

THE COLLECTION OF BOOKS and maps belonging to King's Inns, Dublin, that was sold in England in April and November 1972 was both large and fascinating. Hellmut Feisenberger of Sotheby's had promised the benchers 'a series of important catalogues that would remain as a monument to your non-legal library', and the catalogues which Sotheby's published in London shortly before each of the auctions show that almost 7,000 volumes belonging to the society were put on sale in approximately 1,450 lots. The 7,000 volumes constituted between 2,700 and 2,800 individual titles. Some lots contained just one title, although this might be in two or more parts. An annual series such as *Archaeologia Cambrensis* (lot 400 of 7 November) could run to over one hundred volumes. Other lots contained a number of different titles, not all of which were necessarily identified or even enumerated, and the greatest number of which in any single lot appears to have been in lot 821 of 26 April 1972. This contained 129 volumes, described simply as 'an extensive collection of books published during the second half of the nineteenth century on all aspects of life in India ...'. Maps were also lumped together into single lots.

Until catalogues were published shortly before each sale, it was not possible for the public to ascertain what books were to be auctioned. As was explained earlier, no full list of titles had been made before their removal from King's Inns Library and nobody, including the benchers of that society, knew exactly what was to be auctioned. The somewhat inaccurate list of 255 abbreviated titles which was circulated in 1971 to certain Irish libraries was indicative of what went to London, but it was far from complete. It has been seen that, following protests by An Taisce and by some academics and journalists and librarians, a small number of books were withdrawn from auction by King's Inns and returned to the society's library. Moreover, approximately fifty lots were bought by An Taisce, at or immediately before auction, and brought back to Ireland. Details of these may be found in Appendix Six and Appendix Nine below.

Descriptions of books given in Sotheby's catalogues are usually, but not invariably, quite informative. The following is an example of an entry for a book from King's Inns, in this case lot 372 of 25 April:

CHURCHILL (A. & J.) A COLLECTION OF VOYAGES AND TRAVELS, some now first printed from original manuscripts, 8 vol. (*vol. 7 and 8 contain*: Osborne (Thomas) A collection of voyages and travels ... compiled from the library of the late Earl of Oxford), *maps and plates, calf, worn, hinges weak or cracked*

folio 1732–1747

We know that this particular book was sold for £200 to one 'W.F. Hammond' because, after each of its auctions, Sotheby's also published a standard 'price list', which gives the bare price paid and the name (but not the address or any other details) of each purchaser. King's Inns Library has a full set of catalogues and price lists for the six days in 1972 on which its books were sold. Among the buyers were a number of established London dealers, including Dawson, Francis Edwards, Maggs, Quaritch and Bertram Rota. It is not known to what extent these profited from the decision of the benchers to sell so many volumes at one time and in one place, but the dealers certainly purchased some of the best books.

In truth, not all of the works sold were masterpieces. Many might seem quite humdrum or their contents irrelevant to busy lawyers and others. The prices that they fetched were by no means all substantial, even at their real value then. However, their cultural worth far exceeded their market value. Reading the catalogues is an extraordinary intellectual experience. It is a virtual tour of a collection that has been dispersed beyond recall. Throughout the vicissitudes of Irish history, how many of the volumes sold in 1972 had earlier been relied upon for support or comfort at a time when even the possession of books was quite rare and when there were few libraries in Ireland? How many provided a connection with the eras in which they were published? What insights did they afford into the professional milieu in which they were deemed worthy of acquisition by what was, during the nineteenth century, Dublin's largest library after that of Trinity College?

Besides books put on sale that were of immediate interest to people who objected strongly to the auctions, or which were of obvious relevance to Ireland, there were many other books sold which were either unique in the country or one of only two or three copies found in Irish libraries. Certain incunables, especially those not in the English language, received no attention and were sold at low prices, as though works printed before 1501 could be replaced easily, and as though the reasons for their being in one of Ireland's oldest libraries were themselves irrelevant. Many books dated from the sixteenth, seventeenth or eighteenth century. Sotheby's also auctioned off certain titles which are of relevance to fields of study which have only developed substantially since the sales took place.

The picture of the collection glimpsed through reading titles of books in the footnotes above, and in the appendices below, may be enhanced by reference to a few of the volumes sold which received little attention. The handful of protestors were fully occupied in trying to discover what was going on, and in salvaging particular titles of which they had knowledge and about which they were especially concerned. Mention is made at certain points below of current prices posted on an internet site that is widely used by the international book-trade, this being *www.abebooks.com*. Readers may wish to compare these prices with those fetched by the benchers thirty years ago. Of course, it ought to be borne in mind that price inflation has been rampant for old books generally, that price is affected by the condition of a volume, and that there is a difference between offering for sale and obtaining a sale. When the sales occurred, in 1972, the Republic of Ireland had not yet broken the link between its currency and sterling, so one English pound was equal to one Irish pound. According to the Central Bank, the purchasing power of one pound in 1972 was the equivalent of £8.59 (€10.91) at the end of 2001. In early 2002, one pound sterling buys €1.62 and a United States dollar buys €1.16.

The benchers sold at Sotheby's many works of interest to anthropologists and historians, including studies of native Americans such as Alexander von Humboldt and A. Bonpland's *Vues des cordillères et monuments des peuples indigènes de l'Amérique*, published in two volumes in Paris in 1810 and sold at Sotheby's to Gaston's Alpine Books for £450 (lot 113 of 24 April), or Henry R. Schoolcraft's *Historical and statistical information respecting the history, condition and prospects of the Indian tribes of the United States*, published in six volumes in Philadelphia in 1851 and sold at Sotheby's for £480. The latter study was one of the chief sources of information and inspiration for Longfellow's great romantic poem of 1855, 'Hiawatha'.[1]

Two books by the author of another famous American work of literature also went under the hammer (lots 596a and 597 of 26 April). These were the first English editions of Herman Melville's *Narrative of a four months residence among the natives of a valley of the Marquesas islands or a peep at Polynesian life* (1846) and *Mardi or a voyage hither* (3 vols. 1849). *Mardi* was Melville's first literary treatment of metaphysical, ethical and political problems and is probably his most widely read work with the exception of *Moby Dick*. Only the fact that the catalogue records that there were three volumes indicates that the benchers owned the English edition of *Mardi*, which appeared in print some weeks before the American two-decker. The absence from the catalogue of a place of publication for many volumes was an unfortunate omission by Sotheby's. At the time of writing, Second Story Books of Rockville, Maryland, are asking US$3,500 on the internet for their copy of this same edition, with detached binding and lacking a spine. In 1972 King's Inns sold theirs to Quaritch for £48, less commission. The other book by Melville, *Narrative … of the Marquesas*, was the first written by that author and was published in the 'Colonial and Home Library' series. At the time of writing, Ruton Miller Books are seeking US$3,200 for their copy of this same edition, notwithstanding some staining to its end papers and light scattered foxing. In 1972, King's Inns got £6 from one S. Baker, less Sotheby's commission.

Great numbers of 'travel' books were sold by the benchers and one wonders to what extent the market may have been flooded by the release of so many similar works at one series of sales. In Dublin in 1972, such eighteenth- and nineteenth-century accounts of colonial adventures, expeditions and tours may have seemed as out-of-date and as out of place as that Georgian architecture which was being demolished by the builders of an Ireland striving self-consciously to appear modern. These books were regarded by some as being simply idiosyncratic, being deemed to be what a junior minister in the Dáil had described as mere 'collectors'

1 Underwood, *Longfellow*, pp. 132–4. Schoolcraft was entered as lot 563 of 7 Nov. 1972 but then withdrawn because one volume was still at King's Inns Library. It was re-entered and sold complete as lot 77 of 2 July 1973.

items': a number contained illustrations and coloured plates which made them even more valuable than otherwise as collectors' items and which could, if so desired, be ripped out and framed. They included James Grant's *Narrative of a voyage of discovery performed in H.M. vessel The Lady Nelson … to New South Wales* (published in 1803), which went to Dawson for £200 (lot 461, 25 April) and William Hamilton's *Campi Phlegraei, observations on the volcanoes of the two Sicilies* (3 vols., Naples, 1776–79), sold to J. Salmons for £1,300 (lot 472, 7 November). The latter work contained 59 hand-coloured engraved plates, described in 1972 by Nicholas Robinson as 'original watercolours beautifully executed'. Mornay's *A picture of St Petersburgh*, published between 1815 and 1825 contained 20 hand-coloured aquatints of that Russian city and was sold to one Mrs Wagner for £160 (lot 521 on 7 November). It appears to have lacked only the engraved frontispiece. Some American book dealers, today, are asking for sums in excess of US$8,000 for complete versions. There is also an instructive difference in the prices fetched at Sotheby's for two works by Prince Maximilian of Wied-Neuwied. His *Travels in Brazil* (1820) went to Quaritch for just £24, while his *Travels in the interior of North America* (2 vols., with 81 coloured aquatints, 1843–44) was sold to C. W. Traylen for a remarkable £6,800 (lots 594 and 595 of 26 April, lot 234 of 20 November).

Occasionally, a travel work was withdrawn by the benchers because it was found to have a direct link to Ireland. This might merely be the fact that it was the Dublin imprint of a book originally published elsewhere, and perhaps reprinted in Ireland without the author's permission. An account of voyages by Captain James Cook and other persons, the place of printing of which in 1773–85 was not shown in the catalogue, was sold for £600 (lot 379 of 25 April). The following lot (380) was withdrawn, being also an account of voyages by Cook and others, but having been identified as printed in Dublin in 1775–84. The Copyright Act of 1801, which was of great benefit to King's Inns in allowing the society free books, also helped to put an end to the practice of Irish printers reproducing English books without permission, and this fact alone makes such Dublin imprints historically interesting.

One hopes that not all books containing impressive illustrations were cannibalised, subsequently, for the purpose of framing pictures. Presumably, dealers such as Quaritch, who paid £140 for the first edition of *The history of Java* by Thomas Stamford Raffles (2 vols., 1817, lot 676 of 26 April), must have appreciated the effort which that author had put into his pioneering study and respected its integrity. *The history of Java* contained 66 plates, and there were ten more in *A memoir of the life and public services of Sir Thomas Raffles* by Lady Sophia Raffles (1830), which Quaritch also purchased (lot 675 for £55). A number of volumes of photographs more than one hundred years old were auctioned off, notwithstanding the fact that no export licences appear to have been issued in relation to them. They included, on 7 November, Watson and Kaye's *People of India* (8 vols., 1868–75, lot 595 for £220) and Wilson and Palmer's *Peninsula of Sinai* (5 vols., 1869, lot 597 for £140), the sale of both of which was later raised in the Dáil by Barry Desmond, TD.[2]

The account of the voyage of *The Lady Nelson* mentioned above was one of ten or more titles relating to New South Wales in the catalogues. Two were bought in April by An Taisce's representative (being lots 294 and 731, by Barrington and Strzelecki respectively, the latter on behalf of University College Galway), and one was withdrawn by King's Inns and returned to Dublin (lot 377, Collins), because its description of convict life was deemed to be of sufficient Irish relevance to require its retention. However, at least seven books on New South Wales, which might allow a reader to place the former in a wider context, were simply sold off. There was no attempt to consider why these particular titles were acquired by King's Inns, to determine if they were thought at the time of their acquisition to have some kind of intrinsic relationship to one another or to assess if, in 1972, they might be relevant to any study of Irish migration. In particular, Roderick Flanagan's *History of New South Wales* (*s.l.*, 1862) was sold notwithstanding its identification as a book of interest to Irish academics and librarians. The presence at King's Inns Library of such related titles as these on New South Wales, as well as other groups of related books, may have resulted from their being donated or bequeathed by some particular benefactor, but no effort was made to identify the source of the acquisitions. No research was conducted in the records of the society to discover the terms of any bequest or donation which might have given rise to a trust. If it had been

2 *Dáil Éireann deb.*, vol. 264, col. 1,425 (13 December 1972).

found that certain books came from the library of a significant public figure or lawyer, then such printed sources of intellectual inspiration would have constituted a legitimate subject for scholarly consideration and ought not to have been dispersed carelessly. In this context, it is worth recalling that, as has been pointed out above, at least one of the books put up for sale bore a book-plate indicating that it had belonged to Daniel O'Connell.[3]

Many 'travel' books of the eighteenth and nineteenth centuries are today appreciated by scholars for the remarkable insights which they afford into the development of national identities, international relations and political, social or cultural ideologies. Exciting contemporary works by Anderson, Said and other academics constitute a new field of study, or intellectual perspective, and allow us to read 'travel' books in ways which retrospectively enhance the value of many titles which once graced the shelves of King's Inns Library and which it is now too late to retrieve.[4] Substantial collections of works on the Middle East and Asia, for example, were removed to London and scattered in no particular order throughout Sotheby's catalogues. Nobody seems to have paused to wonder why the benchers had acquired so many books on India, forgetting or not wishing to remember the role which a burgeoning Irish professional middle-class played during the nineteenth century in the 'great game' of colonial expansion. It is not enough that the existence of catalogues allows one to ascertain what had been deemed relevant and worthy of inclusion in what was once Dublin's second greatest library, or that some of the works may still be consulted at other locations in Ireland, or that others can be obtained by means of inter-library loans from abroad or by purchasing reprints. For one thing, there is a special cultural significance in particular institutions, repositories and collections of books; for another, the convenience of inspecting all of the titles under one roof must not be underestimated.

3 Flanagan was sold as lot 433 of 25 Apr. 1972 for £40. Other titles sold in April included Bennett, George. *Wandering in New South Wales* [etc.]. 1834 (lot 314 to T. Thorp, £30) and [O'Hara, J.] *The history of New South Wales*. 1st ed. 1817 (lot 638 to Quaritch, £100). In the *Irish Times*, 21 April 1972, William Dillon had objected to the forthcoming sale of O'Hara. The O'Connell bookplate is on Benyowsky's *Memoirs and travels* (Dublin, 1790), which was sold in April to An Taisce (lot 316, £28), and which may now be viewed in University College Galway.

4 For example, Benedict Anderson, *Imagined communities: reflections on the origin and spread of nationalism* (London, 1983); Edward Said, *Culture and imperialism* (London, 1993).

One example of the manner in which related travel books were separated at auction is provided by reference to the works of Sir Aurel Stein, a British citizen of Hungarian origins, who was arguably the most successful archaeologist to explore the vast area between Iran and the borders of China, and who conducted three major expeditions into Central Asia between 1901 and 1916. His cartographic and ethnographic work is said to offer us 'a glimpse of the tangled relationship between scholarship and international politics'.[5] On 24 April 1972 Sotheby's sold from King's Inns Library his *Serindia, detailed report of explorations in central Asia and Westernmost China* (5 vols., 1921 as lot 234 to F. Edwards for £240) and his *Innermost Asia, detailed report of explorations in central Asia, Kan-Su and Eastern Iran* (2 vols., 1928 as lot 235 to Quaritch for £180). On 26 April they sold his *Sand-buried ruins of Khotan* (1903 as lot 727a to Kegan Paul for £24) and on 7 November, *Les documents Chinois découverts par Sir Aurel Stein dans les sables du Turkestan Oriental, pub. et traduits par Ed. Chavannes* (1913 as lot 575 to Ad Orientem for £24). The first two rare editions had been mentioned in the abbreviated list of books sent to some Irish libraries months before the actual auctions at Sotheby's, along with 'Explorations, illustrations and maps 1929' and 'Western Iran 1940', which four titles were said to constitute 'altogether 19 volumes'. This reference does not appear to correspond to the information in the catalogues published later by Sotheby's where I am able to find neither the last two works nor a total of nineteen volumes by Stein. Such an anomaly underlines the undesirability of allowing books to be removed from King's Inns by Sotheby's without a full list of what was being taken having first been made by the benchers.

Stein was facilitated in his undertakings by George Macartney, Britain's sole diplomatic representative in Chinese Central Asia. When Stein got news of the Boxer uprising, he hastened to deliver a consignment of pistols and ammunition to Macartney, whose home served as a resting place for the explorer. Earlier, another Macartney had played a crucial role in opening up China to Britain and wrote with Sir George Staunton *An authentic account of an embassy from the king of Great Britain to the emperor of China* (1797). However, it and many other works which might help to put Stein's work into an historical or political context were also

---

5 Stanley K. Abe, 'Inside the wonder house: Buddhist art and the West', in Lopez, *Curators of the Buddha*, pp. 85–7; Mirsky, *Stein, passim.*

sold by the benchers in 1972. This was notwithstanding the fact that Macartney was born in Co. Antrim and had been chief secretary for Ireland between 1769 and 1772, and once penned a sketch of the political history of Ireland. He had also been a law student in London. His Irish papers are today in the Public Record Office of Northern Ireland. This book was clearly 'of relevance to Ireland' or 'of Irish interest', but it was a 'poor copy' and one of nine particular volumes about which the benchers consulted An Taisce and which An Taisce adjudged to be not 'of sufficiently outstanding Irish importance to merit special consideration'. At the time of writing no copy of it is for sale on the internet but the asking price for a contemporary French edition is US$1,250. King's Inns got just £30, less commission (lot 575 of 26 April).

There is some irony in the fact that Sotheby's came to Dublin and carried off a valuable cultural asset, this being a collection of volumes from King's Inns Library which included in it works by Aurel Stein. Stein himself purported to be driven by the spectre of impending destruction and loss hovering over the remains of an earlier civilization. In his *Sand-buried ruins of Khotan*, a copy of which was sold by the benchers, Stein wrote (p. xx) that, 'the thought of the grave risks with which nature, and still more, human activity threaten all these relics of antiquity, was ever present to my mind, and formed an urgent incentive to unwearied execution, however trying the conditions of work might be'. He was alarmed, in particular, by the activities of various treasure hunters, these being precisely the sort of people who, in the second half of the twentieth century, have been very active in India, and who have broken that country's laws both by removing antiquities from their ancient locations and by illegally exporting them for sale in European auction houses. Yet, for all of their high aspirations, the work of explorers such as Stein helped colonialists in Europe to gather useful information about other societies. This was advantageous commercially and militarily, allowing imperialists to appropriate cultural authority over the history and identity of other peoples and to define foreign territories politically. For that very reason, the work was assisted by colonial powers. The removal from Ireland of the King's Inns collection may itself be viewed as yet another cold calculation of the material benefits of dealing in culture internationally.

Stein was just one of several important authors whose works were dispersed. Amongst others were the Bernoulli brothers. A collection of all works by John (1667–1748), *Opera omnia* (Lausanne and Geneva, 1742) went for £60 to Dawson's (lot 269 of 13 November), that London dealer for whom Feisenberger himself had earlier worked. John's brother James (or Jacob, 1654–1705) was the professor at Basle who famously introduced a sequence of rational numbers. An Taisce managed to buy the latter's *Opera* [Works], as published in two volumes in Geneva in 1744 (lot 268 of 13 November, for £35). However, a first edition of a collection of correspondence between John Bernoulli and Leibnitz, the great German philosopher and mathematician (mistakenly given in the catalogue as 'G.G.' instead of G.W.), entitled *Commercium philosophicum et mathematicum, 1694–1716* (2 vols., Lausanne and Geneva), was sold to C.W. Traylen for £120 (lot 406 of 14 November 1972). A work by Leibnitz himself, *Essais de Theodicée sur la bonté de Dieu* (new ed., Amsterdam, 1734) was lumped into lot 585 of 7 November 1972 and only withdrawn by King's Inns because one of the other four titles in this lot was by John Toland who, as An Taisce pointed out, had been born in Donegal. Another work edited by Leibnitz (mistakenly given in the catalogue this time as 'G.C.' instead of G.W.), *Novissima Sinica historiam nostri temporis illustratur* ([Hanover?], 1699), was sold for £2 to Pottesman (lot 493 of 7 November). *Novissima Sinica* is a collection of letters and essays by members of the Jesuit Mission in China, first published in 1697. The benchers owned the second, enlarged edition of the book, neither edition giving a publisher or place of publication. According to a note made in 1972 by Nicholas Robinson, this book was marked '*ex libris* Robt. Travers', the latter being perhaps either that Robert who was father of John Moore Travers, barrister, or Robert Travers, the eighteenth-century Irish attorney, both of which lawyers were members of King's Inns. Among other members of the society in the late eighteenth century whose autographs appeared on books sold by the benchers were Matthew Young, BD, attorney in the Exchequer (on Joseph Priestley's *Disquisitions relating to matter and spirit* (1777) and *Doctrine of materialism and philosophical necessity* (1778), being lots 543 and 544 of 7 November) and John Harvey, a barrister (on Edward Reynoldes's *Treatise of the passions and faculties of the soul* (1640), being lot 551 of 7 November).[6]

---

6 It is also possible that Monck Mason had purchased the library's *Novissima Sinica* at an auction which included a copy of the same edition (Sharpe,

A lot bought by An Taisce on 13 November 1972 may be used to illustrate further one aspect of the auction: that books once sold can seldom be retrieved, yet they may come to be valued for reasons which were not apparent at their date of sale. We have seen that the works of Stein and other travellers are now appreciated by scholars because the field of cultural studies has developed greatly since 1972. In the case of Thomas Bewick (1753–1828), who revived the art of wood engraving in Britain, his work is now particularly interesting because he has been identified as a putative ancestor of and influence on Pauline Bewick, recognised since 1972 as one of Ireland's leading painters. The reason An Taisce paid £22 for lot 270, Bewick's *History of British birds* (2 vols., Newcastle upon Tyne, 1822), was that he is also remembered as the illustrator of Goldsmith's 'Deserted Village' and 'The Traveller'. Yet his *History of British quadrupeds* (8th ed., Newcastle upon Tyne, 1824) was lumped in with six miscellaneous titles on natural history, in a lot sold to Wheldon & Wesley for £22 (lot 566 of 14 November).[7]

One might have argued somewhat facetiously that Bewick's 'British birds' were perhaps partly of Irish descent, or at least 'of interest to Ireland' or 'of Irish relevance' if migrating across this island. Indeed, whence came the birds and butterflies and little fishes, whatever about the bees, seems to have been a matter of occasional significance for the benchers and for An Taisce. So, although on 14 November 1972 another *History of British birds*, this by Rev. F. O. Morris (3rd ed., 6 vols., 1891 as lot 434), took flight and was bought by G. Walford for £55, a fine *History of British butterflies* by Morris (6th ed., 1891, as lot 435) was pinned down for Ireland by An Taisce for £12. That same day, the benchers withdrew Francis Day's *Fishes of Great Britain and Ireland* (2 vols., 1880–84, as lot 328). The British birds in Selby's *Illustrations of British ornithology* (4 vols., London, 1841, as lot 489) appear to have been racially pure because it was sold for a full £3,000 to Quaritch, perhaps thanks to its 218 hand-coloured engraved plates rather than to the quality of its text.

Catalogue of the library of Robert Travers, p. 41). The Toland title was *Nazarenus or Jewish, Gentile and Mahometan christianity* (1718). In the same lot were *Four treatises concerning the doctrine … of the Mahometans* (1712), listed as possibly being by Toland. For a recent appreciation of the significance of this Irish philosopher see Champion, 'John Toland', 321–42.

7 White, *Bewick*, pp. 11, 72.

In 1960, Pauline Bewick herself had visited Sotheby's, where she tried to buy some woodcuts by her putative ancestor, but failed, she says, when the auctioneer would not permit the large collection to be sold except in one lot. At the same auction house, related titles from King's Inns Library were split up. A striking example was a substantial number of works connected with the Jesuits and published during four centuries, one of which works was edited by Leibnitz as has been mentioned. These books could be argued to have been of direct relevance to the King's Inns in particular and to Ireland in general. For, in the seventeenth century, a chapel on the eastern boundary of the lands then occupied by King's Inns near the River Liffey appears to have been used by the Jesuit order, and one Jesuit was chaplain to King James II. In 1689, James addressed the Irish 'patriot parliament' at King's Inns, and thus became the only monarch known to have visited the society's premises.[8] Moreover, the role of the Jesuits in Irish history is a long and honourable one, and the existence of so many related works at King's Inns immediately begs the question of how they came to be there. One wonders if some of the religious volumes sold in 1972 had been in circulation among recusant Irish lawyers, or among their detractors. John Oldham's *Satyrs upon the Jesuits* (1682–84) actually bore the signature of one of its former owners, 'Thomas Johnson 1685'. It was sold to Howes Bookshop for £12 (lot 518 of 7 November), notwithstanding that in 1628 one Thomas Johnson had been admitted to King's Inns as an attorney. The mere possibility that such tracts and books may have been in Irish families for hundreds of years, before finding their way onto the benchers' shelves, ought to have been sufficient to deter the benchers from selling them. These volumes included a first edition of *In librum duodecim prophetarum commentarii*, by Franciscus Ribera, SJ, published in Salamanca in 1587 and sold to one 'Dr Sargent' for £10 (lot 553 on 7 Nov.). They included, also, two works of 1679 by Blaise Pascal which were bound in one volume. These were *The mystery of Jesuitism, discovered in certain letters* (engraved frontispiece) and *Additionals to the mystery of Jesuitism*. This volume by Pascal was part of lot 530 of 7 November 1972 which, remarkably, also contained two works by Archbishop James Ussher

8 White, *Bewick*, p. 60; Kenny, *King's Inns*, pp. 146–8, 227, 306. Leibnitz's *Novissima Sinica* was the result of the links he established with members of the Jesuit Mission, following his meeting in Rome with Francesco Grimaldi.

of Dublin that were bound in another single volume. The latter were *An answer to a challenge made by a Jesuite in Ireland* (4th ed., 1686), and *A discourse of the religion anciently professed by the Irish and British* (4th ed., 1687). The lot, completed by Thomas Fitzherbert's *Treatise concerning policy and religion* (1652), was recorded as having been sold to the Export Book Company for £6. However, although I have seen no evidence of a public objection to the inclusion of Ussher's works in the auction, they do appear to have been withdrawn from lot 530 immediately prior to sale. The entry in the catalogues of any work by Ussher, being of manifest Irish interest, seems quite extraordinary, taking into account the various public assurances that such works would not be sold. Indeed, Duhigg has stated that Ussher was once chaplain to King's Inns, although his suggestion is supported only by a suspect interposition in the society's Black Book. Nevertheless, ought the benchers have attempted to sell a work by an author who was even possibly their own chaplain, and who was certainly a figure of some importance in Irish history?[9]

Another notable item, with connections both Jesuitical and Irish, was a set of 13 volumes of the entire works of Duns Scotus. This *Opera omnia collecta ... a PP. Hibernis, Collegii Romani S. Isidori ...* was published by Luke Wadding at Lyons in 1639. The benchers' copy, which Sotheby's noted came from the Jesuit College in Antwerp, was sold to Howes Bookshop for £70 (lot 447 of 7 November). A contemporary note by Nicholas Robinson states that this copy had once belonged to the University of Louvain and that it contained a preface by Luke Wadding himself. Few Irish people were publishing books in 1639, especially important philosophical works, and even if there existed at other Irish libraries copies of this same edition of the writings of Duns Scotus, it is regrettable that the benchers' copy was lost to Ireland.

---

9 Duhigg, *King's Inns*, pp. 97, 346–51; Kenny, *King's Inns*, p. 351. Sotheby's relevant 'Price list' gives lot 530 (Pascal/Ussher) as having been sold at auction. However, a hand-written list at King's Inns gives it as 'excluded from sales by the committee but sold', presumably less Ussher. Another King's Inns list gives Ussher's *Answer* as received back at the library from Sotheby's in February 1973. Other titles sold, by or relating to Jesuits, included lots 7, 48, 120, 172, 201, 227–30, 434, 736 and 755 of 24 April; 396, 401, 428, 454, 487 (episcopal bookplate), 493, 518, 528–30 and 553 of 7 Nov.; 396 of 14 Nov.; 230 of 20 Nov. The benchers also sold tracts concerning recusancy, including, on 7 November, seven titles in lot 586 and another seven in lot 599 (both lots to T. Thorp for £10 each).

AN

ANSWER

TO A

CHALLENGE

Made by a *JESUITE*

In IRELAND.

WHEREIN,

The Judgment of Antiquity in the points
queftioned is truly delivered, and the Novelty of the now ROMISH Doctrine plainly difcovered.

To which is added
A Difcourfe of the Religion anciently profeffed by the
IRISH and BRITISH,

By the moft Reverend and Learned

JAMES USHER,

late Lord Arch-Bifhop of *Ardmagh*, and Primate of all *Ireland.*

Matth. 19. 8. *From the beginning it was not fo.*

The Fourth Edition Corrected and Augmented from a Copy
left under the Authors own hand.

London Printed for *Benjamin Tooke*, at the *Ship* in St.
Pauls Church-Yard, MDCLXXXVI.

Title page of King's Inns copy of James Ussher's *Answer to a challenge made by a
Jesuite in Ireland* (4th ed., 1686). Withdrawn from sale and returned to King's
Inns. Duhigg claimed that Ussher, who delivered the oration at John Selden's
funeral, was chaplain to King's Inns. Courtesy of King's Inns.

At the very least it was an ornament to their collection. Other works written by Wadding and by his nephew, Peter Walsh, were also in the catalogue that same day, notwithstanding earlier promises that nothing of Irish relevance would be put up for auction, but these were subsequently withdrawn by the benchers (lots 592, 593). One wonders at the failure of the benchers to give effect to their own expressed wishes in the matter of works of relevance to Ireland.

The sale included many other religious or philosophical works which it is difficult to regard as being of no 'interest' or no 'relevance' to Ireland. There were, for example, the Latin section of Martin Luther's entire works (*Opera omnia*, published 1564–58, sold as lot 499 on 7 November to F.L. Cunningham for £75); Calvin's collected works (published Amsterdam, 1671–1667, said by An Taisce to include 'manuscript notes at length inside cover', specifically desired by University College Dublin but let go as lot 427 on 7 November to J.Thin for £25); a decree addressed by the Bishop of Haarlem to the church, confirming that the decisions of the Council of Trent were binding (Venice, 1564), sold as lot 436 on 7 November to Maggs for £120. A bible in Latin, published by Andreas Cratander at Basle in 1526, went to A.G. Thomas for £65 (lot 414 of 7 November), notwithstanding the fact that it was the first separate edition of a Latin translation of the Greek Septuagint and that it bore an inscription on the title prohibiting it to be read, as the printer was a heretic. Among psalters sold were an edition of *The psalms of King David*, translated by King James and published in 1636, and psalms in Anglo-Saxon published in 1640 (lots 547 and 548 of 7 November, for £20 and £18 respectively).

Nobody appears to have objected that a first edition of Spinoza's *Opera posthuma* (including the 'Ethics'), published in 1677 and bound with his *Renati Descartes principiorum philosophiae pars I et II, more geometrico demonstratae* (Amsterdam, 1663), was sold as lot 573 to H.H. Koch for £140. Descartes was one of the three dominant influences on Spinoza and, one week later, on 14 November, a work by Descartes himself, *Principia matheseos universalis seu introductio ad geometriae methodum* (Amsterdam, 1661–1656) was sold as lot 330 to Blackwell for £60. There seems to be no trace of the latter work ever having been entered in the catalogue of King's Inns.

At the last moment the benchers withdrew their copy of the first printing of *Historia ecclesiastica*, written by Eusebius of Caesarea and providing the chief primary source for the history of the Christian church up to the year 324. It was published in 1497 and their copy had been in Oxford during the sixteenth century (lot 455 of 7 Nov. 1972). They also withdrew *Moriae encomium* [*In praise of folly*] by Erasmus (*c*.1466–1536), the greatest figure of the northern Renaissance. This work, published in Basle in 1517, contains pictures of contemporary life, wittily observed, and the Breughel-like quality of its writing is said to anticipate the style of a new age (lot 453 of 7 November).

In some cases the benchers withdrew an extraordinary work only to sell it subsequently. Of at least one such work there was no other copy in Britain, Ireland or America. This was Augustinus Datus, *Elegantiolae* (Daventer, 1489). Having been withdrawn on 24 April (lot 70), the Datus volume, which included twenty leaves and a large woodcut of a lecturer and pupils, was then re-entered and sold at Sotheby's on 7 November (lot 442). Corresponding with King's Inns in 1994 about the society's incunables, the curator of incunables at the British Library wrote, 'I would particularly like to know if you still have the Augustinus Datus item on the list.' In fact it had been sold in 1972 to T. Thorp for just £140. Only two other copies were known to exist, one in The Hague and one in Copenhagen.[10]

Another work withdrawn but later sold was a fine edition of Ptolemy's *Geographiae*, bound in one volume with an atlas and maps by Mercator, published in the late sixteenth century (lot 201 of 20 November 1972, sold finally to N. Israel for £1,300). Sotheby's noted that this was 'the first appearance of what became afterwards the Mercator Atlas'. One week earlier, the London auction house had also sold a first edition of Ptolemy's *Liber de analemmate* ... (Rome, 1562) from King's Inns Library (lot 466 of 14 November, to T. Thorpe for just £60). Ptolemy's *Geographiae* itself had been on the list circulated to university libraries by the benchers, and was one of the titles in which the librarian of University College Dublin had expressed an interest, albeit an interest in receiving it as a gift because the university could not afford to bid for this and other works. Also, notwithstanding a similar expression of interest from University College Dublin,

---

10 J. Goldfinch to J. Armstrong, 19 May 1994.

Kepler's *Astronomia Nova* ([Heidelberg], 1609) was bought by a dealer (lot 395 of 14 November to Dawson's for £1,400). Eighteenth century scientific works by Leonhard Euler and Isaac Newton and nineteenth century first editions of Charles Darwin went under the hammer without any objection (lots 319–22, 340–42 and 440–4 of 14 November 1972). Nobody appears to have objected to the sale of Hermes Tristmegistus, *Mercurii Tristmegisti* ... (Bordeaux, 1574), which G. Walford picked up for £50 (lot 367, 14 November). Only T.P. O'Neill appears to have voiced concern about the sale that same day of the very rare *Concise account of the origin and progress of the rocket system* by Sir William Congreve, which appeared in 1807 two years before the rocket was actually launched for the first time at sea, and which was sold as lot 307 to Dawson's for £180. Did anyone care that *A new booke of destillatyon of waters, called the treasure of Euonymus, containing the wonderful hid secrets of nature touching ... medicines for the conservation of health,* by Conrad Gesner, the great Swiss physicist and naturalist, was sold to W.F. Hammond for £250 (lot 355 of 14 November)? This English edition was published in 1565, the year of the author's death, and included 58 woodcuts of apparatus and plants. Gesner's innovative use of woodcuts was significant in fixing the accuracy of his data, and is said to have made possible the eventual emergence of a scientific zoology and botany. Early editions of his works are sold today for thousands of dollars. Sold to Quaritch for £300, in the face of an objection by T.P. O'Neill, was the first unillustrated edition of *De Humani corporis fabrica librorum epitome* by Andreas Vesalius, instigator of the modern study of anatomy (lot 520 of 14 November to Quaritch). This is one of the two most famous texts in the history of medicine. One dealer today is seeking more than £100,000 for a copy of the earlier illustrated edition. The unillustrated edition of 1560, published in Paris, is worth considerably less than that financially, but is still a precious item, and one which deserved to be appreciated by King's Inns for more than its monetary value. The benchers also sold works of natural history, including Sir Hans Sloane's *Voyage to the islands Madeira, Barbadoes, Nieves, St Christophers and Jamaica* (published in 1707–25, containing 284 double-engraved plates). This was a first edition of the first published descriptions and illustrations of the flora and fauna of Jamaica, and is said to be a fundamental work for West Indian botany. At the time of writing, on the internet, two U.S. booksellers are each offering a copy of the first edition, one for $19,000 and one for $37,500. On

24 April 1972, the King's Inns copy went at auction to Quaritch for £920 (lot 225a).

Some books appear at first sight to have no relevance to King's Inns but may have been in the library for a particular reason. One of them is Repton's *Fragments of the theory and practice of landscape gardening*, which was sold for £500 (lot 199a of 24 April). Given that it was published in 1816, it was almost certainly acquired by the benchers with a view to helping them to determine how to lay out their grounds at Constitution Hill, where Gandon's fine edifice was then nearing completion. Also sold was Countess Blessington's *The idler in France* (2 vols., 1841, lot 817 of 26 April), notwithstanding the fact that Blessington House stood directly across Henrietta Street from King's Inns Library. It is now a convent but formerly served also both as the home of Luke Gardiner and, later, the location of Tristram Kennedy's Dublin Law Institute. The Countess of Blessington's own correspondence was edited by R. R. Madden, historian of the United Irishmen, whose *Travels in Turkey* … (1829) and *Turkish empire* (2 vols,, 1862) were also sold by the benchers (lots 609 and 829 of 26 April).

There were other books sold at Sotheby's which might well be described in that phrase used in the Dáil by a junior minister as 'collectors' items', but which it seems a pity to have lost from an old library such as that of King's Inns. They included a set of three works on the game of chess published between 1819 and 1822 and sold with Murray, *History of chess* (Oxford, 1913) for £32 (lot 431 of 7 November 1972); Tomas Reid's *Treatise on clock and watch making* (Edinburgh, 1826) which had twenty plates and which was sold for £35 (lot 469 of 14 November); Henry Holland's *Treatise against witchcraft* (Cambridge, 1590) which went to F. Edwards for £160 (lot 478 of 7 November); Heinrich Grellman, *Dissertation on the gipsies* (1787), bound with another title and sold for £42 to Wheldon and Wesley (lot 526 of 14 November); Pierre Muret's *Rites of funeral ancient and modern, in use throughout the known world*, which was published in 1683 and which had some manuscript annotations, but which was sold bound with another volume to Pottesman for just £6 (lot 512 of 7 November). According to a note made in 1972 by Nicholas Robinson, the society's copy of Muret's *Rites* was signed by one 'Rich. Strong'. This suggests that it had once belonged to the Rev. Richard Strong, rector of Rathdrum, Co. Wicklow, whose son Charles was admitted to King's Inns in 1808. Also bearing this autograph was John Spencer's *Discourse concerning prodigies, second edition to which is added a short treatise concerning vulgar prophecies* (1665), which was sold for £16 to T. Thorp (lot 572 of 7 November).

Increasingly valuable today, as the study of sports becomes an academic pursuit, are books such as Thomas Williamson's *Oriental field sports* (2 vols., 1808) which Hartnoll & Eyre bought for £14 (lot 260 of 24 April) and the Rev. William Daniel's *Rural sports* (3 vols., including hand-coloured plates, 1805), which was withdrawn on 24 April (lot 64) but later sold on 7 November to Aladdin Bookshop for £60 (lot 441). Today, one dealer is asking £750 for a copy of *Rural sports*. The work includes an account of the rivers and loughs of Ireland. Whatever about such ephemera, it is surprising that books referring in any way to the House of Orange were not withdrawn as being 'of relevance to Ireland' or 'of Irish interest'. A 'rather worn' copy of J. Rousset and Jean Dumont, *Histoire militaire du Prince Eugène, du Duc de Marlborough et du Prince d'Orange et de Nassau-Frise* (3 vols., The Hague, 1729–45) was sold to Marcus for £240 (lot 209 of 24 April), while a copy of a sermon preached by the Dean of Peterborough before the prince of Orange on 20 January 1688 was one of seven works in one volume sold to T. Thorp for £10 (lot 599 of 7 November). Other curiosities of some interest were a pair of official papers from the reign of Elizabeth I, printed in 1600 and sold for £12 (lot 451 of 7 November 1972), and the 'new' enlarged edition of *An essay on the principle of population* ... (1803) by Malthus, which had appeared in its original form in 1798 and which had a significant influence on political thinking in the decades before the Irish Great Famine. This pioneering work was sold to G. Walford for £80 (lot 503 of 7 November).

Although law books were not entered in the auction, a copy of *Contemplations moral and divine* by Sir Matthew Hale (1699) was put into lot 470 of 7 November along with two other somewhat damaged items, Gale's *Court of the gentiles* (1677) and [Prynne's] *Perpetuitie of a regenerate man's estate* (1626/7). They were sold together and 'not subject to return' to K. Kirk for £10. Today, on its own, such a work by Hale, the great historian of the common law, would be likely to fetch at least twenty times that amount.

Between 1839 and 1886, King's Inns Library had accumulated the first 51 volumes of the *Journal of the Statistical Society* of London. These were sold on 7 November 1972 for £70 (lot 574), being no longer as appreciated as they once were. During the mid-nineteenth century, many Irish lawyers were prominent in the

Statistical and Social Inquiry Society of Ireland. Among barristers who joined it were William Littledale, its long-standing secretary and the author of an informed critique of King's Inns, and J.A. Lawson, one of a succession of brilliant young lawyers who occupied the new chair of political economy at Trinity College Dublin, and Tristram Kennedy, founder of the Dublin Law Institute.[11]

Many hundreds of wonderful maps, loose and bound into books, were sold in 1972 for a fraction of their value today. Inflation in the price paid for maps, including those by Abraham Ortelius and Thomas Jefferys, has been substantially in excess of the rate of inflation generally. King's Inns once owned a treasure trove of such beautiful work, of immense cultural and intellectual importance.

Those who inspect the catalogues of books from King's Inns Library sold by Sotheby's may have their own particular regrets about the loss of specific titles. Two which caught this writer's eye, and which were bound together for some unknown reason (lot 252 of 13 November), appear to have attracted the attention of only T. P. O'Neill. They were a first edition in Greek and Latin of works by Archimedes with a commentary by Eutocius (Basle, 1544) and Albert Dürer's *Etliche underricht zu befestigung der Stett, Schloss und Flecken* (Arnhem, 1603). The latter had large wooden arms on its title, woodcut plates and plans (some folding or double-page). I would like to hold this in my hands and explore it for any indication of how and when it made its way to Ireland. There is not a surfeit of such early prints in this country, and the export of this lot merited special consideration. However, in 1972, the sole consideration involved in its sale was the sum of £280 received by King's Inns from E. Morris, less standard commission to Sotheby's.

Only by reading the catalogues does one come to a full appreciation of the range and quality of books which were sold from the library of King's Inns. The brief and necessarily selective review which I have undertaken above serves merely to mark the fact that, while a few dozen books were withdrawn and returned to King's Inns or bought by An Taisce and lodged in other Irish libraries, very many books were sold which were important in their own right.

11 Kenny, *Tristram Kennedy*, pp. 153n, 175, 180; Littledale, *King's Inns, passim.*

CHAPTER FOURTEEN

Another storm brews

REVIEWING THE CONTROVERSIAL events of the year 1972, benchers George Murnaghan and Raymond O'Neill stated, in February 1973, that much remained to be done to bring the library up to the standards required by the legal profession, particularly in respect of reports of foreign courts and tribunals. They said that, 'whilst some progress has been made in recent years towards remedying this deficiency, much remains to be done'. They eyed what was left on their shelves and observed that,

The books sold comprise a relatively small proportion of the books in the library. There are still in the library many rare and valuable non-legal books which are of no Irish interest. The number of books in the library is approximately 90,000, of which 50 per cent are law books or of legal interest.[1]

They reported that the society maintained fire insurance cover in respect of its books of a legal character but that 'it could not afford to do so, and does not do so, in respect of its non-legal books many of which are of very considerable value and irreplaceable'. They could not be entirely sure what was in the society's possession:

Whilst there is a catalogue of books in the library, this is of very rudimentary character and does not cover the majority of the non-legal books of antiquity and value. Manifestly, a complete catalogue is highly desirable, and to that end an assistant to the librarian has been employed since February 1972 with the primary duty of cataloguing the library. The preparation of a complete catalogue will cost a substantial sum.[2]

Although the assistant to whom the benchers referred did commence cataloguing and prepared certain shelf lists, work on a complete catalogue did not proceed. Moreover, it appears that if the benchers had been bruised by the controversy of 1972, they were certainly not entirely deterred from considering the possibility of

1 FS, paragraphs 44, 49.
2 FS, paragraphs 45–6.

further sales. In November 1975, they agreed that the society 'should seek an appraisal of books of non-legal interest in the library which the society might possibly sell with a view to applying the proceeds to the establishment of a library of European law and other general purposes of King's Inns'.[3] On foot of this decision, Murnaghan again took up the running and wrote to Sotheby's. As a result of his letter the head of that firm's book department and the man who had presided in the sales rooms in 1972, Lord John Kerr, visited King's Inns on 20 and 21 January 1976 and made a preliminary appraisal of its books. Within a week of his visit Kerr fired off a one-page report to the benchers. In it he acknowledged firstly that 'it has been decided to retain all the legal books and the books of predominantly Irish interest'. He recommended that all of the books in the 'Committee Room' and in 'Room A' which did not fall into these categories should be sold off in London. He said that the books in the library proper presented more of a problem because there were many 'in poor condition'. Kerr indicated that the volumes which he thought ought to be sold included titles on art, architecture, history, English topography, bibliography, music, heraldry and genealogy, America and linguistics, as well as incunables and books of classical and European literature:

None of these categories however is represented in such depth that they are of major importance for scholarship, and for someone to acquire the books en bloc to add to an existing library would in my opinion inevitably result in wasteful duplication.

Given the strength of feeling among Irish librarians concerning the sales of 1972, it was certainly audacious for the auctioneer who benefited from those sales to venture an opinion on the possible value of the collection to Irish or other libraries. Having done so, he turned his attention to the large collection of pamphlets, of which he said there were 'I understand about 7,000', bound in several hundred volumes. The figure of 7,000 pamphlets coincided with that given by Richard Hayes in his report to the benchers in 1960 and not the '1,000' which Sotheby's own Hellmut Feisenberger had previously typed in his report for the benchers of 1969. If Kerr was aware of this disparity he did not deem it worthy of comment. He estimated the collection of

3 BMB, 1975–80, p. 8 (8 Nov. 1975).

pamphlets to be worth £30,000 on the open market, adding the qualification that,

I was not able to examine the collection in detail, but most of the volumes I did look at included, but were not confined to, pamphlets printed in Dublin, some of Irish interest, others Dublin reprints of what were originally English pamphlets.

He said that without a proper catalogue the pamphlet collection 'is of little practical use', but 'judging from my cursory examination it is not so solely of Irish interest that it should be incumbent on the Society to undertake the expense of preparing a catalogue as part of its Irish collection'. He suggested that the benchers sell the pamphlets to the Government of Ireland at a proper valuation, which sale 'should absolve them from any possible odium arising from a sale of any other books on the open market'. Otherwise, if it be decided that it be not of sufficiently specific Irish interest, 'it would make an extremely attractive sale in London'. Kerr did not explain how one might arrive at 'a proper valuation' of the collection in the absence of 'a proper catalogue', and perhaps underestimated the likelihood of 'any possible odium arising from a sale of any other books on the open market'.[4]

However, word got out that another sale was being contemplated by the benchers. Once again T.P. O'Neill of Galway and Mary Pollard of Dublin wielded their pens, as they had done in 1972, while Senator Mary Robinson, barrister-at-law, tabled a motion which was passed at a special meeting of the Bar and which requested further information from King's Inns. The editor of the *Irish Times* accused the benchers of 'behaving in an intolerably arrogant fashion', while academics such as Denis Donoghue, Séamus Deane, Gus Martin and Art Cosgrove protested. The Library Association of Ireland deplored the benchers' attitude 'in treating books which should be a national asset as a source of income'. Mary Pollard, of the library at Trinity College Dublin, denied that the King's Inns collection was 'unused by scholars because it is inadequately catalogued'. She claimed that the number of scholarly reference works in which the King's Inns had been included as a location for specific titles proved that its library

4 Report of John Kerr, Jan. 1976 (Library correspondence files (King's Inns MS)).

had been well used in the past, 'in spite of the great difficulties'.[5] A question was then tabled in the Dáil by John Wilson, TD, of Fianna Fáil, asking if the Minister for Education intended to take any steps 'to prevent rare books from the library of the benchers of the King's Inns from being exported'. Replying on 11 February 1976, John Bruton, TD, of Fine Gael, then parliamentary secretary to the Minister for Education and later to become taoiseach, pointed out that the owners of rare books were at liberty to dispose of them but added that the terms of the Act of 1945 which allowed this were being reviewed. He understood that the benchers had not yet made a decision to sell.[6]

By now, Cearbhall Ó Dálaigh had become president of Ireland. In 1972, when chief justice, he had not voiced publicly his private reservations about aspects of the sale at Sotheby's. In 1976, when president, he was even more reserved. In a letter which is a fine specimen of diplomacy, President Ó Dálaigh replied to Muriel McCarthy, then deputy keeper at Marsh's Library in Dublin:

The Constitution and the limitations surrounding the office of President do not allow me to attempt to intervene publicly, or even privately, in controversies, Everyone who has sat up here has had views on matters that have passed on the public scene and, doubtless, has, on occasion, felt he could propound a satisfactory solution. But the penalty of being President is silence on controversial issues. He can – and does – wish for certain solutions to certain controversies, but he may not break silence.[7]

The Bar Council invited the benchers to consider the feasibility of imposing an annual charge on all barristers, whether practising or not, for the right to use the King's Inns Library:

It was felt that a proposal along this line (which it is believed the benchers may have previously considered) might be more acceptable to the Bar as a means of solving the financial problems faced by the benchers than any further disposal of books or pamphlets.

The benchers readily agreed that this might be a good idea.[8] They did not attempt to proceed to another auction. However, as a

---

5 *Ir. Times*, 27–31 Jan. 1976 for articles by Don Buckley and editorial (30 Jan); *Ir. Times*, 12 Feb. 1976.
6 *Dáil Éireann deb.*, vol. 287, col. 1,709 (11 February 1976).
7 Ó Dálaigh to McCarthy, 19 Feb. 1976. I am grateful to Mrs McCarthy for permission to reproduce this letter.
8 Coyle, secretary of Bar Council, to Doyle, under-treasurer of King's Inns, 6 May 1976; Doyle to Coyle, 28 May 1976.

recent exchange in Dáil Eireann indicates, there remains the possibility that at some future date the benchers could again find themselves in an auction room. On 4 April 2000 the Select Committee on
Enterprise and Small Business convened in one of a continuing
series of sessions being devoted by it to the consideration of the
Copyright Bill then before the Dáil. Deputy Pat Rabbitte of
Labour was intrigued by clause 190 of the bill, which proposed to
re-enact section 58 of the Copyright Act 1963. If it did not do so,
as he was informed by Mr Tom Kitt, minister of state at the
Department of Enterprise, Trade and Employment, then 'the
repeal of the 1963 Act could give rise to doubt as to the power of
the benchers to dispose of books in the King's Inns Library,
including those obtained under the depository provisions of the
pre-1836 legislation':

Mr T. Kitt: However, my Department was uncertain as to the necessity for
section 190 and consulted with the Attorney General, who confirmed the
necessity for such a section in the Bill.

Mr Rabbitte: He would. I support this enthusiastically, lest there be any
question otherwise, but are these legal tomes only or is *David Copperfield* [the
Victorian novel by Charles Dickens] included?

Mr T. Kitt: I understand there are a lot of books of no particular national
heritage value, whatever about developing legal education.

Mr Rabbitte: I presume the implication here is that the King's Inns may sell
them outside the country. Do they have to comply with any heritage
requirements from the Department of Arts, Heritage, Gaeltacht and the
Islands?

Mr T. Kitt: Not that I am aware of, but I can find out ... The heritage aspect
is relevant and I will have it checked out.

The clause in which Deputy Rabbitte was interested was later
passed and became section 201 of the Copyright and Related
Rights Act (no. 28 of 2000), thereby ensuring that the benchers
might, if they wish to do so, again dispose of books from their
library. It reads,

Notwithstanding anything contained in the King's Inns Library Act, 1945,
or the enactments referred to in that Act or the Copyright Act, 1801, or the
Copyright Act, 1836, the Benchers of the Honorable Society of King's Inns
may sell or exchange any books of the King's Inns Library, Dublin, whether
acquired before or after the commencement of this section.

It is not evident on what basis the junior minister informed the Dáil in 2000 that 'there are a lot of books of no particular national heritage value' at King's Inns. His opinion appears to be no more founded on a comprehensive assessment of the benchers' collection than was the earlier judgement of another junior minister who, as we saw above, told the Dáil in 1972 that the society's volumes sent for auction at Sotheby's were 'more collectors' items than books of any special interest to Ireland'. While it is undeniably the case that some volumes in the King's Inns Library are of minor cultural interest, the broad sweep of Mr Kitt's statement is worrying in the light of what happened the last time that the benchers embarked on a sale. These recent exchanges in the Dáil are a reminder that the owners of valuable books remain free to send their volumes abroad for auction and that politicians remain free to react as they will to the possibility of such sales. Although the experiences of the past are no guarantee of behaviour in the future, they may provide lessons from which we can learn to avoid repeating mistakes and to manage better the assets of the nation.

CHAPTER FIFTEEN

Lessons for the future

THE CREATION OF A LIBRARY is an act of faith in the future and a mark of respect for the past. A library is a repository of learning and of information, where people go in order to equip themselves better, intellectually and emotionally, for both the ordinary and the extraordinary challenges that face them in their daily lives. A library is one of the hallmarks of civilisation, its foundation being worthy of note. One simple observation by Strabo, describing the city of Smyrna, in Asia Minor, echoes reassuringly down the ages. Writing at the time of Christ, about what he thought was the 'most beautiful city in Ionia', he remarked evocatively, 'And there is a library [ἐστι δε και βιβλιοθηκη] ...'[1]

The volumes sold abroad from King's Inns Library will never be recovered. They are spread far and wide, and are appreciated elsewhere today for their cultural and monetary value. It is clear from information given above about particular works that, since 1972, there has been considerable inflation in the value of rare books. This fact exacerbates any sense of cultural loss inherent in a review of what was sold by King's Inns. Hellmut Feisenberger advised the chief justice and other benchers that 'the books proposed for sale would be a diminishing asset, if retained'. However, to date, the benchers might have suffered little or no loss had they rejected Feisenberger's advice and kept their books, even supposing some further deterioration in the condition of their volumes. In real terms, their collection might even have gained in value. However, the benchers wanted cash immediately and the sale proceeded, earning a sum in the range that had been anticipated by Feisenberger when he promised 'a memorable series' of auctions which would yield 'somewhere between £100,000 and £200,000 at least'. Including sales to An Taisce, the net figure realised for the benchers by the three days of sales in April 1972 was £53,672 after the deduction of Sotheby's commission, The net figure realised by the

1 Strabo, *Geography*, book xiv, ch. 1, paragraph 37; Strabo, *Rerum geographicarum*, ii, 925.

subsequent three days of sales in November 1972 was £65,303, making a grand net total of £138,975. That amount, equivalent at the start of 2002 to approximately IR£1.2m, or more than €1.5m, would have been higher had the benchers not been forced to withdraw some valuable works and to sell others at the reserve price. Sotheby's had charged their standard commission of 15 per cent and earned themselves approximately £24,000 on the whole deal.[2] When one sees how much commission the auction house stood to earn, and did earn from the transaction, it makes it all the more remarkable that Sotheby's was not expected to compete in any way for the privilege of being the benchers' agent, and that its representative had been allowed to attend in person at the crucial meeting of the Library Committee on 21 June 1971 and to argue strongly in favour of selling the books.

There is still a library on Henrietta Street in Dublin. Its shelves are adorned with a wonderful collection of volumes, including many that are unlikely to be cited frequently in a court of law. Among them are the works of John Milton, the English poet and activist, in one of which he remarks that 'books … do preserve as in a vial the purest efficacy and extraction of that living intellect that bred them'. Lawyers and other authors who long ago penned the volumes in King's Inns Library still proffer, thereby, the fruits of their labour. However, the care of such a collection presents many challenges to those who own it. Even if they can afford to conserve it as perfectly as possible, and that is not an assumption that will be rashly made by anyone familiar with the costs of book conservation or building maintenance, it is worth asking from time to time what purposes a library serves. One former librarian at the great Newberry Library in Chicago has recently made the obvious but cautionary point that,

A research library does not exist for the pride of the collector, the enhance-ment of the rare book dealer, or indeed for the vanity of the librarian … To preserve the records of the past and to make them available for scholarly research are the real uses of a research library.[3]

A library may serve many purposes, some of them more obviously utilitarian than others. It is, most immediately, a store of occupa-tional or practical information. In the case of King's Inns Library,

2 FS, paragraphs 34, 40.
3 Milton, *Areopagitica*; at Milton, *Works*, i, 142–3; Towner, *Past imperfect,* p. 126.

founded by and for lawyers, the librarian must strive first and foremost to ensure that its shelves contain all law books that are essential to students and to practitioners, and that its users have access also to fundamental on-line data. Such visitors will also need a broad range of reference works, to enable them to interpret matters to which law books refer. The provision of such manifestly useful materials, alone, is a costly exercise. Some lawyers believe that it is sufficient for a law library to confine its acquisitions to such works. They might agree that general works provide the basis for a sort of 'absorbing parlour game', as one character in a work of contemporary fiction concedes condescendingly of literature, adding that 'reading books and having opinions about them [is] the desirable adjunct to a civilised existence'.[4] However, their appreciation of the ornamental value of such books would probably not extend to financially supporting their acquisition in great numbers.

It is primarily, but not only, for financial reasons that librarians must be selective in acquiring stock. They are usually inclined to concentrate on shelving works that are not 'out-of-scope' for those who frequent the library. Never have more books been produced. If writers in biblical times were prolific, it being said then that '... of making many books there is no end ...' (*Ecclesiastes*, 12:12), what can one say today? Before the invention of printing, and even still up to the seventeenth century, the biggest library that had existed in the western world was almost certainly that of the city of Alexandria in Egypt. Yet, its collection of manuscripts is thought to have numbered only, at the height of its fame, 40,000 books or documents, or much less than half the number of printed volumes now held by King's Inns Library.[5] Vast numbers of works are being published internationally each year, including a stream of new journals that purport to be relevant to specific professional requirements. Thus, even in the unlikely event of there being no financial restraint on its purchasing, a modern library could easily be overwhelmed by unrestrained acquisition. Indeed, not only is the exercise of discrimination in relation to the selection of new works and types of work desirable, but librarians may also deem it necessary to dispose of existing stock because of the need for shelf space. This is most likely to occur where such stock is thought to be redundant in the light of current policy.

4 Ian McEwan, *Atonement* (London, 2001), p. 91.
5 Hobson, *Great libraries*, p. 10.

The concept of 'relevance' is today an influential one in determining the policy of, and towards, educational or professional institutions. It is by no means new. We have seen above a forceful observation, made in 1891 by one of the society's former librarians, James McIvor, that a large proportion of the books in King's Inns were '*useless*'. Indeed, it would be futile and foolish to argue that a library that is dependant on a professional body for its existence ought not to be seen to be relevant and useful to the member of that profession. However, a law library may serve other purposes besides meeting the most immediate and obvious professional needs of its readers. If 'information is power', as a contemporary cliché has it, the nature of power itself is complex. Only those who are ignorant of legal matters assume that the rule of law is a fixed thing. Those who are acquainted with legal principles know that precedent and practice depend on many variables that cannot be understood without a fair knowledge of how human nature and society tend to work. For this reason, amongst others, educators of lawyers have traditionally recognised the need for practitioners to be equipped not only with the tools of their trade but also with a broader understanding of their culture. The Irish brehons and the benchers of the English inns of court, in their heyday, would have been contemptuous of any suggestion that they confine either their educational aspirations or their professional practices to a recitation of statute and precedent, or to sophistry.

Those who founded King's Inns Library, more than two centuries ago, believed that their library might also be a place of aspiration and dreams, and of honouring the written word. For more than two centuries before then, Irish lawyers had been prevented from having an independent inn of court and had failed to build themselves a library of any kind, never mind a general one comparable to that enjoyed by their Scottish counterparts. Those benchers, whose determination led to the construction of the present King's Inns premises, had no doubts about the benefits to their profession of a dedicated library that included many works which could not be catalogued simply as books of law. They, and most of their successors in the nineteenth century who reaffirmed the desirability of a broad collection, created a legacy that became a financial burden but that may only be truly appreciated in its historical context. It is both a service and a symbol.

In 1957, as we have seen, the secretary of the Department of Justice suggested that the benchers might like to be rid of their library. After all, since the foundation of King's Inns Library, there had come into existence, for practising barristers, a considerable law library at the Four Courts itself, and solicitors had departed King's Inns to found their own society with its own library. Yet, the benchers themselves only very slowly and very reluctantly made the decision to sell off even some of their books. The broad ideals of the Renaissance and of the Enlightenment had percolated down through their profession and through their education at school and college. Moreover, practising judges knew what civil servants might not, that adjudicating upon human affairs in court is not a simple matter of legal formulas. The 'relevance' of a book is not always instantly apparent, as Raymond Irwin noted in his enjoyable review of the origins of English libraries:

… we must beware of judging a library only by its visible and immediate fruits. The provenance of recorded thought is too complex a web for us to unravel every thread to its source … The fruits of research may be hidden or lost, perhaps to be disinterred by chance centuries later.[6]

Just as workmen, clearing away the cellar of an older building to make room for the foundation of King's Inns Library, found in a blocked-up cellar both wine and money, as we saw earlier, so readers may discover in the catalogue of a particular collection certain non-legal works that inspire juridical insights and compassionate solutions to legal problems.

Yet, even if King's Inns were to surrender its collection to the National Library, its maintenance on Henrietta Street would pose no fewer problems of finance and conservation than before. Did the civil servants who raised that option, in 1957 and 1966, assume that the library building itself was to be abandoned and left to its fate as disgracefully as most of the rest of Henrietta Street has been left to decay, by the city and by the state? At the start of the twenty-first century, it is difficult to imagine any other society in western Europe allowing a place of such architectural and historical importance as Henrietta Street just to rot away. Moreover, if the King's Inns Library premises were to be abandoned, the National Library would require considerable funding to keep the collection elsewhere. There was little in the government's response to the benchers' sale of 1972, or in its general attitude towards financing

6 Irwin, *The English library*, p. 189.

the National Library itself down the years, to suggest that ministers might be inclined to award a very substantial grant to build new accommodation for books from King's Inns. Perhaps, in reality, the civil servants and government were pleased to see the benchers selling off their books. Certainly, Taoiseach Jack Lynch himself seems to have been indifferent to the fate of those volumes.

There were those, undoubtedly, to whom the institution of King's Inns itself was an unwelcome reminder of an era before independence – as was, too, even the decaying Georgian architecture of the capital city. Of the demolition of two houses in Kildare Place, in 1957, one government minister is said to have remarked: 'I was glad to see them go. They stood for everything I hate.'[7] Just as it took pitched battles between builders and preservationists in Hume Street and Wood Quay to alter public opinion on Dublin's architectural heritage, so it took the battle of the books at King's Inns to alert people to the intrinsic cultural value of that collection.

However, not all of the criticisms levelled against the benchers and their establishment in connection with the sale of books were unfair. How the benchers handled their financial crisis in the two decades leading up to the sales at Sotheby's was almost quaint, if not perverse. At one point, it drove the secretary of the Department of Justice to declare that the benchers were, in his opinion, 'the most unbusinesslike people in the world'.[8] The benchers then being mainly judges, and judges usually being reluctant to court controversy or publicity, they made little attempt to sway public opinion in the matter. Had people known more of the attempts made by benchers to interest the taoiseach and others in the future of the books, they might not have judged King's Inns quite so harshly.

Since 1972, the way in which King's Inns is governed has been reformed and there have been improvements in its provision of legal training. There have also been a number of improvements and changes at King's Inns Library itself. Manuscripts belonging to the benchers are now kept in much better conditions than in the 1980s, when this writer was undertaking research for a history of King's Inns, and when many documents were piled on the floor or tossed into tea chests.[9] In 1989, a summary descriptive list of the

7 McDonald, *The destruction of Dublin*, p. 12.
8 King's Inns grant, etc., 1957–59 (National Archives), for Thomas Coyne's memorandum, 31 July 1957.
9 Cochrane, 'Archives and manuscripts of King's Inns', 27–8; Kenny, 'Records of King's Inns', 231–47.

society's records was prepared for the benchers by Ms Julitta Clancy, an archivist, and a number of typed copies of it circulated. Since then, shelving and boxes have been provided and the papers are now arranged neatly, while the cataloguing of manuscripts continues. However, notwithstanding the events of 1972, the catalogue of the collection of books is still comprised largely of a series of 13 great guard-books, into which for over a century successive librarians have written details of their acquisitions and losses. Recently, the benchers agreed to commission an electronic database in order to allow readers, eventually, to see precisely what is held in the library. Work on this has begun with the entering of data on the most recently published law books belonging to the society. The library of King's Inns is thought to contain a total of about 100,000 printed volumes, of which very many are of general interest and at least 25,000 were printed before 1851. Casteleyn describes it as 'particularly rich in historical materials'. Clearly, in 1972, the benchers and their agents did not strip the collection of all of its books of relevance to fields of study other than law, nor even of all of its general books of great monetary worth. For example, since 1995, nineteen of the society's incunables have been recorded in the British Library's 'Incunable Short-Title Catalogue [ISTC]'.[10]

An unsigned note on the files of King's Inns Library reports an estimate by Sotheby's, in 1971, of the monetary value of four particular works that are still, today, owned by the society. These include Cicero's *De officiis* (Lyons, undated, fifteenth century), which Sotheby's then considered to be 'perhaps the most valuable book in the library' and of which there is only one other copy known to exist in Britain or Ireland. The other three books then singled out by Sotheby's were Joseph Turner's *Liber studiorum* (2 vols., London, 1808–19), William Lewin's *Birds of Great Britain* (7 vols., London, 1789–94), and certain 'Decretals of Gregory IX' (no title page). Such rare volumes belonging to the society are secured in a special place. The library is a veritable treasure-trove, its shelves laden with great and unusual works. These include,

---

10 Jessop and Nudds, *Dublin libraries*, p. 17; Casteleyn, *Literacy and libraries in Ireland*, p. 139. King's Inns Library has a list of its books that are on the ISTC, and related correspondence, from the 1990s, between its own librarian and John Goldfinch, curator of incunables at the British Library. Goldsmith expressed interest in the fate of twenty-two incunables sent for sale at Sotheby's in 1972. The ESTC also includes data on King's Inns Library (see p. 38, n. 7 above).

1 Portrait of Henrietta Somerset (1690–1726), by Enoch Seeman (*c*.1694–1744). Henrietta Street, Dublin, is thought to have been named by Luke Gardiner in her honour. She was married to the second duke of Grafton, lord lieutenant of Ireland, 1724–7.

2 Oval portrait of a man, seated, with books, 1771. By the Dublin artist,
Francis Robert West (*c*.1749–1809).

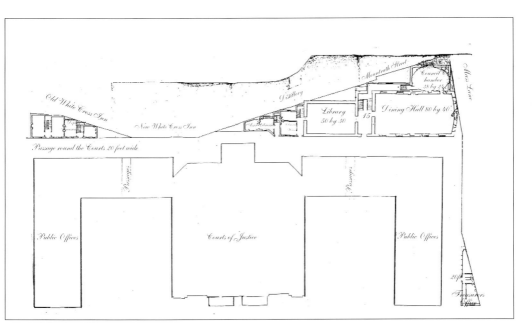

3a *Above*: Plan of buildings intended for the King's Inns, proposed but never built behind the Four Courts, 1790. The plan is unsigned, but appears to be by James Gandon (both from its style and from Duhigg, *History of King's Inns,* p. 511). Note the 'Treasurer's office' in bottom right corner, and an office for the 'Deputy Treasurer' at top left. **3b** *Below*: Detail of same plan, showing library (50 x 30 feet), with rooms for the librarian and his assistant. (King's Inns MS H4/6–1).

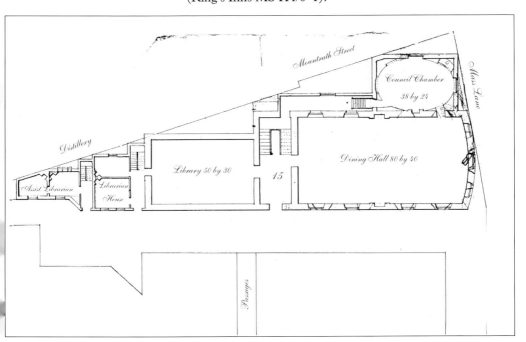

4. Benchers' Council Room, King's Inns, photographed in 1958.
This room served as the society's temporary and overcrowded library
from 1811 until 1832.

Elevation.

5a *Above:* Elevation of King's Inns, 1813. The south-east wing (on the right) was intended to house the society's library (from *Rec. comm. Ire. Reps*). **5b** *Right:* Entrance to the intended library of King's Inns, taken instead for the Registry of Deeds. This entrance and that to the north-west wing of the King's Inns building are ornamented by the only 'caryatids' or draped stone figures in Dublin. By the door to the Registry of Deeds, as seen here, stand Security and Law, holding a key, scroll and book. Before the vestibule of the society's dining room are Plenty with her cornucopia and a Bacchante with wine goblet.

6a *Above:* King's Inns Library, Henrietta Street, 1981, showing also the back of the wing now housing the Registry of Deeds but originally intended to house the library.
6b *Below:* Ground floor of King's Inns Library, 1981, showing the entrance to rooms formerly used by librarians as a private residence, *c.*1832–65.

7a *Above:* King's Inns Library, reading room with catalogues on table, 1981.
7b *Below:* King's Inns Library, 1981, showing both the entry to the annex, completed in 1892, and the gallery.

8 Richard Hayes, director, National Library of Ireland (1940–67). Hayes
also served as director of the Chester Beatty Library, Dublin (1967–76).
He advised the benchers of King's Inns on the sale of their books.

9 Portrait of Conor A. Maguire, by David Hone, 1963. Maguire, chief justice from 1946 until 1961, discussed with Richard Hayes the future of King's Inns Library, and entertained the possibility of selling some books.

a

b

10a Portrait of George Murnaghan, by Thomas Ryan, 1979.
10b Hellmut Feisenberger, 1967.
10c T.P. O'Neill.   **10d** Portrait of Cearbhall Ó Dálaigh, by Thomas Ryan, 1968.

c

d

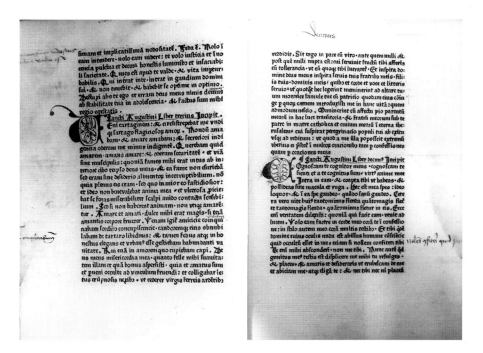

11a and **b** *Above:* Pages of the benchers' copy of a rare edition of Saint Augustine's *Confessiones*, printed about 1470. This was the most valuable book from King's Inns to go for sale at Sotheby's in 1972. Now in University College Galway.

11c *Below:* Details of *Scenes from the life of St Augustine*, by 'The Master of the Silver Windows'. Flemish School, about 1500. National Gallery of Ireland.

12 Sotheby's auction rooms, 34 and 35 New Bond Street, London.

13a *Above:* Pages from the very rare 'Waterford, 1555' imprint of Olde's *Acquital*, showing some manuscript notes. This copy belonged to King's Inns until 1972, when it was sent to Sotheby's without an export licence and bought by An Taisce. Now in University College Galway. 13b *Below:* Nicholas Robinson at Dublin airport, April 1972, showing to Noel Jameson (left) books which Robinson had just purchased at Sotheby's on behalf of An Taisce.

14 Maura Neylon, librarian of King's Inns, with her assistant,
Christine Lysaght, 1981.

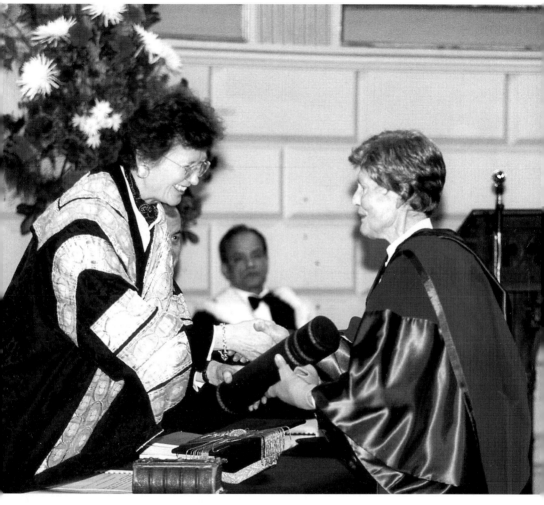

15 Mary Robinson, chancellor of the University of Dublin, presenting a certificate to Mary Paul Pollard, on the occasion of her being awarded an honorary doctorate in letters, December 2001. Pollard was described in the oration as 'Ireland's greatest living historical bibliographer'. Both Robinson and Pollard were among those who, in 1972, actively opposed the sale of books from King's Inns Library.

16 Jonathan Armstrong, librarian of King's Inns,
with Isabel Duggan, assistant-librarian. January 2002.

among five editions of the works of Aesop, one published in Basle in 1524 (*Fabellae Graece et Latine*), and three editions of letters attributed to Phalaris. It may be noted that Aesop and Phalaris were, in particular, among those whose defence by William Temple and Charles Boyle at the end of the seventeenth century sparked off a bitter dispute with advocates of the supposedly superior virtues of more recent writers. This led to Jonathan Swift penning, in the late 1690s, his satirical 'Full and true account of the battle fought last Friday between the ancient and modern books in St James's Library'. The same William Temple provided humble employment for Swift, long before the latter became dean of St Patrick's Cathedral in Dublin, and may even have been his half-brother. For, although Dean Swift's nominal father was briefly an attorney and the steward of King's Inns (1666–7), which was a position equivalent in some ways to that of under-treasurer today, it has been suggested that his actual father was Sir John Temple, William's parent. John Temple was both the treasurer of King's Inns and master of the rolls in Ireland. King's Inns Library owns many books by and about Swift himself, the benchers having sought to sell none of these in 1972. It even possesses two small volumes, by other authors, which Jonathan Swift appears to have signed on the title pages and which, one assumes, formerly belonged to him. One is *A collection of the several statutes now in force, relating to high treason* (London, 1709) and the second a collection of essays and other works translated into French. Those who complain about the inconveniences of going on circuit may take some consolation from the reported circumstances of the death of Swift the elder, steward of King's Inns. Some things do appear to have improved, for he was said by Mrs Pilkington to have died early, from a condition known as 'the Itch'. She wrote that, 'The account I have frequently heard the Dean give of himself was that his father was a lawyer, and returning from the Circuit, he unfortunately brought home the Itch with him, which he got by lying in some foul bed on the road.'[11]

---

11 *Oeuvres diverses du Sieur D****, *avec le traité du sublime ou du merveilleux dans le discourse …, traduit du grec de Longin* (new ed., Amsterdam, 1692). Swift's satire was first published, in one volume with *A Tale of the Tub*, as *The battle of the books* (London, 1704). Its title was respectfully borrowed by W. J. McCormack for his own study of two decades of contemporary cultural debate related to the 'Troubles' in Northern Ireland. For the theory on Swift's parentage see Johnston, *In search of Swift, passim*, where entries relevant to

It is clear that the preparation of a fully computerised catalogue will be a worthwhile addition to King's Inns Library, provided that the cost of preparing it does not entirely drain the benchers' budget for other library purposes. Those purposes include repairs to and rebinding of existing holdings and the provision of sufficient space for a range of new acquisitions. The recent installation of computers for students in a room on the ground-floor of the library has resulted in a reduction in shelving, and books previously kept there had to be moved elsewhere. Because the society's holdings continue to increase, it may become necessary either to build a new extension to the library or to remove the society's offices from the library building to another location on Henrietta Street. Perhaps the benchers might even begin negotiations for the acquisition, for educational and other purposes, of the south-west wing of Gandon's building. This is still occupied by the Registry of Deeds but was, as noted earlier, originally intended to house the society's library.

The benchers may also wish to consider disposing of some of their existing stock to other libraries. One ought not to make of a library either a fetish or a mausoleum. While it is understandable that intellectuals tend to be deeply concerned about any precipitate disposal of cultural assets, especially if the auctioneer likely to be retained is also involved in the decision to dispose of them, it cannot be made a rule that no old book is to be sold or disposed of by a library.

One argument in favour of retention and conservation depends solely on a ritualistic invocation of 'heritage', as though the possession of books that are highly regarded by the learned classes of western civilisation necessarily enhances the cultural or social standing of those who possess them. Such 'heritage' may be appreciated for its material value when it is displayed as a commodity, for paying visitors to admire and enjoy. However, there is a more admirable way in which the heritage of learning can be appreciated, and that is as a source of inspiration and information for subsequent generations. Are lawyers who have confined their reading to legal texts as likely to be as wise and as compassionate as those whose study has extended to other fields of human

Jonathan Swift, the elder, are reproduced *facsimile* from the society's 'Black Book'; ibid., p.54, for Pilkington. William Temple was also appointed master of the rolls in Ireland, but under him the position became a sinecure (Ball, *Judges in Ireland*, i, 294–5).

knowledge? It may be noted that, in 1972, the benchers of King's Inns by no means set out to denude their library of all books unrelated directly to legal practice. Moreover, the King's Inns Library is an important national institution, being one of Ireland's oldest libraries and, formerly, the second biggest repository of books in the city of Dublin. Given the prominent role that members of King's Inns have played in public life down the centuries, when it proved very difficult to sustain libraries of any kind in Ireland, a collection that was founded more than two centuries ago, and carefully built up over time, ought not to be carelessly dispersed. Each and every book therein deserves consideration before being sold or otherwise removed, both for its intrinsic merits and for its historical associations. Such volumes cannot be considered quite dead, although their authors may be deceased. Jonathan Swift was not being excessively fanciful when he wrote that,

I believe it is with libraries as it is with other cemeteries, where some philosophers affirm that a certain spirit, which they call *brutum hominis*, hovers over the monument, till the body is corrupted and turns to dust or to worms, but then vanishes or dissolves; so we may say a restless spirit haunts over every book, till dust or worms have seized upon it, which to some may happen in a few days, but to others later ...[12]

However, one cannot rule out the possibility that some volumes belonging to the benchers are entirely moribund and no longer serve any useful purpose, either cultural or professional. In such cases, the option of selective disposal may be preferable to having books double-shelved, one row in front of another. Moreover, apart from the challenge of finding enough space for their holdings to be displayed appropriately, the benchers are aware of their responsibilities for the upkeep and repair of books in their possession. If they have thousands of volumes which are seldom or never consulted at their premises, and if other Irish libraries would like to have these books and are prepared to maintain them, then it seems unnecessary to insist that the benchers hold on to such volumes. By giving them to other Irish libraries the benchers may make considerable savings on future maintenance and create space for further acquisitions that are required today. If no other library wants a particular volume, then the benchers may wish to sell it.

12 Swift, *Battle of the books*, p. 7.

If painful memories of the battle of the books in 1972 deter the benchers from actively and intelligently considering the best manner of managing their library, then that protest will have had an undesirable and unforeseen consequence. Those who opposed the sales did so in the national interest, and it may be in the national interest to consider all options in relation to the books of King's Inns. Admittedly, there is a danger that if the benchers choose again to sell, or even to give away, some of their collection, then their decision will become both a tempting precedent and the option of least resistance when contemplating further economies or methods of raising funds in the future. This was, to a certain extent, the experience of the Signet Library in Edinburgh. There, the lawyers felt compelled by financial difficulties to sell part of their collection between 1958 and 1964, but resolved, thereafter, to recommence the purchase of a limited number of general books. However, in the late 1970s, books from the Signet Library were again sold. Within twenty years, there had been 'two drastic reductions' in the stock of that renowned Scottish institution.[13]

The question arises as to what might be an appropriate way for the benchers to manage any possible relocation or sale of parts of their collection, if that is deemed necessary or desirable at some point. In the light of what occurred in 1972, it seems essential to ensure as a minimum that the following steps are taken before disposing of books or pamphlets:

1) A comprehensive electronic database or catalogue of holdings should be completed as quickly as possible. This ought to include information on the author, title, subject and place and date of publication of each work, as well as a note on visible peculiarities such as manuscript annotations, indications of provenance or unusual insertions. The cataloguer should also rate the condition of the binding and the body of each volume. For example a rating of the binding in the range 1–4 would mean that it is 'very poor' to 'poor' and needs immediate attention. A rough attempt to place a monetary value on each non-law book might also be made, if it does not unduly delay the process of cataloguing. For reasons of security, such valuations of particular volumes ought not to be disclosed on the general catalogue.

13 Ballantyne, *Signet Library*, pp. 180–1.

2) While the database is being completed, the benchers ought to employ a qualified archivist or historian to undertake a search of the records of the society in order to find any evidence of bequests or donations to the library which might be thought to constitute a legal or moral trust, and to make such information available to interested parties.

3) While the database is being completed, the benchers also ought to determine their own policy in relation both to the retention and to the acquisition of works. Where it was once considered appropriate and necessary to create and maintain a general library, it is not practical to do so now due to the sheer number of books being published. For professional libraries, it seems, the Enlightenment ideal may have been over-whelmed by specialism and prolixity. In any event, beyond King's Inns, law students and barristers today are likely to encounter much general and scientific literature elsewhere. There are now many more libraries in Dublin than when that of King's Inns was founded, paperbacks are both widely available and relatively cheap compared to the price of books in the nineteenth century, and attendance at college or university provides many opportunities for reading. There is also the novelty of 'on-line' sources of information.

4) It must be determined what types of book, other than law texts, are most directly relevant to the professional needs of students and members of King's Inns. Clearly, there has been a growth of interest in legal history, underlining the value of some of the society's existing history books as well as the need to continue to keep abreast of general trends in historical writings, especially those relating to Ireland. Similarly, the science of jurisprudence requires some acquaintance with philosophy, ethics, politics and sociology. In assessing the condition and value of their collections in these areas, as well as of certain other works of cultural merit, the benchers will need to make provision for the acquisition of new and related stock. In 1890, in his outline of the history of the Signet Library in Edinburgh, T.G. Law made the point that 'a library which ceases to grow soon becomes a collection of curiosities, interesting mainly to the antiquary. Old books are useful and profitable in proportion as they can be brought into contact

with the newest and the freshest'.[14] Lawyers who are friendly to the King's Inns Library may, or may not, be persuaded to contribute annually to a special fund for general acquisitions.

5) While the electronic database is being completed, the benchers ought to write to Irish librarians and to invite them to state if they have any interest in receiving books from King's Inns that the benchers specifically determine are redundant to their requirements as the keepers of a professional library. The benchers may even deem it desirable to shed some of their old law books from time to time, and will need to consider a means of identifying works of lasting value or interest. The test of redundancy has been adopted in Britain as one of the grounds on which it is reasonable for the owners of a library to dispose of their assets, and a former keeper of Newberry Library in Chicago makes no apology for the sale at Sotheby's of its duplicate and 'out-of-scope' materials.[15]

6) When the database has been completed, the benchers should extract a shorter version containing any titles they no longer wish to keep at King's Inns. This shorter version should be made available for public inspection for a period of at least four months and should be circulated in either electronic or hard-copy form to relevant libraries. Requests from the public to view particular holdings should be facilitated by the benchers as far as is reasonably possible.

7) In the event of a full database not being prepared for any reason, a complete list of books proposed to be removed from King's Inns Library should be made and circulated in the manner proposed above.

8) No book should be sold which is requested by the National Library of Ireland or by an Irish university library. Any such book should only be transferred to the library requesting it if and when that library agrees, at the very least, to meet any expenses involved in its transfer, including repairing and/or rebinding the volume/s should the benchers deem that to be

14 Cited at Ballantyne, *Signet Library*, p. 61.
15 *In re St. Mary's Warwick* [1981] Fam. 170, concerning the sale of a parochial library to the University of Birmingham. This judgement also stressed the importance of obtaining independent expert advice when a library is to be sold; Towner, *Past imperfect*, p. 139.

necessary. The library which receives free such a book, or books, must also pledge not to sell any book received from King's Inns for a specified number of years, and to keep it in a good condition and in such manner that its individual origin will be easily identifiable, both from the receiving library's catalogue and from an inspection of the particular book itself.

9) In transferring any books to other libraries, the benchers should take into account the particular strengths of each library and, as far as possible, should avoid fragmenting their collection. Preference should be given to the wishes of the National Library of Ireland. It may be noted that books of general interest belonging to the Faculty of Advocates became the foundation of the National Library of Scotland.[16]

10) Only upon completion of this process, if at all, should the benchers proceed to sell books or pamphlets. They should invite more than one auction house to make proposals to them relating to the sale or auction of books, so as to ensure that they will obtain the best value. No auction house should be permitted to make reports or representations to the benchers other than in writing. No work which is written or published by an Irish person, or which is known to be the only copy of a title existing in Ireland, or the subject matter of which relates substantially to Ireland should be sold. Whether being sold or otherwise relocated, no book or pamphlet should be removed from King's Inns Library unless and until full details of it and of its destination have been recorded in a special file to be created and retained indefinitely by the benchers for public inspection.

It may be objected by some benchers that all of their books are their own private property, and that to adopt restrictive procedures would result in other libraries gaining, and King's Inns Library losing, valuable assets which belong to the society. Moreover, there is no guarantee that these procedures would ensure that the benchers avoid further criticism for selling books or breaking up their old collection.

Some citizens may say that, rather than ever disposing of volumes, the benchers should ask members of the profession to contribute

16 National Library of Scotland Act 1925 (*Acts parl. U.K.*, 15 & 16 Geo. V, c.73).

to a special library fund. A number of barristers have been seen to earn very large amounts of money in recent years, especially from tribunals and civil proceedings, and it is reasonable for the public to expect the profession to give generously for the maintenance of its professional heritage. Indeed, the Bar Council itself appeared to countenance some form of annual charge on its members relating to King's Inns Library when, as we have seen, it wrote to the benchers concerning the possible sale of books in 1976.

Above all, in the event of their ever deciding that they must again sell volumes from King's Inns Library, the benchers ought to be seen to act in a way that is considerate of the cultural value of books and sensitive to the type of fair criticism that was voiced in 1972.

APPENDICES

Books of special concern to protestors against the sales

THE LOT NUMBERS, which are given in brackets below before the authors' names, are from the sales catalogues that Sotheby's published in London in 1972. The names of purchasers are as they appear on Sotheby's printed price lists, in King's Inns Library. A place of publication is shown if it was included in the information about lots published in Sotheby's catalogues for the auctions.

APPENDIX ONE

Books desired for the library of University College Dublin

On 27 July 1971 Ellen Power, the librarian of University College Dublin, wrote to Chief Justice Cearbhall Ó Dálaigh in connection with the short list of titles that the benchers had circulated to some libraries. She informed him that her institution would like the following 29 works, in particular, but could not afford to bid for them at Sotheby's. She later saw 24 of the items sold at auction, and another five withdrawn by King's Inns. What she had wanted were:

(Lot 130 of 24 April) Layard, (Sir) Austen Henry. *Monuments of Nineveh from drawings made on the spot.* 2 vols. 171 plates, a few coloured. Sold to Maggs, £140.

(11 of 24 April) *Archaeologia or miscellaneous tracts relating to antiquity.* 101 vols. 1804–1779–1921. Sold to Quaritch, £190.

(27 of 24 April) Bellin, Jacques Nicholas. *Le petit atlas maritime.* 5 vols. 575 engraved maps and plans coloured in outline. Paris, 1764. Sold to F. Edwards, £900.

(80 of 24 April). Erasmus (Desiderius), *Opera omnia* [Complete works]. 10 vols. Leiden, 1703–06. Sold to F. Edwards, £85.

(218 of 24 April) Schedel, Hartmann. *Liber chronicarum cum figuris et imaginibus ab initio mundi.* ['*Nuremberg chronicle/s*'.] 1st ed., including 1,809 woodcuts. Nuremberg, 1493. Sold to Maggs, £2,100.

(395 of 7 November) Alberta Magnus, *Opera* [Works]. 21 vols. Lyons, 1651. Sold to Howes Bookshop, £40.

151

(399 of 7 November) *Analecta Bollandia*. 48 vols. Paris and Brussels, 1882–1923. Although recorded by Sotheby's as sold 'not subject to return' to J. Salmons for £130, these volumes are on a list of books which were recorded as having been returned to King's Inns in February 1973 (King's Inns Library sales files), but they appear offered for sale again as lot 124 on 9 April 1973.

(402 of 7 November) *Asiatic journal and monthly register for British and foreign India, China and Australasia*. 62 vols. 1816–45. Sold to Dr J. Bastin, £30.

(406 of 7 November) Augustine (Saint). *Opera omnia*. 11 vols. Paris, 1836–38. Sold to Howes Bookshop, £45.

 (?417 of 7 November). Given on the benchers' short list as 'Bolandius Bibliotheca', this may be Bollandus, Joannes. *Acta sanctorum*. 66 vols. Paris, Rome and Brussels, [1863]–1910. Sold to Howes Bookshop, £150.

(424 of 7 November) *Bullarum privilegiorum* (papal bulls). 54 vols. Rome, 1739–1857. Sold to H. Brass, £70, but perhaps returned as defective, because it appears to have been put up for sale again at Sotheby's as lot 104 of 9 April 1973, when it was possibly not sold.

(427 of 7 November) Calvin, Johannes. *Opera omnia*. 9 vols. Amsterdam, 1671–67. Sold to J. Thin, £25.

(447 of 7 November) Duns Scotus, Johannes. *Opera omnia*. Lyons, 1639. From the Irish College, Rome. Published by Luke Wadding. Sold to Howes Bookshop, £70.

(450 of 7 November) Egypt Exploration Fund. Various publications in 59 vols. 1885–1941. Including Naville, Ed., *The temple of Deir El Bahari*, 174 maps and plates. All sold to Ars Artis for £110.

(521 of 7 November) Orme, Edward and Mornay (Count of). *A picture of St Petersburgh*. 20 hand-coloured aquatints. No date but plates water-marked 1825. Sold to Mrs Wagner, £160.

(284 of 14 November) British Association for the advancement of science. *Reports*. 95 vols. 1833–1926. Included meetings in Ireland and reports by Irish scholars. Sold at auction to Whitehart, £30.

(371 of 14 November) *Hippocratis medicorum omnium principis Epidemion liber sextus, a Leonardo Fuchsio medico latinitate donatus*, etc. Basle, 1537. Sold to Blackwell, £120 including a title by Beatus Rhenanus with which it was bound. See p. 58 above.

(395 of 14 November) Kepler, Johannes. *Astronomia Nova*. 1st ed. Heidelberg, 1609. Sold to Dawson, £1,400.

(467 of 14 November) Ray Society. *Publications*. 147 vols. 1845–1965. Sold to Wheldon & Wesley, £900.

(473 of 14 November) *Philosophical Trans. Roy. Soc.* 181 vols. 1781–1923. Sold to Dawson, £400.

(487 of 14 November) Scultetus, Johannes. *The churgeon's storehouse …
together with a hundred choice observations on famous cures performed.*
1674. Sold to Dawson, £150.

(201 of 20 November) Ptolemaeus, Claudius. *Geographie libri octo
recogniti jam* … The first edition of Ptolemy with maps by Mercator,
1584. Included inserted map of Europe by Mercator, possibly 1595;
also Mercator, Gerard. *Atlas.* 1st ed. 3 vols. 1585–9. Apparently all
bound together in one volume. Sold to N. Israel, £1,300.

(226 of 20 November) Hakluyt Society. *Publications.* 251 vols, with maps
and plates. 1847–1970. Sold to T. Thorp, £800.

(250 of 20 November) *Jn. Royal Geographical Soc.* Vols. 1–50. 1831–90.
Sold to F. Edwards, £160.

The following works mentioned by Power were withdrawn from sale by
the benchers:

(422 of 7 November) Bradshaw Society. *Publications.* Vols. 1–96 except
88. 1891–1969. Returned to King's Inns.

(507 of 14 November) Stokes, William. *Diseases of the heart and the aorta.*
Dublin, 1854. Returned to King's Inns.

(562 of 14 November) Carmichael, Richard. *Observations on … venereal
disease.* 1813. Location unknown.

(Absent from catalogues) *Materia Medica.* Identity unknown.

(Absent from catalogues) *Journal of Roman Studies.* In King's Inns.

APPENDIX TWO

*Certain 'items recommended for withdrawal' on an annotated list
furnished to the benchers by their librarian, 21 April 1972*

Eight of the 16 items were tagged by Maura Neylon as 'IR', ostensibly
indicating an Irish author. There were 17 items if that listed between lot
423 and lot 575 below is not a repetition of 423 itself. Only one of the 16
items (lot 423) was not sold by King's Inns.

(15) Augustine, *Confessiones.* 1st ed. Strasbourg, *c.* 1470. Withdrawn. Re-
entered 7 November 1972 (lot 404). Withdrawn again and sold to An
Taisce for £4,000. Now in the library of University College Galway.

('IR'/22) Barry, Sir Edward (educ. TCD, MP for Charleville, Co. Cork).
*Observations historical, critical and medical on the wines of the ancients,
and the analogy between them and modern wines.* 1775. Sold to E.
Joseph, £24.

(117) Paulus Jovius. *Libellus de legatione Basilii magni principis Moschoviae
ad Clementem VII.* Basle, 1527. Sold to Quaritch, £35.

('IR'/150) Murphy, James Cavanagh (born Blackrock, Co. Cork). *The
Arabian antiquities of Spain.* 98 plates. 1815. The benchers were

informed by the librarian that this was the 'item referred to in Mr McParland's letter'. Sold to E. Nebenzahl, £130.

('IR'/163) [Olde, John]. *The acquital or purgation of the most Catholyke Christen Prince, Edwarde the VI, king of England, France and Irelande … against all suche as blasphemously … infame hym or the sayd Church of heresie.* 'Waterford, 1555' imprint [really Zurich?]. 'Very rare' (Sotheby's). Bought at auction by An Taisce for £380. Now in UCG.

(180) [Pope] Pius II. *Epistola ad Mahumetem* (Letter to the Muslims). Treviso, 1475. Withdrawn, having been sold before auction to An Taisce for £800. Now in National Library of Ireland.

(181) [Pope] Pius II. A collection of seven works in one volume (details in catalogue), 1488–92. Binding signed by Mullen, Dublin. Withdrawn, having been sold before auction to An Taisce for £550. Now in Trinity College Dublin.

('IR'/184) Pococke, Richard (precentor of Waterford). *A description of the East and some other countries.* 2 vols. 1743–5. Sold at auction to Dawson, £55.

(218) Schedel, Hartmann. *Liber chronicarum cum figuris et imaginibus ab initio mundi.* ['Nuremberg chronicle/s'.] 1st ed., including 1,809 woodcuts. Nuremberg, 1493. Especially indicated as desirable by the librarian of University College Dublin, which lacked a copy, in her letter to the benchers. Sold to Maggs, £2,100.

(256) *The weekly pacquet of advice from Rome on the history of popery … to each being added the Popish Courant, vol. 1 to 3.* 1679–82. The librarian told the benchers that this was 'the item on the Popish plot referred to in newspaper correspondence'. Sold to Pottesman, £10.

('IR'/264) [Wood, Robert]. *The ruins of Palmyra.* 57 plates. 1753. Sold to Quaritch for £50.

('IR'/265) [Wood, Robert]. *The ruins of Balbec otherwise Heliopolis in Coelosyria.* 1757. Sold with one other book in this lot to Quaritch, £70.

(423) *Letters,* from England in a number of volumes by various authors including F. von Raumer (1836). Raumer made references to Ireland and the benchers were informed by the librarian that this was 'the von Raumer referrred to in Mr O'Neill's letter'. Withdrawn and returned to King's Inns.

'423 (tour includes Ireland)' (*sic*), being probably Raumer repeated (423 above), or perhaps meant to be lot 424: [Clarke, Edward D.]. *A tour through the south of England, Wales and part of Ireland … 1791.* Minerva Press, 1793. Withdrawn and returned to King's Inns. Other titles in lot 424 were sold together to Quaritch, £12.

(575) Macartney, George (Earl of), and Staunton, George. *An authentic account of an embassy from the king of Great Britain to the emperor of China.* 2 vols. 1797. Said by Nicholas Robinson to be a poor copy. Sold to Export Book Co., £30.

('IR'/602) Francis Beaufort. *Karamania or a brief description of the South Coast of Asia Minor and of the remains of antiquity.* 1817. The librarian of King's Inns noted that the author was 'Beaufort inventor of the Beaufort scales'. This lot, which included three other volumes, was sold to Maggs, £80.

('IR'/789) Weld, Isaac. *Travels through the states of North America and the provinces of Upper and Lower Canada during the years 1795–97.* 1st ed. 1799. Withdrawn. Re–entered 20 Novemner 1972 (lot 259). Withdrawn again then and sold to An Taisce for £50.

APPENDIX THREE

Books identified to the newspapers by a group of protestors

On 21 April 1972 a letter appeared in the morning newspapers objecting to the sale of books by King's Inns. It was signed by Séan Corkery (librarian at Maynooth), Mary Pollard (keeper of early printed books at Trinity College Dublin), Neville Figgis (bookseller), Jean Paul Pittion (of the French Department. Trinity College Dublin), M. O'Neill Walshe and Noel Jameson. Pollard, Figgis, Walshe and Jameson were also acting as advisors to An Taisce. Included with the letter was a list of books, concerning the possible sale of which the signatories were particularly exercised. Their list was as follows:

(15) Augustine, *Confessiones.* 1st ed. Strasbourg, *c.*1470. Withdrawn. Re-entered 7 November 1972 (lot 404). Withdrawn again and sold to An Taisce for £4,000. Now in the library of University College Galway.

(22) Barry, Sir Edward (educ. TCD, MP for Charleville, Co. Cork). *Observations historical, critical and medical on the wines of the ancients, and the analogy between them and modern wines.* 1775. Sold to E. Joseph, £24

(141) Marsden, William (born Co. Wicklow). *Numismata Orientalia illustrata, the oriental coins ancient and modern.* 2 vols. 1823–5. Sold at auction to Quaritch, £55.

(150) Murphy, James Cavanagh (born Blackrock, Co. Cork). *The Arabian antiquities of Spain.* 98 plates. 1815. Sold to E. Nebenzahl, £130.

(157) *New Testament.* Dublin, 1801. Withdrawn. Received back at King's Inns on 25 May 1972.

(163) [Olde, John]. *The acquital or purgation of the most Catholyke Christen Prince, Edwarde the VI, king of England, France and Irelande ... against all suche as blasphemously ... infame hym or the sayd Church of heresie.* 'Waterford, 1555' imprint [really Zurich?]. 'Very rare' (Sotheby's). Bought by An Taisce for £380. Now in UCG.

(184) Pococke, Richard (precentor of Waterford). *A description of the East and some other countries*. 2 vols. 1743–45. Sold to Dawson, £55.

(225A) Sloane, Sir Hans (born White's Castle, Co. Down. Founder of the British Museum). *A voyage to the islands Madera, Barbadoes, Nieves, St Christophers and Jamaica; with the natural history*. 2 vols. 284 double engraved plates. 1707–25. Sold to Quaritch, £920.

(294) Barrington, G. (born Co. Kildare). *An account of a voyage to* [a history of] *New South Wales*. 2 vols. 1810. Bought by An Taisce for £150. Now in UCG.

(297) Barrow, Sir John. *Some account of the public life and a selection from the unpublished writings of the earl of Macartney* (an Irish earl). 2 vol., portrait. 1807. Withdrawn and returned to King's Inns.

(318) Blainville, M. de. *Travels through Holland, Germany* ... 3 vols. Dublin, 1743. Withdrawn and returned to King's Inns. The other four titles in this lot were sold to T. Thorp, £14.

(357) Carver, Jonathan. *Travels through the interior parts of North America in the years 1766–68*. Dublin, 1779. Withdrawn. Recorded as returned to King's Inns, but apparently entered for sale again on 20 November 1972 as lot 210, when it was again withdrawn and returned to King's Inns.

(377) Collins, David. *An account of the English colony in New South Wales ... to which are added some particulars of New Zealand*. 1808. Withdrawn. Returned to King's Inns. Includes information on Irish political prisoners.

(380) Hawkesworth, John. *An account of the voyages undertaken ... for making discoveries in the southern hemisphere* [principally from the journals of Captain James Cook]. With seven related volumes concerning Cook's voyages. Dublin. 1775–84. Withdrawn and returned to King's Inns.

(404) Dillon, Capt. P. (born and died Ireland, 1785–1847). *Narrative and successful result of a voyage ... to ascertain the actual fate of La Pérouse's expedition*. 2 vols. 1829. Sold to N. Israel, £180.

(424) [Clarke, Edward D.]. *A tour through the South of England, Wales and part of Ireland ... 1791*. Minerva Press, 1793. Withdrawn and returned to King's Inns. Other titles in lot sold to Quaritch, £12.

(433) Flanagan, Roderick (born Co. Roscommon). *The history of New South Wales*. 2 vols. 1862. Sold to W. F. Hammond, £40.

(441) Various authors, including Morgan (Lady). *France*. 2 vols. 4th ed. 1818; O'Conor, M. *Picturesque ... recollections during a tour through Belgium, Germany ... in 1835*. 7 vols. 1814–37. Withdrawn. Returned to King's Inns.

(511(a)) Various works relating to India, in two volumes, including Burke, Edmund. *Articles of charges ... against Warren Hastings*. 1776; Sheridan, Richard Brinsley. *Speech ... on a charge ... against Warren Hastings*. 1787. Withdrawn and returned to King's Inns.

(525) Keatinge, Colonel Maurice (MP for Co. Kildare). *Travels in Europe and Africa*. 1816. Sold to An Taisce, £38. Now in UCG.

(620) Moryson, Fynes. *An itinerary … through the twelve dominions of Germany … England, Scotland and Ireland*. 1st ed. 1617. This volume had had the distinction of being singled out in the Dáil for salvation. Withdrawn. Returned to King's Inns. See p. 75 above.

(636) O' Bryan, W (of Irish descent). *A narrative of travels in the United States of America*. 1836. Withdrawn on 26 April and kept in London. Re-entered and withdrawn again 20 November. Sold to An Taisce for £35. Now in UCG.

(658) Percival, Robert (1765–1828: Irish soldier and traveller). *An account of the island of Ceylon*. 2nd ed. 1805. Withdrawn. Re-entered on 20 November 1972 as lot 244. Withdrawn again. Sold to An Taisce for £35. Now in UCG.

(789) Weld, Isaac. *Travels through the states of North America and the provinces of Upper and Lower Canada during the years 1795–97*. 1st ed. 1799. Withdrawn. Re-entered on 20 November 1972 as lot 244. Sold to An Taisce, £50. Now in UCG.

(804) Young, Arthur. *Travel during the years 1787–89 [in] France to which is added the register of a tour to Spain*. Dublin, 1793. Withdrawn. Returned to King's Inns.

APPENDIX FOUR

William Dillon's April choice

On 21 April 1972, an article by William Dillon appeared in the *Irish Times*. He objected to the sale and highlighted particular books which he did not wish to see being sold. Mentioned by Dillon were:

(14) *Atlas*. Collection of 605 engraved maps. Amsterdam. *c.* 1700–1750. A 'magnificent collection' (Sotheby's). Sold at auction on 20 November 1972 (lot 183) to Reader, £17,000.

(15) Augustine, *Confessiones*. 1st ed. Strasbourg, *c.*1470. Withdrawn. Re-entered 7 November 1972 (lot 404). Withdrawn again and sold to An Taisce for £4,000. Now in UCG.

(45) *Calabria*. A series of 66 (of 70) hand-coloured engraved plates illustrating the earthquake in Calabria in 1783. [?Naples, after 1783]. Withdrawn on 24 April but subsequently sold at auction on 7 November (lot 426) to Traylen, £420.

(55) (Comte de) Choiseul-Gouffier, M. G. F. A. *Voyage pittoresque de la Grèce*. 2 vols. bound in 3, including maps and 284 engraved views. Finely bound with the arms of Marie Caroline de Bourbon-Sicile, Duchesse de Berry. Paris, 1782–1809–1822. Sotheby's notes, 'The

1837 Rosny sale catalogue records volume 1 only (lot 1264); this set must have been included in another of her sales'. Sold at auction to S. Matantos, £1,400.

(158) Nodier, Ch., Taylor, J. and De Cailleux, Alph. *Voyages pittoresques et romantiques dans l'ancienne France, Ancienne Normandie.* 2 vols. with 232 plates. Finely bound with arms of Marie Caroline de Bourbon-Sicile, Duchesse de Berry. Signed in vol. 1, 'Simier, relieur de son A. R. Madame Duchesse de Berry'. Paris 1820–25. Sold at auction to Quaritch, £280.

(116) Johnson, Samuel. *Diary of a journey into North Wales in the year 1774.* Ed. R. Duppa. 1st ed. 1816. Sold at auction to P. H. Williams, £22.

(163) [Olde, John]. *The acquital or purgation of the most Catholyke Christen prince, Edwarde the VI, king of England, France and Irelande ... against all suche as blasphemously ... infame hym or the sayd Church of heresie.* 'Waterford, 1555' imprint [really Zurich?]. 'Very rare' (Sotheby's). Bought by An Taisce for £380. Now in UCG.

(180) [Pope] Pius II. *Epistola ad Mahumetem* (Letter to the Muslims). Treviso, 1475. Withdrawn, having been sold before auction to An Taisce for £800. Now in National Library of Ireland.

(181) [Pope] Pius II. A collection of seven works in one volume (details in catalogue), 1488–92. Binding signed by Mullen, Dublin. Withdrawn, having been sold before auction to An Taisce for £550. Now in Trinity College Dublin.

(218) Schedel, Hartmann. *Liber chronicarum cum figuris et imaginibus ab initio mundi.* ['*Nuremberg chronicle/s*'.] 1st ed., including 1,809 woodcuts. Nuremberg, 1493. Sold to Maggs, £2,100.

(266) Wurzburg. *Statuta Synodalia Herbipolensia.* Wurzburg, c.1486. Bishops' decrees. The benchers' copy included a decree that was not in the British Museum copy in 1972. Re–entered as lot 600 on 7 November 1972 and then sold to An Taisce for £30. Now in UCG.

(?). 'A history of the colony of NSW 1804'. This is perhaps lot (377) Collins, David. *An account of the English colony in New South Wales.* 1808. The latter includes information on Irish political prisoners and was withdrawn and returned to King's Inns. I have not located a relevant title for 1804 but this may be a misprint in Dillon's article.

(636) O'Bryan, W. (of Irish descent). *A narrative of travels in the United States of America.* 1836. Withdrawn on 26 April and kept in London. Re–entered and withdrawn again 20 November. Then sold to An Taisce for £35. Now in UCG.

(638) [O'Hara, J.] *The history of New South Wales.* 1st ed. 1817. Sold at auction to Quaritch, £100.

(640) O'Reilly, Bernard. *Greenland, the adjacent seas and the north-west passage to the Pacific Ocean ... 1817.* Illustrated. 1818. Sold at auction to Gaston's Alpine Books, £95.

APPENDIX FIVE

T.P. O'Neill's November choice

Entered for auction on 13 and 14 November 1972, and mentioned by T. P. O'Neill in a report in the *Irish Times*, 13 November 1972.

(284) British Association for the advancement of science. *Reports*. 95 vols. 1833–1926. ('among which is ... Charles Bianconi's account of the transport service which he established in Ireland', wrote O'Neill). Sold at auction to Whitehart, £30.

(328) Day, Francis. *The fishes of Great Britain and Ireland*. 2 vols. 1880–84. Withdrawn and returned to King's Inns.

(507) Stokes, William. *Diseases of the heart and the aorta*. Dublin, 1854. An Taisce had earlier written, 'Very important medical work by the most eminent Irish specialist of his time'. Withdrawn and returned to King's Inns.

(509) Kirwan, Richard. *Geological essays*. Dublin, 1797. Bought by An Taisce in this lot which included four other titles, all five in one volume. £32. Now in University College Galway.

(513) Turner, Dawson. *Muscologiae Hibernicae spicilegium*. Coloured plates. Yarmouth and London, 1804. O'Neill noted it was 'the first book on Irish mosses'. Withdrawn and returned to King's Inns. During 1973 the benchers sold this to the Royal Irish Academy for £20 (King's Inns Library minutes 1954–81, pp. 226, 230).

(514–7) Tyndall, John. Various mathematical works. See p. 162 below for these. Withdrawn and returned to King's Inns.

(252) Archimedes. *Works*. In Greek and Latin. Diagrams. 1st ed. Basle, 1544. Bound with a work by Albert Dürer which was published in Arnhem, 1603. Sold to E. Morris, £280.

(307) Congreve, (Sir) William. *A concise account of the origin and progress of the rocket system*. 1807. 'Very rare. Congreve's first publication published two years before the rocket was actually launched for the first time at sea in 1809' (Sotheby's). Sold to Dawson, £180.

(371) *Hippocratis medicorum omnium principis Epidemion liber sextus, a Leonardo Fuchsio medico latinitate donatus*, etc. Basle, 1537. Sold to Blackwell, £120 including a title by Beatus Rhenanus with which it was bound. See p. 58 above.

(520) Vesalius, Andreas. *De humani corporis fabrica librorum epitome*. 1st unillustrated edition. Paris, 1560. Sold to Quaritch, £300.

APPENDIX SIX

Lots withdrawn by the benchers and returned to King's Inns Library

April 1972

In April 1972, 43 books were withdrawn from auction by King's Inns. Six were so withdrawn only because An Taisce had agreed to purchase them on behalf of Maynooth College, Trinity College Dublin and the National Library. For these (lots 33, 76, 115, 126, 180 and 181) see Appendix Nine below. Another 21 of the 44 lots withdrawn were kept in London and sold in November, five to An Taisce and 16 to other bidders. The remaining 16 lots withdrawn in April were returned to King's Inns Library. A typed note on the sales files of King's Inns Library records that the following 16 titles were 'Books received from Sotheby's on 25 May 1972':

(157) *New Testament*. Dublin, 1801.

(232) Speed, John. *England, Wales, Scotland and Ireland described.* 1668.

(297) Barrow, (Sir) John. *Some account of the public life and a selection from the unpublished writings of the earl of Macartney.* 2 vols, portrait. 1807.

(318) Blainville, M. de. *Travels through Holland, Germany* ... 2 vols. Dublin, 1743. The remaining three titles in this lot were sold together to T. Thorp for £14.

(357) Carver, Jonathan. *Travels through the interior parts of North America in the years 1766–68.* Dublin, 1779. Subsequently returned to London and entered for sale on 20 November 1972 (lot 210), but then again withdrawn and brought back to Dublin.

(377) Collins, David. *An account of the English colony in New South Wales ... to which are added some particulars of New Zealand.* 1808.

(380) Hawkesworth, John. *An account of the voyages undertaken ... for making discoveries in the southern hemisphere* [principally from the journals of Captain James Cook]. With seven related volumes concerning Cook's voyages. Dublin. 1775–84.

(423) *Letters*, from England in a number of volumes by various authors including F. von Raumer (1836).

(424) [Clarke, Edward D.] *A tour through the South of England, Wales and part of Ireland ... 1791.* Minerva Press, 1793. Withdrawn and returned to King's Inns. The other titles in this lot were sold.

(436) Forrest, Thomas. *A voyage to New Guinea and the Moluccas from Balambangan.* Dublin, 1779.

(437) Forster, John R. *History of the voyage and discoveries made in the North.* Dublin, 1786.

(441) Various authors, including Morgan (Lady). *France.* 2 vols. 4th ed. 1818; O'Conor, M. *Picturesque ... recollections during a tour through Belgium, Germany ... in 1835.* 7 vols. 1814–37.

(511(a)) Various works relating to India, in two volumes, including *Original papers relative Tanjore*. Dublin, 1777; Burke, Edmund. *Articles of charges ... against Warren Hastings*. 1776; Sheridan, Richard Brinsley. *Speech ... on a charge ... against Warren Hastings*. 1787.

(620) Moryson, Fynes. *An itinerary ... through the twelve dominions of Germany ... England, Scotland and Ireland*. 1st ed. 1617. This volume had had the distinction of being singled out in the Dáil for salvation. See p. 75 above.

(756) Troil, Uno von. *Letters on Iceland*. Dublin, 1780.

(804) Young, Arthur. *Travel during the years 1787–89 [in] France to which is added the register of a tour to Spain*. Dublin, 1793.

November 1972

The following titles were withdrawn in November 1972 and are recorded on the files at King's Inns as having been 'received from Sotheby's 28th Feb. 1973':

(7 November)

(399)? Forty-eight volumes of *Analecta Bollandiana*, 1882–1923. On Sotheby's price list this is recorded as sold 'not subject to return' to J. Salmons for £130, but it was returned to King's Inns in February 1973 along with the Bradshaw Society, *Publications* (next below, lot 422). However, the benchers' set of *Analecta Bollandiana*, 1882–1923 was again put up for sale at Sotheby's on 9 April 1973.

(422) Bradshaw Society. *Publications*, vols. 1–96 except 88. 1891–1969. An Taisce wrote, 'Bradshaw (1851–1886) was born in Co. Antrim and these publications are of the greatest importance for Celtic studies'.

(430) Palmer, (T[homas Hibernicus]). *Flores doctorem*. Cologne. 1606.

(468) *Great Exhibition: official catalogue*. 5 vols. 1851; *Illustrated record and catalogue of the Dublin international exhibition, 1865*. 1866.

(484) Kingsborough, (Viscount) Edward. *Antiquities of Mexico*. 9 vols. 1830–48. An Taisce described this as 'One of the most scholarly works to come out of Ireland in the 19th century. Kingsborough was born in Cork in 1795, became MP for Cork county and died in the sheriff's jail in Dublin in 1837.'

(522) O'Rourke, (Count) John. *A treatise on the art of war*. 1778. Born in Woodford, Co. Leitrim, *c*.1710.

(530) Ussher (Archbishop) James. *An answer to a challenge made by a Jesuite in Ireland*. 4th ed. 1686. See p. 123 above.

(542) Prichard, James C. *The eastern origin of the Celtic nations*. Oxford, 1831; Parker, John. *The passengers [sic] containing the Celtic annals, a*

poem. 1831; Price, T. *An essay on ... physiognomy.* 1829; Beugnot, A. *Histoire de la destruction du paganisme en Occident.* 2 vols. Paris, 1835.

(585) Toland J. *Nazarenus or Jewish, Gentile and Mahometan christianity.* 1718; Mangey, T. *Remarks upon Nazarenus.* 1719; [?Toland, J.]. *Four treatises concerning the doctrine ... of the Mahometans.* 1712; Toulmin, G.H. *The eternity of the world.* 1785; Leibnitz, G.W. *Essais de Theodicée sur la bonté de Dieu.* New edition. Amsterdam, 1734. An Taisce wrote that Toland was born in Inishowen, Co. Donegal, 1670, and that this book was not in the National Library.

(592) Wadding, Luke. *Epitome annalium ordinis Minorum.* Ed. Franciscus Haroldus. 2 vols. Rome, 1662.

(593) Walsh, Peter. *A letter to the Catholicks of England, Ireland, Scotland and all other dominions under ... Charles II.* 1674.

(14 November)

(294) Walsh, Francis. *The antediluvian world or a new theory of the earth.* 1743. An Taisce wrote to King's Inns, 23 Oct. 1972, 'Irish author. Almost certainly printed in Dublin; the British Museum *Catalogue* records only a Dublin edition'.

(328) Day, Francis. *The fishes of Great Britain and Ireland.* 2 vols. 1880–84.

(456)? Includes Berkeley, (Bishop) George. *Siris, a chain of philosophical reflexions.* 1744. According to the *Irish Times,* 14 November 1972, this item was withdrawn. It was one of the works that An Taisce wished to remain in Ireland (Appendix Eight below).

(507) Stokes, William. *The diseases of the heart and the aorta.* 1st ed. Dublin, 1854. An Taisce wrote, 'Very important medical work by the most eminent Irish specialist of his time'.

(513) Turner, Dawson. *Muscologiae Hibernicae spicilegium.* Coloured plates. Yarmouth and London, 1804. During 1973 the benchers sold this to the Royal Irish Academy for £20 (King's Inns Library minutes 1954–81, pp. 226, 230).

(514) Tyndall, John. *Researches on diamagnetism ...* 1st ed. 1870. Born Leighlinbridge, Co. Carlow.

(515) Tyndall, John. *Contributions to molecular physics in the domain of radiant heat.* 1st ed. 1872.

(516) Tyndall, John. *Essays on the floating matter in the air.* 1st ed. 1881.

(517) Tyndall, John. *Fragments of science.* 1st ed. 1871; *New fragments.* 2nd ed. 1892; *Six lectures on light.* 1st ed. 1873; *Heat, a mode of motion.* 6th ed. 1880; *Sound.* 4th ed. 1883.

(523) Weld, Charles R. *A history of the Royal Society with memoirs of the presidents.* 2 vols. 1848. An Taisce wrote, 'The author is a son of Isaac Weld and member of the noted Dublin family. Educated at Trinity College Dublin'.

(542) Muller, H. *The fertilisation of flowers*, translated by D'Arcy W. Thompson. 1883. An Taisce described D'Arcy Thompson as 'an Irishman who was a professor at Galway'.
(552) Breen, H. *A treatise on the summation of series.* Belfast, 1827.
(561) Cheyne, John. *Essays on partial derangement of the mind in supposed connexion with religion.* Dublin, 1843; Hayden, G.T. *An essay on the wear and tear of human life.* Dublin, 1846. An Taisce wrote that Cheyne was a practitioner in Dublin who collaborated with William Stokes.
(562) Carmichael, Richard. *Observations on … venereal disease.* 1813.
(574) Fitzgerald, George Francis. *The scientific writings.* 1902. An Taisce wrote that the author was educated at TCD, became Erasmus Smith Professor there and was prominent in Irish educational affairs.
(575) Lairdner, Dionysius. *The steam engine explained and illustrated.* 1836. An Taisce wrote that the author was born in Dublin (1793), educated at TCD and married Henry Flood's grand-daughter.
(577) Gwynn, St. *Burgundy.* 1934; Tennent, James E. *Wine, its uses and taxation.* 1855. An Taisce described Gwynn as a 'well-known man of letters' and said Tennent was 'born Belfast 1804, educated TCD and MP for Lisburn'.

(20 November)

(172) Rocque, John. *A collection of plans of the principal cities of Great Britain and Ireland.* 41 engraved maps and plans, coloured in outline. [1764].
(210) Carver, Jonathan. *Travels through the interior parts of North America in the years 1766–68.* Dublin, 1779. Earlier withdrawn on 25 April (lot 357), and recorded as having been received at King's Inns on 25 May 1972.

APPENDIX SEVEN

Lots withdrawn by the benchers but subsequently sold to An Taisce and various other buyers

In April and November 1972, a total of 34 lots were withdrawn from auction, but were subsequently sold. Of these, 17 were sold to An Taisce. Thus, in April, An Taisce bought the withdrawn lots 33, 76, 115, 126, 180 and 181. They also, eventually, bought lots 15, 82, 636, 658 and 789, which were withdrawn in April only to be re-entered for auction in November as lots 404 (7 November), 455 (7 November), 243 (20 November), 244 (20 November) and 259 (20 November), before again being withdrawn and then sold to An Taisce. That November, too, six other lots (not previously entered in any sale) were withdrawn from auction in order to be sold to An Taisce. These were lots 453, 498, 535 and 577 (all on 7 November) and 246 and 254 (both on 20 November). An Taisce successfully bid for certain other books which had not been withdrawn from auction. For details of all books bought by An Taisce, and for their current locations, see Appendix Nine below.

April-November 1972

The following sixteen lots, withdrawn in April, were kept in London and subsequently re-entered in the November auctions and sold to various bidders other than An Taisce (export licences for each of them, and for lots 15 and 82 above, having been issued):

(14) *Atlas.* A collection of 605 engraved maps. Amsterdam. *c.*1700–1750. A 'magnificent collection' (Sotheby's). Sold on 20 November 1972 (lot 183) to Reader, £17,000.

(34) *Bible* in Latin. Basle. 1526. The first separate edition of a Latin translation of the Greek Septuagint. 'The copy has an inscription on the title signed "Capucinorum Aeriensium" prohibiting this translation to be read as the printer is a heretic' (Sotheby's). Sold on 7 November 1972 (lot 414) to A. G. Thomas, £65.

(45) *Calabria.* 66 hand-coloured plates illustrating the earthquake in Calabria in 1783. Possibly Naples, after 1783. 'Remarkable and rare' (Sotheby's). Sold on 7 November 1972 (lot 426) to Traylen, £420.

(60) Council of Trent. *Canones et decreta.* Venice, 1564. Sold on 7 November 1972 (lot 436) to Maggs, £120.

(64) Daniel, (Rev.) Wm. *Rural sports.* Engraved. 3 vols. 1805. Sold on 7 November 1972 (lot 441) to Aladdin Bookshop, £60.

(70) Datus, Augustinus. *Elegantiolae.* Daventer. 1489. 'Only two copies are recorded (The Hague and Copenhagen)' (Sotheby's). Large woodcut of lecturer and pupils on title. Sold on 7 November 1972 (lot 443) to T. Thorp, £140. See p. 125 above.

(85) Fellowes, W.D. *A visit to the monastery of La Trappe in 1817.* 1st ed. Stockdale, 1818. Sold on 7 November 1972 (lot 456) to Heffer, £18.

(101) Hamilton, (Sir) Wm. *Campi Phlegraei, observations on the volcanoes of the two Sicilies.* 59 hand-coloured engraved plates. 3 vols. Naples, 1776–9. Sold on 7 November 1972 (lot 472) to J. Salmons, £1,300.

(165) Orme, Edward and Mornay (Count of). *A picture of St Petersburgh.* 20 hand-coloured aquatints. No date but plates water-marked 1825. Sold on 7 November 1972 (lot 521) to Mrs Wagner, £160.

(167) Ortelius, Abraham. *Théatre de l'univers.* 112 double-page engraved maps, all hand-coloured. Antwerp, 1587. Sold on 20 November 1972 (lot 200) to B. Schram, £2,800.

(171) Paratus. *Sermones de tempore et de sanctis*. Possibly Paris, 1518. Re-entered as lot 526 on 7 November 1972 and then sold to An Taisce for £32.

(189) Ptolemaeus, Claudius. *Geographie libri octo recogniti jam* ... The first edition of Ptolemy with the maps by Mercator, 1584, but includes inserted map of Europe by Mercator, possibly 1595; also Mercator, Gerard. *Atlas*. 1st ed. 3 vols. 1585–9. Apparently all bound together in one volume. Sold on 20 November 1972 (lot 201) to N. Israel, £1,300.

(205) Rolewinck, Werner. *Fasciculus temporum*. Cologne, *c*.1483. Sold on 7 November 1972 (lot 556) to F. Bondi, £100.

(266) Wurzburg. *Statuta Synodalia Herbipolensia*. Wurzburg, *c*.1486. Bishops' decrees. The benchers' copy included a decree that, in 1972, was not in the British Museum copy. Re-entered as lot 600 on 7 November 1972 and then sold at auction to An Taisce for £30. Now in UCG.

(439) Foxe, Luke. *North-West Fox or Fox from the North-West passage* ... [with abstracts of others' voyages]. Signature on title possibly that of Lord North (1637–85), lord chancellor. 1635. Sold on 20 November 1972 (lot 218) to Gaston's Alpine Books, £180.

(595) (Prince) Maximilian of Wied-Neuwied. *Travels in the interior of North America*. Aquatints. 2 vols. 1843–4. Sold on 20 November 1972 (lot 234) to C. W. Traylen, £6,800.

(7 November)

One book which was withdrawn for the first time in November was subsequently re-entered at auction and sold to a bidder. It was:

(563) Schoolcraft, Henry R. *Historical and statistical information respecting the history, condition and prospects of the Indian tribes of the United States*. Vols. 1–5 (of 6). Philadelphia, 1851–5. Later sold with the sixth volume (1857), on 2 July 1973 (lot 77), £480.

The fate or whereabouts of two other lots withdrawn on 7 November is unknown. These were:

(483) No entry in catalogue, but noted at King's Inns as 'withdrawn'.
(507) *Miscellaneous letters, giving an account of the works of the learned, both home and abroad. To be published weekly*. Vol. 1, nos. 1–22. 1694–96.

APPENDIX EIGHT

The fate of those books which An Taisce wanted saved
for Ireland as a priority

Having been provided with proof catalogues of the forthcoming November sales, An Taisce wrote to the benchers on 23 October 1972, enclosing the following two lists, with comments.

LIST I

An Taisce wrote of this list that, 'The following items are, we submit, of distinct Irish interest and should be excluded from sale together with works already withdrawn by the Benchers on this ground'. An Taisce added further comments about individual titles and those comments are included below:

(A: 7 November 1972)

(399) *Analecta Bollandia*. 48 vols. Paris and Brussels, 1882–1923. 'The Bollandists produced the definitive lives of the Christian saints and this work contains a great amount of material about the men and women of the Irish Church'. Although recorded by Sotheby's as sold 'not subject to return' to J. Salmons for £130, these volumes are found on a list of books said to have been returned to King's Inns in February 1973 (King's Inns Library sales files), but then appear offered for sale again on 9 April 1973.

(410) (The Venerable) Bede. *Complete works*. 1843–44. 'Much concerned with the Celtic Church'. Sold at auction to F. Edwards, £75.

(417) Bollandus, J. *Acta Sanctorum*. 66 vols. Paris, Rome and Brussels. [1863]–1910. Sold at auction to Howes Bookshop, £150.

(422) Bradshaw Society, *Publications*. 96 vols. 1891–1969. 'Bradshaw (1831–1886) was born in Co. Antrim and these publications of the greatest importance for Celtic studies'. Withdrawn and returned to King's Inns. This is also on List 2 below.

(461) Gams, P. *Series Episcoporum*. Regensburg, 1873–. 'Contains succession lists of Irish bishops'. Sold at auction to Howes Bookshop, £22.

(463) Gillow, J. *Biographical dict. of the English Catholics*. 5 vols. 1885. 'Contains many Irish biographies'. Sold at auction to Jenkins Rare Books, £60.

(466) Goa, Dellon. *History of the Inquisition*. Dublin. Reprinted for Robert Owen. 1732. Sold at auction to F. Edwards, £24.

(475) *History of the works of the learned*. 24 vols. 1699–1710 and 1737–1742. 'A very important bibliographical work containing Irish material'. Sold at auction to C. W. Traylen, £160.

(484) Kingsborough, (Viscount) Edward. *Antiquities of Mexico.* 9 vols. 1830–48. 'King was born in Cork in 1795, was MP for Co. Cork and became bankrupt as a result of publishing this work. He died in the Sheriff's Jail, Dublin, in 1837. This is one of the most scholarly works to come out of Ireland in the nineteenth century and has been described as "noble, colossal and magnificent" (Alibone)'. Withdrawn and returned to King's Inns. This is also on List 2 below.

(522) O'Rourke, (Count) John. *A treatise on the art of war.* 1778. This lot included three other titles by other authors. That by O'Rourke, 'born in Woodford, Co. Leitrim, *c.*1710', appears to have been withdrawn.

(527) Parker Society. *Publications.* 32 vols. 1841–49. 'Contains Irish material'. Sold at auction to T. Thorp, £62.

(542) Prichard, J.C. *The eastern origin of the Celtic nations.* Oxford, 1831; Parker, J. *Celtic annals* (a poem). 1831; with two other titles by two other authors. Withdrawn.

(577) Stern, Ludwig. *Epistolae Beati Pauli.* Halle, 1910. 'Contains facsimile plates of the Würzburg interlinear Irish glosses. Of the greatest importance for the study of Old Irish'. Withdrawn and sold to An Taisce, £30, for St Patrick's College, Maynooth, where 'Father O Fiannachta is avid to see it' (Séan Corkery to Nicholas Robinson, 20 November 1972 (Robinson family papers); Murnaghan to Shaffrey, 27 Jan. 1973 (An Taisce MS)).

(585) Includes Toland, J. *Nazarenus.* 1718 and [?Toland, J.], *Four treatises concerning the doctrine … of the Mahometans.* 1712. 'Neither are in the National Library. Toland was born in Inishowen, Co. Donegal, in 1670'. Entire lot withdrawn and returned to King's Inns.

(B: 13 and 14 November 1972).

(284) British Association for the advancement of science. *Reports.* 95 vols. 1833–1926. 'Includes meetings in Ireland and reports to them by Irish scholars'. Sold at auction to Whitehart, £30.

(294) Includes Walsh, Francis. *New theory of the earth.* 1743. Irish author. Almost certainly printed in Dublin. The British Museum catalogue recorded only a Dublin edition. Withdrawn and returned to King's Inns.

(328) Day, Francis. *The fishes of Great Britain and Ireland.* 2 vols. 1880–84. Withdrawn and returned to King's Inns.

(361) Harrington, Robert. *Letters and experiments.* In 1 vol. 1788–98. Correspondents include Kirwan, a noted Irish scientist. Sold at auction to Whitehart, £95.

(456) Includes Berkeley, (Bishop) George. *Siris, a chain of philosophical reflexions.* 1744. Lot sold at auction to Covendell Books, £38, but the *Irish Times* of 14 November 1972 suggests that the Berkeley item was first withdrawn from the lot.

(473) Royal Society of London. *Philosophical transactions*. 181 vols. 1781–1923. 'Among the RSL transactions are papers by distinguished Irish scholars and scientists'. Sold at auction to Dawson, £400.

(475) Royal Society of London. *Catalogue of scientific papers, 1800–1863*. 1867–1879. 'Companion volume to lot 473' above. Sold at auction to Whipple Museum, Cambridge, £50.

(507) Stokes, William. *Diseases of the heart*. Dublin, 1854. 'Very important medical work by the most eminent Irish specialist of his time'. Withdrawn and returned to King's Inns.

(513) Turner, Dawson. *Muscologiae Hibernicae spicilegium*. Yarmouth and London, 1804. Withdrawn and returned to King's Inns. During 1973 the benchers sold this to the Royal Irish Academy for £20 (King's Inns Library minutes 1954–81, pp. 226, 230).

(514–7) Four lots of scientific works by John Tyndall, an Irish natural philosopher born in Leighlinbridge, Co. Carlow. See p. 162 above for these. Withdrawn and returned to King's Inns.

(523) Weld, C. R. *History of the Royal Society*. 2 vols. 1848. 'The author is the son of Isaac Weld and member of the noted Dublin family. Educated at Trinity College Dublin'. Withdrawn and returned to King's Inns.

(542) Includes Muller, H. *The fertilisation of flowers*, translated by D'Arcy W. Thompson. 1883. 'D'Arcy Thompson, an Irishman who was a professor at Galway'. This item withdrawn and returned to King's Inns. Rest of lot sold at auction to Wheldon & Wesley, £35.

(552) Includes Breen, H. *Summation of series*. 1827. This item withdrawn and returned to King's Inns. Rest of lot sold at auction to Weinreb, £20.

(561) Includes Cheyne, John. *Essays on partial derangement of the mind in supposed connexion with religion*. Dublin, 1843 (Cheyne was 'a practitioner in Dublin who collaborated with William Stokes'); Hayden, G.T. *An essay on the wear and tear of human life*. Dublin, 1846; Phelan, D. *Accommodation for the lunatic poor of Ireland*. Dublin, 1846. Cheyne and Hayden withdrawn and returned to King's Inns. Rest of lot apparently sold at auction to B. Rota, £95.

(574) Includes Fitzgerald, George F. *The scientific writings*. 1902. 'Educated at TCD he became Erasmus Smith Professor at that university and was prominent in Irish educational affairs'. Item withdrawn and returned to King's Inns. Rest of lot sold at auction to G. Walford, £95.

(575) Includes Lairdner, D. *Steam engine explained*. 1836. 'Author was born in Dublin (1793), educated at TCD and married Henry Flood's grand-daughter'. Item withdrawn and returned to King's Inns. Rest of lot sold at auction to G. Walford, £48.

(577) Includes Tennent, Sir James E. *Wine, its use and taxation*. 1855; Gwynn, Stephen. *Burgundy* [wine]. 1934. Tennent was 'born Belfast

1804, educated TCD and active in Irish politics. He was M.P. for Lisburn'. Gwynn was a 'well known Irish man of letters'. Items withdrawn and returned to King's Inns. Rest of lot sold at auction to Skelsey, £20.

(C: 20 November 1972)

(210) Carver, Jonathan. *Travels through the interior parts of North America in the years 1766–68*. Dublin, 1779. Withdrawn and returned to King's Inns.

LIST 2

An Taisce wrote that, 'The sale abroad of the following items we would regard as a major cultural loss to the country as a whole.'

(A: 7 November 1972)

(404) Augustine, *Confessiones*. 1st ed. Strasbourg, *c*.1470. 'The first great autobiography ever printed. This copy is bound by George Bellew, a leading Irish bookbinder. A work of major importance in world literature unique in this country. If it goes abroad it will probably never be replaced.' Withdrawn before sale when An Taisce agreed to buy it for £4,000. Donated to University College Galway.
(422) Bradshaw Society. *Publications*. See List 1 above for details. Withdrawn and returned to King's Inns.
(484) Kingsborough, *Mexico*. See List 1 above for details. Withdrawn and returned to King's Inns.

(B: 20 November 1972)

(183) *Atlas*. Collection of 605 engraved maps, fully hand-coloured. Amsterdam, [*c*.1700–1750]. 'A magnificent and unique collection, quite irreplaceable'. Sold at auction to Reader, £17,000.
(200) Ortelius, Abraham. *Théatre de l'universe*. Antwerp, 1587. 'Another magnificent atlas containing 112 double-page engraved maps all hand-coloured'. Sold at auction to B. Schram, £2,800.
(201) Ptolemaeus, Claudius. *Geographiae*. Duisburg, 1585–89. 'The first edition of Ptolemy's "Geographiae' with maps by Mercator, together with the first appearance of what became afterwards the Mercator Atlas. Both works are of the greatest importance.' Sold at auction to N. Israel, £1,300.
(234) (Prince) Maximilian of Wied-Neuwied. *Travels in the interior of North America*. Including 81 coloured aquatints. 2 vols. 1843–4. 'A major work'. Sold at auction to C.W. Traylen, £6,800.

APPENDIX NINE

Books of King's Inns bought by An Taisce, 1972

Almost all of the books purchased by An Taisce from the benchers were subsequently deposited by An Taisce in the library of University College Galway. Except where it is otherwise indicated below, that is where the books may be inspected today.

April

Immediately before the April sales, An Taisce negotiated six major purchases in order to save the following lots for Ireland. The prices paid were halfway between the higher and lower possible prices estimated by Sotheby's:

(33) *Biblia Latina*. Basle. 1487. £140. Russell Library, NUI Maynooth.

(76) Duranti, Gulielmus. *Rationale divinorum*. Vicenca. 1478. £50. Russell Library, NUI Maynooth.

(115) Johannes Gallensis. *Summa collationum*. 1st ed. Cologne, *c.*1470. £120. Russell Library, NUI Maynooth.

(126) Lamsheim (or Lampsheym, Johann). *Speculum conscientiae et novissimorum* (with other tracts). Speier, 1446 (*recte* 1496). £90. Russell Library, NUI Maynooth.

(180) [Pope] Pius II. *Epistola ad Mahumetem* (Letter to the Muslims). Treviso, 1475. £800. National Library of Ireland.

(181) [Pope] Pius II. A collection of seven works in one volume (details in catalogue), 1488–92. Binding signed by Mullen, Dublin. £550. Trinity College Dublin.

At the April sales the following nine lots were bought by An Taisce:

(163) [Olde, John]. *The acquital or purgation of the most Catholyke Christen Prince, Edwarde the VI, king of England, France and Irelande … against all suche as blasphemously … infame hym or the sayd Church of heresie.* 'Waterford, 1555' imprint [really Zurich?]. 'Very rare' (Sotheby's). £380.

(202) (Cardinal) Richelieu, Armand. *A Christian instruction*. Paris, 1662. 'The only other known copy … is housed in Yale' (Nicholas Robinson in *Hibernia*, 26 May 1972). £62.

(294) Barrington, G. *An account of a voyage to* [a history of] *New South Wales*. 2 vols. 1810. £150.

(316) (Count) Benyowsky, Mauritius. *Memoirs and travels*. Dublin, 1790. £28. Bookplate [Daniel] 'O'Connell'.

(525) Keatinge, Maurice. *Travels in Europe and Africa*. Aquatints. 1816. £38.

(533) Knox, John. *A tour through the highlands of Scotland and the Hebride islands.* 1787; Pichot, Amedée. *Historical and literary tour of a foreigner in England and Scotland.* 1825; Vega, Juan de. *Journal of a tour made by Juan de Vega, the Spanish minstrel through Great Britain and Ireland.* 2 vols. 1830. £18.

(542) La Martinière, P. M. de. *A new voyage into the Northern countries.* 1674; Villaut, Nicolas. *A relation of the coasts of Africk called Guinee, faithfully Englished.* 1st ed. 1670. Two works in one volume. £150.

(580) Marigny, Abbé de. *The history of the Arabians under the government of the Caliphs.* Dublin, 1758. £30.

(731) Strzelecki, P. E. de. *Physical description of New South Wales.* 1845. £55. Specifically bought on behalf of University College Galway.

Contributions for purchases made by An Taisce in April had come to £2,165, being £500 each from Trinity College Dublin, Maynooth and the National Library and £200 from Friends of National Collections, £55 from University College Galway for lot 731 (Strzelecki), £150 from Falkner Grierson, £100 from Nicholas Robinson, £50 from Michael Keohane, £50 from an anonymous donor, £25 from Mary Pollard, £20 from 'G.U.', barrister-at-law, £10 from T. P. O'Neill and £5 from Dr T.J. O'Driscoll. The total in contributions fell hundreds of pounds short of what An Taisce actually spent.

November

During the sales of November 1972, An Taisce made some further purchases in order to save the following lots for Ireland:

(7 November)

Withdrawn and sold to An Taisce prior to the auction of 7 November were:

(404) Augustine, *Confessiones*. 1st ed. Strasburg, *c.*1470. 'Of the greatest rarity' (Sotheby's). £4,000.

(453) Erasmus (Desiderius). *Moriae encomium ...* Basle, 1517. Sold to An Taisce, £50 (Murnaghan to Shaffrey, 27 January 1973 (An Taisce files)).

(455) Eusebius. *Historia Ecclesiastica.* Paris, 1497. Previously withdrawn on 24 April 1972 (lot 82). £150 (Murnaghan to Shaffrey, 27 January 1973 (An Taisce files)).

(498) Lipsius, Justus. *Six bookes of politickes ... in Latin ... done into English by William Jones*. 1594. Withdrawn and apparently sold to An Taisce, £30 (Murnaghan to Shaffrey, 27 January 1973 (An Taisce files)). Although a note on the UCG files shows that the college expected to receive this, it is not in that college's catalogue. Nor is it to be found in King's Inns Library.

(535) Pico della Mirandula. *Opera omnia*. Basle. [1557]. Sold to An Taisce, £20 (Murnaghan to Shaffrey, 27 January 1973 (An Taisce files)).

(577) Stern, Ludwig (ed.). *Epistolae Beati Pauli ... Codex*. Halle, 1910. An Taisce wrote that this edition of the epistles of St Paul 'contains facsimile plates of the Würzburg interlinear Irish glosses. Of the greatest importance for the study of Old Irish'. Sold to An Taisce, £30 (Murnaghan to Shaffrey, 27 Jan. 1973 (An Taisce files)). Russell Library, NUI Maynooth.

The total price of £280 for lots 453, 455, 498, 535 and 577 above was thought by An Taisce to be 'highly satisfactory', according to an internal memo by Nicholas Robinson (An Taisce MS).

Bought by An Taisce at auction on 7 November were:

(428) Campion, Edmund – Hanmer, Meredith. *The great bragge and challenge of M. Chapion, a Jesuit, commonly called Edmunde Campion*. 1581. With four further pamphlets on religion by other authors. £120. For Mr Dan Nolan of *The Kerryman*, Tralee, 'who had guaranteed that anything bought on his behalf would remain in Ireland' (*Irish Press*, 8 November 1972). Nolan asked An Taisce to spend up to £300 on his behalf. See, also, last entry for 20 November below, pp. 174–5.

(454) Estius, Guilielmus. *Historiae martyrum Gorcomiensum*. Namur, 1655; Hasenmuller, Elias. *Jesuiticum Jeiunium ... Frankfurt, 1595; Vargas, Alphonso de. *Relation ad reges et principes ... Societatis Jesu ...*, pt. 1. [Padua or Rome], 1636; *The moral practice of the Jesuits*. London, 1670; Lelarge, Jos. A. *Avis paternelle d'un militaire à son fils Jesuite* [Paris], 1760. £12.

(526) Paratus. *Sermones de tempore et de sanctis*. Possibly Paris, 1518. Withdrawn previously by King's Inns (lot 171 of 24 April 1972) but re-entered on this date. £32.

(537) Pineda, Juan de. *Los treyntos libros de la monarchia ecclesiastica o historia universal*. 4 vols. in 5. Salamanca, 1588. £35.

(600) Wurzburg. *Statuta Synodalia Herbipolensia*. Wurzburg, c.1486. Withdrawn previously by King's Inns (lot 266 of 24 April 1972), but re-entered on this date. £30. For St Patrick's College, Maynooth (*Irish Press*, 8 November 1972).

(13 November)
(See *Irish Independent* and *Irish Times*, 14 November 1972)

Bought by An Taisce at auction on 13 November were:

(258) Bacon, (Sir) Francis. *Instauratio Magna.* 1st ed. 1620; *De dignitate et augmentis scientiarum* ... (excerpt from *Operum moralium.* 1638); *Sylva sylvarum or a natural history.* 7th ed. 1658. All bound in one volume. £20.

(268) Bernoulli, Jacob. *Opera.* 2 vols. Geneva, 1744. £35.

(270) Bewick, Thomas. *A history of British birds.* 2 vols. Newcastle, 1822. £22.

(14 November)

Bought by An Taisce at auction on 14 November were:

(296) C[arleton], G[eorge]. *Astrologomania: the madness of astrologers.* 1624. £8.

(403) Lawrence, John. *The history and delineation of the horse* ... 1809. £18.

(411) Lorgna, A. M. *A dissertation on the summation of infinite converging series* ... 1779, with a *supplement* by Henry Clarke. 1782. £5.

(419) Maclaurin, Colin. *Sir Isaac Newton's discoveries.* 1st ed. 4 vols., 1748. £35.

(435) Morris, F. O. *A history of British butterflies.* 6th ed. 72 coloured plates. 1891. £12.

(438) Napier, John. *A description of the admirable table of logarithms, translated into English by Edward Wright.* 2nd edition in English. 1618. £48. 'This copy has the rare leaf A10 with the verses to the author by Thomas Bretnor' (Sotheby's).

(472) Rohault, Jacques. *Traité de physique.* 3rd ed. 2 vols. Paris, 1675; [Papin, Isaac]. *La vanité des sciences.* Amsterdam, 1688; Werenfels, Samuel. *Dissertation de logomachiis* ... Amsterdam, 1702; Obsequens, Julius. *De prodigiis liber.* Amsterdam, 1679. £20.

(499) Sprat, Thomas. *The history of the Royal Society.* 4th ed. 1734. £24. Contains bookplate of the Dublin Library Society and is inscribed, 'For the Dublin Library Society, 22 January 1791. Rich. Merier'.

(509) Tilesius (Dr). *On the mammoth or fossil elephant found in the ice at the mouth of the river Lena, in Siberia.* 1819. Lithographic plate; Kirwan, Richard. *Geological essays.* Dublin, 1797; three further works, all five in one volume. £32.

(530) Wing, Vincent. *An ephemeris of the coelestial motions for the year 1659 (–71).* 1657. £4.

(20 November)

Withdrawn and sold to An Taisce prior to the auction of 20 November were:

(243) O'Bryan, W. *A narrative of travels in the United States of America.* 1836. Re-entered for 20 November 1972, having been withdrawn 26 April (lot 636). £35.

(244) Percival, Robert. *An account of the island of Ceylon.* 2nd ed. 1805. Re-entered for 20 November, having been withdrawn on 26 April (lot 658). £35. However, sold at auction to J. Thin for £65 was Robert Percival's *Account of the Cape of Good Hope* (1804), which was one of nine books in relation to which An Taisce had been asked for an opinion as to whether they were of 'sufficiently outstanding Irish importance to merit special consideration', and responded in the negative (see Appendix Ten below).

(246) Porter, (Sir) Robert K. *Travels in Georgia, Persia, Armenia, Ancient Babylonia, etc … 1817–20.* 2 vols. with many plates. 1821–22. £50.

(254) Thomson, C. W. *The depths of the sea.* 1873; Moseley, H.N. *Notes by a naturalist on the 'Challenger'.* 1879; Stuart, Villiers (of Lismore, Co. Waterford). *Adventures amidst equatorial forests and rivers … South America … West Indies … Florida.* 1891. Sold to An Taisce, £30 (Murnaghan to Shaffrey, 27 Jan. 1973 (An Taisce MS)).

(259) Weld, Isaac. *Travels through the states of North America and the provinces of Upper and Lower Canada during the years 1795–97.* 1st ed. 1799. Re-entered on 20 November, having been withdrawn on 26 April (lot 789). £50.

Bought by An Taisce at auction on 20 November were:

(233) Martin, Robert M. *Statistics of the colonies of the British empires in the West Indies, South America, North America, Asia, Australasia, Africa and Europe.* 1839. £35. Martin was born in Tyrone in 1803.

(248) Rennell, James. *An investigation of the currents of the Atlantic Ocean* (A volume of text and an atlas, 1832). £2. Present location unknown.

On 20 November 1972 An Taisce also bought at Sotheby's two lots which were not part of the King's Inns collection. They did so on behalf of Dan Nolan (in addition to Lot 428 of 7 November above). These two additional lots, described by Sotheby's as 'the property of a gentleman', were:

(350) Burton, (Sir) Richard Francis. *Abeokta and the Camaroons Mountains.* 2 vols. 1st ed. Signed by Burton's sister, Lady Maria Stisted, with a note by Isabel Burton. 1863. £110.

(373) Speke, John M. *Journal of the discovery of the source of the Nile.* 1st ed. 1863. £90. Another copy of this same edition, which copy had belonged to King's Inns, had been sold on 26 April to Kegan Paul for £35 (lot 721).

APPENDIX TEN

Books 'of substantial Irish interest' sold

According to Nicholas Robinson, An Taisce was asked by the benchers to say if the following books in the April sales were 'of sufficiently outstanding Irish importance to merit special consideration'. In the opinion of An Taisce they were not, although they were judged to be 'of substantial Irish interest'. The books were then sold off at auction (Robinson papers, two notes):

(569) (Marquis of) Londonderry (Charles William Stewart, afterwards Vane). *Recollections of a tour in the North of Europe in 1836–7.* 2 vols. in one. 1838. Sold, with six other titles in this lot, to Germundson, £35.

(575) Macartney, George (Earl of), and Staunton, George. *An authentic account of an embassy from the king of Great Britain to the emperor of China.* 2 vols. 1797. Said by Nicholas Robinson to be a poor copy, and sold to Export Book Co., £30.

(601) Mariti (Abbé). *Travels through Cyprus, Syria and Palestine, with a general history of the Levant.* 2 vols. Dublin, 1792. Sold, with two other titles on the Middle East in this lot, to Dr Habibis, £40.

(605) Burton, Nathaniel. *Narrative of a voyage from Liverpool to Alexandria.* Dublin, 1838. Sold, with four other titles on the same general region in this lot, to Kegan Paul, £10.

(609) Madden, R.R. *Travels in Turkey, Egypt, Nubia and Palestine.* 1829. Sold, with three other titles on the Middle East in this lot, to N.E.I. Wood, £70.

(621) Moryson, Fynes. *Itinerary.* Glasgow, 1907–8. Sold to Quaritch, £18.

(657a) Percival, (Captain) Robert. *Account of the Cape of Good Hope.* 1804. Sold to J. Thin, £65.

(808) Walker, Samuel A. *Missions in Western Africa.* Dublin, 1845. Sold, with more than seven other titles on Africa in this lot, to P. W. Frances, £85.

(818) Ormonde, (Marquis of). *An autumn in Sicily.* Dublin, 1850. Sold, with four other titles on Europe in this lot, to Gaston's Alpine Books, £16.

Also then identified as being 'of substantial Irish interest', in the opinion of An Taisce, were lots 22, 141, 150, 184, 225A, 404, 433. See pp. 155–6 above for details of these, all sold to bidders.

Librarians of King's Inns, 1792–2002

IN 1788, THE BENCHERS of the society of King's Inns purchased books that had belonged to Christopher Robinson, a recently deceased judge. These became the nucleus of their new library. Subsequently, the benchers employed George Hart, their first known librarian.

By 21 January 1792	George Hart
21 November 1793	Stephen Dickson
6 November 1815	Henry Monck Mason
10 June 1851	John Bermingham Miller
13 June 1856	James Haig
27 May 1862	Francis R. Stewart*
8 December 1862	Joseph La Barte
18 January 1882	James MacIvor
11 January 1901	Joseph Carton
3 July 1935	Hubert Carr
1 June 1944	Bridget Walsh (McMenamin)
1 January 1970	Maura Neylon
1 August 1984	Jonathan Armstrong

Among assistants to the librarians of King's Inns has been Bartholomew Duhigg. He was styled 'deputy librarian' between 1794 and 1801, and 'junior librarian' from 1801 until his death in 1813. Duhigg wrote *History of the King's Inns* (Dublin, 1806) and other works. A number of those listed above acted in an assistant capacity prior to their appointments as principal librarians.

---

* Less than six months after his appointment, Stewart died of an unspecified 'dangerous illness'. This led to the library being closed for some weeks, and the benchers ordering that it be kept 'properly ventilated and disinfected' and that fires be kept burning there (Benchers' minute book, 1856–69, pp. 137, 139).

KING'S INNS LIBRARY ABOUT 1910

The library, once reached, was a comfortable building, and well supplied with books and reports, although I never discovered much space for their storage. Almost any afternoon one might stumble upon Archbishop Walsh, the notable prelate who exposed the Pigott forgeries, immersed in a study of the law relating to charities.* But half a dozen students, and, on Saturday afternoons, a few industrious barristers, formed the entire body of beneficiaries of this valuable institution. Two servants in knee breeches and buckled shoes were on duty daily: one of them appeared to have no charge beyond seeing that nobody ran away with the attendance book in the hall, but, the other, a genius named Horner, fetched and carried books all day, and entertained the neophytes with a vast fund of inaccurate information. Horner was as mad as a hatter, and pursued an implacable vendetta against the assistant-librarian, one Shrimpton. The librarian, Joe Carton, did his work unobtrusively, and kept an amused eye upon the warfare between his subordinates.

Maurice Healy, *The old Munster Circuit*, pp. 62–3.

---

* William J. Walsh, Catholic archbishop of Dublin, chancellor of University College Dublin and former librarian of Maynooth College. He researched over many years the celebrated case involving Daniel O'Connell, Bishop Murray and the Board of Charitable Bequests, and his pamphlet on that case was published in 1918 (Morrissey, *Walsh*, pp. 13, 122–3, 231, 298). When Chief Baron Christopher Palles died, Walsh bought his collection of law books for University College Dublin.

Bibliography

MANUSCRIPTS

An Taisce
Files relating to the sale of books by King's Inns, 1972.

King's Inns
Admission of benchers, 1741–92 (MS B1/3–2).
Benchers' minute books, 1792–1956 (MSS B1/5–14).
Benchers' minute books, 1957–89 (MSS UT/1/A/1–4).
Books entered at Stationers' Hall (MSS M2/1–4).
Caterer's account book, 1793–1846 (MS E9/1).
Charter and bye-laws of King's Inns, 1793 (MS A 1/3).
Committees of benchers, 1844–1975 (MSS B2/1).
Copyright Act, opinion of Francis Blackburne, 1830 (MS M16/2).
Draft of bye-laws, printed 1792 (MS A2/1–2).
Factual statement in regard to the sale of certain books, by George Murnaghan and Raymond O'Neill, 7 February 1973 (MS C/1/2–6).
Free State grant to King's Inns Library (MS M16/4).
Librarian: rules for selection, list of candidates, 1856 (MS F1/1–1).
Librarian: applications etc., 1881–82 (MS F1/1–2).
Library: arson files (MS C/4/1–2).
Library catalogues (MS M9/1–6).
Library construction, contracts, accounts, etc., 1822–35 (MSS H3/1 to H3/2–1).
Library Committee minute books, 1844–1981 (MSS M1/1–10 and M1/2–6).
Library correspondence files, 1957–2001, including re Sotheby's (MS C/4/1).
Library extension: agreement between the society and James and William Beckett, May 1891 (MS M8/6).
Library: plans for a circular extension, by James Franklin Fuller, nineteenth century, undated (MSS M8/1 and M8/4).
Library premises: papers including abstract of title, copies of wills and opinion of Francis Blackburne as to title, 1824–5 (MS G3/2–1).
Longitudinal section of front of gallery, King's Inns Library, by Frederick Darley jnr. [*c*.1827] (MS H4/3–1).
Northern Ireland Bar: transfer of books from King's Inns Library, 1922 (MS M16/3).

Plan of courts and society's [proposed] buildings at Inns Quay [unsigned but attributed to James Gandon], 1790 (MS H4/6–1).
Receipt book, 1781–99 (MS E24/1).
Rules of King's Inns, 1793 (MS A2/1).
Sale by auction of building materials, 1811 (MS H2/1–5).
Standing Committee minute books, 1929–60 (MS B2/1–8).
Standing Committee minute book, 1960–75 (MS 1/C/1).
Standing Committee report on the library, etc., June 1822 (MS B1/5–2, ff. 130–32).
Treasurers' account books, 1789–1803 (MSS E2/1).
Tristram Kennedy papers: assignment of house and premises, Henrietta St., 1865 (MS G3/2–2).

National Archives
King's Inns grant, 1945 (Taoiseach's office, S.13641A).
King's Inns grant, 1957–59 (Taoiseach's office, S.13641B).
King's Inns grant, 1966 (Taoiseach's office, 98/6/169, formerly S.13641C).

National Library of Ireland
Correspondence relating to the sale of books by King's Inns (Director's office).

Robinson family
Papers in the possession of Mary and Nicholas Robinson relating to the sale of books by King's Inns. 1972.

University College Dublin
King's Inns books 1972 (Librarian's office).

University College Galway
King's Inns books, files 2–7 (Librarian's office).
Text of the introductory address delivered by Dr Colm Ó hEocha on June 26, 1995, in University College Galway, on the occasion of the conferring of the degree of Doctor of Laws, *honoris causa*, on Nicholas Robinson (Registrar and Deputy President's office).

ACTS AND STATUTES

An Act to regulate the admission of barristers at law (*Stat. Ire.*, 21 & 22 Geo III, c.32 (1781–2)).
An Act for confirming the powers of the society of King's-Inns, Dublin, and to repeal an Act entitled An Act to regulate the admission of barristers at law (*Stat. Ire.*, 32 Geo III, c.18 (1792)).

An Act to repeal so much of an Act passed in the thirty-second year of His Majesty, entitled, An Act for confirming the powers of the society of King's-Inns, Dublin, and to repeal an Act entitled An Act to regulate the Admission of barristers at law, as confirms the charter of the said society (*Stat. Ire.*, 33 Geo III, c.44 (1792)).

An Act to enable the dean and chapter of Christ Church, Dublin, and other persons therein named to grant certain grounds in the city of Dublin, to the society of King's Inns, 1798 (*Stat. Ire.*, 38 Geo III, c.49 (1798)).

An Act for the further encouragement of learning in the United Kingdom of Great Britain and Ireland, by securing the copies and copyright of printed books, to the authors of such books, or their assigns, for the time herein mentioned [Copyright Act 1801] (*Stat. Parl. U.K.*, 41 Geo III, c.107).

An Act to vest in his majesty, his heirs and successors, for ever, part of the ground and buildings now belonging to the society of King's Inns, Dublin, for the erecting thereon a repository for public records in Ireland (*Stat. Parl. U.K.*, 54 Geo III, c.113 (1814)).

An Act to amend the several Acts for the encouragement of learning by securing the copies and the copyright of printed books to the authors of such books or their assigns [Copyright Act 1814] (*Stat. Parl. U.K.*, 54 Geo III, c.156).

An Act to alter and amend an Act passed in the fifty-fourth year of the reign of his late majesty King George III, for vesting in his majesty, his heirs and successors, for ever, part of the ground and buildings now belonging to the society of King's Inns, Dublin, for erecting thereon a repository for public records in Ireland, 1826 (*Stat. Parl. U.K.*, 7 Geo IV, c.13).

An Act to repeal so much of the Act of the fifty-fourth year of King George III, respecting copyrights, as requires the delivery of a copy of every published book to the libraries of Sion College, the four universities of Scotland, and of the King's Inns in Dublin [Copyright Act 1836] (*Stat. Parl. U.K.*, 6 & 7 Will IV, c.110).

Copyright Act 1911 (*Acts parl. U.K.*, 1 & 2 Geo V, c.46).

An Act to establish a National Library in Scotland on the foundation of the library gifted for that purpose by the Faculty of Advocates, and for purposes connected therewith [National Library of Scotland Act 1925] (*Acts parl. U.K.*, 15 & 16 Geo V, c.73).

Industrial and Commercial Property (Protection) Act 1927 (*Acts Oireachtas*, no. 16).

King's Inns Library Act 1945 (*Acts Oireachtas*, no. 22).

Documents and Pictures (Regulation of Export) Act 1945 (*Acts Oireachtas*, no. 29).

Funds of Suitors Act 1959 (*Acts Oireachtas*, no. 32).

Copyright and Related Rights Act 2000 (*Acts Oireachtas*, no. 28).

PARLIAMENTARY DEBATES AND PAPERS

Dáil Éireann deb. (Dáil Éireann ..., díosbóireachtaí páirliminte (parliamentary debates); tuairisg oifigiúil (official report), iml. i (vol. i), 1922 [etc.] (Dublin Stationery Office)).

Report from the select committee on public libraries. H.C. 1849 (548), xvii. 1.

Return on public libraries. H.C. 1849 (18), xlv. 199.

Report from the select committee on legal education, together with the minutes of evidence. H.C. 1846 (686), x.1.

BOOKS AND ARTICLES

Abbot, Charles (ed.). *Diary and correspondence of Charles Abbot, Lord Colchester.* 3 vols. London, 1861.

Anon. (1). Henrietta Street. In *Irish Builder*, 15 June -15 August 1893.

Anon. (2). Henrietta Street. In *Irish Times*, 19 Nov. 1896.

Ball, F. Elrington. *Judges in Ireland.* 2 vols. London, 1926.

Ballantyne, G.H. *The Signet Library Edinburgh and its librarians 1722–1972.* Glasgow, 1979.

Boylan, Henry. *Dictionary of Irish Biography.* 3rd ed., Dublin, 1998.

Casteleyn, Mary. *A history of literacy and libraries in Ireland.* Aldershot, 1984.

Champion, J.A.I. John Toland, the druids and the politics of Celtic scholarship. In *I.H.S.*, xxxii, no. 127 (May, 2001).

Cochrane, Nigel. The archives and manuscripts of the King's Inns Library. In *Ir. Archives*, i (1989).

Connor, Henry. *Juridical catalogue of the library of the King's Inns, Dublin.* Dublin, 1846.

Cosgrave, Liam. The King's Inns. In *Dublin Hist. Rec*, xxi, no. 2 (March, 1964).

Craig, Maurice. *Dublin 1660–1860.* Dublin, 1952.

de Brún, Pádraig. *Catalogue of Irish manuscripts in King's Inns Library Dublin.* Dublin, 1972.

Dillon, William. King's Inns rarities. In *Irish Times*, 21 April 1972.

Dillon, William. The King's Inns sales. In *Irish Times*, 20 November 1972.

Duffy, D.J. The King's Inns. In *Irish Times*, 16 and 17 September 1957.

[Duhigg, Bartholomew]. *A catalogue of the library belonging to the honorable society of King's Inns, Dublin, to Trinity term 1801.* Dublin, 1801.

Duhigg, Bartholomew. *King's Inns remembrances.* Dublin, 1805.

Duhigg, Bartholomew. *History of the King's Inns.* Dublin, 1806.

DNB (Dictionary of National Biography).

Edwards, Edward. *Memoirs of libraries.* 2 vols. London, 1859.

Georgian Society records of domestic architecture (Strickland, W.G. and Mahaffy, J.P. (eds). *Georgian Society Dublin: records of eighteenth* century domestic architecture and decoration in Dublin. 5 vols. Dublin, 1909–13. Reprinted Shannon, 1969).

Haig, J.D. *A list of books printed in England prior to the year MDC in the library of the Honorable Society of King's Inns, Dublin.* Dublin, 1858.

Healy, Maurice. *The old Munster Circuit: a book of memories and traditions.* Dublin, 1939. Reprinted London, 2001, with a new introduction by Charles Lysaght.

Henchy, Patrick. *The National Library of Ireland, 1941–1976.* Dublin, 1986.

Hobson, Anthony. *Great libraries.* London, 1970.

Hogan, Daire. *The legal profession in Ireland 1789–1922.* Dublin, 1986.

Hogan, Daire and Osborough, W.N. (eds). *Brehons, serjeants and attorneys: studies in the history of the Irish legal profession.* Dublin, 1990.

Inis Cealtra. The proselytisers and Irish: their plans a hundred years ago. In *Catholic Bulletin,* xxv (Jan.–June 1935).

Irwin, Raymond. *The origins of the English library.* London, 1958.

Jessop, Norma and Nudds, Christine (eds). *Guide to collections in Dublin libraries: printed books before 1850 and special collections.* Dublin, 1982.

Johnston, Denis. *In search of Swift.* Dublin, 1959.

Kennedy, Maev. Great Irish libraries: the King's Inns. In *Irish Times,* 10 March 1981.

Kenny, Colum. Counsellor Duhigg — antiquarian and activist. In *Ir. Jurist, n.s.,* xxi (Winter, 1986).

Kenny, Colum. The records of King's Inns, Dublin. In Hogan and Osborough, *Brehons, serjeants and attorneys.*

Kenny, Colum. *King's Inns and the kingdom of Ireland: the Irish 'inn of court' 1541–1800.* Dublin, 1992.

Kenny, Colum. *Tristram Kennedy and the revival of Irish legal training 1835–1885.* Dublin, 1996.

Kinane, Vincent. Legal deposit, 1801–1922. In Kinane, Vincent and Walsh, Anne (eds). *Essays on the history of Trinity College Library Dublin.* Dublin, 2000.

King's Inns admissions (Keane, Edward, Phair, P. B. and Sadlier, T.U. *King's Inns admission papers 1607–1867.* Dublin, 1982).

Lacey, Robert. *Sotheby's: bidding for class.* London, 1998.

Littledale, William F. *The society of King's Inns, Dublin, its origins and progress, and the present results of its assumed control over the legal profession in Ireland.* Dublin, 1859.

Lopez, Donald S. *Curators of the Buddha: the study of Buddhism under colonialism.* Chicago and London, 1995.

McCarthy, Muriel. *Archbishop Marsh and his library.* Dublin, 1977.

McCormack, W.J. *The battle of the books: two decades of Irish cultural debate.* Mullingar, 1986.

McDonald, Frank. *The destruction of Dublin.* Dublin, 1985.

McParland, Edward. *James Gandon: Vitruvius Hibernicus*. London, 1985.

McParland, Edward (and others). *The architecture of Richard Morrison (1767–1849) and William Vitruvius Morrison (1794–1838)*. Irish Architectural Archive, Dublin, 1989.

Milton, John. Areopagitica: a speech for the liberty of unlicensed printing. In John Milton, *A complete collection of the historical, political and miscellaneous works of John Milton* (2 vols., London, 1738).

Mirsky, Jeannette. *Sir Aurel Stein*. Chicago, 1977.

Monck Mason, Henry J. *Essay on the antiquity and constitution of parliaments in Ireland*. Dublin, 1891.

Morrissey, Thomas J. *William J. Walsh, archbishop of Dublin, 1841–1921*. Dublin 2000.

Neylon, Mary [Maura] J. King's Inns Library, Dublin. In *Law Librarian*, iv (1973).

Neylon, Maura, and Henchy, Monica. *Public libraries in Ireland*. Dublin, 1966.

O'Brien, Jacqueline and Guinness, Desmond. *Dublin: a grand tour*. London, 1994.

O.E.D. (*Oxford English Dictionary*, ed. 1901).

O'Mahony, Eoin. Some Henrietta Street residents. In *Ir Georgian Soc. Bull.*, ii, no. 2 (April-June 1959).

O'Neill, T. P. International Book Sale Year? In *Ir. Press*, 23 Nov. 1972.

Osborough, W.N. In praise of law books. In *Ir. Jurist, n.s.*, xxi (1986).

Osborough, W. N. On selling cathedral libraries: reflections on a recent cy-près application. In *Ir. Jurist, n.s.*, xxiv (Summer, 1989).

Pollard, Mary. *A list of members of the Dublin Book Trade 1550–1800*. Oxford, 2000.

Ruane, Blathna. An assessment of the independence of the Irish Supreme Court in the context of constitutional law with particular reference to the system of judicial appointments. Ph. D thesis, University of Cambridge, September 1993.

St Clair, John and Craik, Roger. *The Advocates' Library: 300 years of a national institution 1689–1989*. Edinburgh, 1989.

Sharpe, Charles. *Catalogue of the library of Robert Travers Esq., A.M., Bachelor of Physics, T.C.D.* Dublin, 1836.

Strabo. *Strabonis rerum geographicum*. In Greek and Latin. Ed. Thomas Falconer. 2 vols. Oxford, 1807.

Strabo. *The geography of Strabo*. Translated by H. C. Hamilton and W. Falconer. 3 vols. London, 1854–7.

Strickland, Walter G. *Dictionary of Irish artists*. 2 vols. Dublin, 1913.

Swift, Jonathan. *Battle of the books*. Ed. A. Guthkelch. London, 1908.

Towner, Lawrence. *Past imperfect: essays on history, libraries and the humanities*. Chicago, 1993.

Underwood, Francis. *Henry Wadsworth Longfellow*. London, 1882.

Warburton, John, Whitelaw, James and Walsh, Robert. *History of the city of Dublin.* 2 vols. London, 1818.

Watson, Peter. *Sotheby's: inside story.* London, ed. 1998.

White, James. *Pauline Bewick: painting a life.* Dublin, 1985.

Wheeler, W. G. Libraries in Ireland before 1855: a bibliographical essay (Diploma in Librarianship thesis, University of London, May 1957. Copy in Early Printed Books section, Trinity College Dublin, 'revised to May 1965').

Wright, G. N. *A historical guide to ancient and modern Dublin.* London, 1821.

NEWSPAPERS AND PERIODICALS

Connacht Tribune

Evening Press

Evening Herald

Hibernia

Illustrated London News

Irish Book Lover

Irish Builder

Irish Press

Irish Independent

Irish Times

Saunders's Newsletter

Sunday Independent

Sunday Press

The Times

Index

Excluded, because of their frequency, are King's Inns, Sotheby's and An Taisce. Also excluded are authors of books sold at auction except where special references are made to them.

The Irish Legal History Society

Established in 1988 to encourage the study and advance the knowledge of the history of Irish law, especially by the publication of original documents and of works relating to the history of Irish law, including its institutions, doctrines and personalities, and the reprinting or editing of works of sufficient rarity or importance.